# Into the Fantastical Spaces of Contemporary Japanese Literature

# Into the Fantastical Spaces of Contemporary Japanese Literature

Edited by Mina Qiao

LEXINGTON BOOKS
*Lanham • Boulder • New York • London*

Published by Lexington Books
An imprint of The Rowman & Littlefield Publishing Group, Inc.
4501 Forbes Boulevard, Suite 200, Lanham, Maryland 20706
www.rowman.com

6 Tinworth Street, London SE11 5AL, United Kingdom

Copyright © 2022 The Rowman & Littlefield Publishing Group, Inc.

*All rights reserved.* No part of this book may be reproduced in any form or by any electronic or mechanical means, including information storage and retrieval systems, without written permission from the publisher, except by a reviewer who may quote passages in a review.

British Library Cataloguing in Publication Information Available

**Library of Congress Cataloging-in-Publication Data**

Names: Qiao, Mina, 1989- editor.
Title: Into the fantastical spaces of contemporary Japanese literature / edited by Mina Qiao.
Description: Lanham : Lexington Books, [2022] | Includes bibliographical references and index. | Summary: "Into the Fantastical Spaces of Contemporary Japanese Literature examines selected contemporary Japanese writers and their use of fantastical spaces. Such spaces grant access to phenomena occluded from everyday life, including the geographically peripheral, the culturally marginalized, the psychologically liminal, and the physically intangible"-- Provided by publisher.
Identifiers: LCCN 2021055709 (print) | LCCN 2021055710 (ebook) | ISBN 9781793646125 (cloth) | ISBN 9781793646149 (paper) | ISBN 9781793646132 (ebook)
Subjects: LCSH: Japanese literature--History and criticism. | Space in literature. | Liminality in literature. | Space perception in literature. | Place (Philosophy) in literature. | LCGFT: Literary criticism.
Classification: LCC PL721.S65 I58 2022  (print) | LCC PL721.S65  (ebook) | DDC 895.609/006--dc23/eng/20220112
LC record available at https://lccn.loc.gov/2021055709
LC ebook record available at https://lccn.loc.gov/2021055710

# Contents

Into the Fantastical Spaces of Contemporary Japanese Literature:
   An Introduction     1
   *Mina Qiao*

Chapter One: The Layered Everyspace in the Fiction of Murakami
   Haruki     15
   *Matthew C. Strecher*

Chapter Two: Shōjo, Mother, and the Uncanny Space in Ogawa
   Yōko's Writings     31
   *Mina Qiao*

Chapter Three: Textual, Liminal, Fantastical Spaces in Kanai
   Mieko's Early Writings     51
   *Anthony Bekirov*

Chapter Four: Cannibalistic Space and Reproduction in Japanese
   Speculative Fiction     71
   *Kazue Harada*

Chapter Five: Ports in a Storm: The Poetics of Space in Hino Keizō     95
   *Amanda C. Seaman*

Chapter Six: The Foreign Land outside Japan: An Attempted
   Solution to Abjection in Murakami Ryū's Fiction     115
   *Francesca Bianco*

Chapter Seven: The Fantastical Space of Exile in Tawada Yōko's
   *Memoirs of a Polar Bear*     137
   *Barbara Hartley*

Chapter Eight: Minding the Gap in Kawakami Hiromi     163
   *Mina Qiao and Matthew C. Strecher*

| | |
|---|---:|
| Index | 189 |
| Index of Works | 193 |
| About the Contributors | 195 |

# Into the Fantastical Spaces of Contemporary Japanese Literature: An Introduction

## Mina Qiao

"Is a snail without its shell homeless or naked?"

This joke popped up during a recent classroom discussion of Ogawa Yōko's "Danjiki katatsumuri" (2013; "The Fasting Snails"). The short story features an unnamed female narrator's travels between a secluded "starvation treatment" hospital and her spiritual lighthouse, a windmill where the isolated attendant keeps colonies of pet snails.[1] The humor comes from the absurdity of the mental imagery, but also because it destabilizes the relationship between space and body. Our perception of space cannot be divorced from the physical sensations or an awareness of the body, and thus our definition of self-identity. The question then becomes, "Is a snail without its shell still a snail?" The image helps us visualize the sociopsychological distance between the physical space we inhabit to the core of the self—in other words, from our identities to our *ibasho* (Japanese notion for a place of belongingness). In "Fasting Snails," the windmill is a physical manifestation of the narrator's desires for food (and by extension, sex), which has been oppressed by the hospital. As she climbs the staircase leading up to the windmill, she gradually awakens to her own body and its cravings. Ogawa's short story incorporates the exploration of space and embodied cognition and typifies a broader tendency among her generation of Japanese writers: namely, the dissolving margins between the fantastical space and the fantastical body.

Japan has a long textual history of connecting space to the body. Indeed, there can be no sense of space before the self-cognition of the body and its functions: only formlessness and chaos. In the Japanese creation myth described in the *Kojiki*, the archipelago was born from the female deity's body as a result of sexual intercourse:[2]

Izanagi asked his spouse Izanami, "How is your body formed?" She replied, "My body, formed though it be formed, has one place that is formed insufficiently." Then Izanagi said, "My body, formed though it may be formed, has one place that is formed to excess. Therefore, I thought I would like to take that place in my body that is formed to excess and insert it into that place in your body that is formed insufficiently and give birth to the land. How would this be?" Izanami replied, "This would be good."[3]

In this traditional cosmology, the origin point of space is regarded as a literal extension of the body. The association of body, spirit, and nature in premodern Japanese aesthetics is central to the evolution of haiku, tanka, and fiction (e.g., *The Tale of Genji*).

Modernity presented the first epistemological challenge to this understanding of contiguity between self and space. According to Karatani Kōjin, the Meiji period saw a "perspectival inversion" among artists, leading to a new distinction between landscape and interiority.[4] As Karatani puts it:

> Landscapes, [. . .] which seem to exist before our very eyes were only discovered as "landscapes" in the third decade of the Meiji period by writers whose "interiority" rejected what up until then had been the external world. Since this time, landscape has been perceived as what exists objectively, while realism has been seen, either as the tracing of that objective existence or as the capturing of a landscape, which is even more "real." Yet there was a time when "landscape" did not exist, and its discovery was predicated on an inversion.[5]

Modernity collapsed the boundaries of the self to the individual corporeal unit. Under modernity, the thinking-feeling self no longer extends into the natural world. The written language reforms of the *genbun itchi* movement, the wave of Naturalism, and the popularity of the confessional genre "I-novel" abandoned affection and adornment in literary expression and encouraged writers to look inward as part of the project of modernizing Japan.[6] Put another way, modernization cultivated a newfound sense of inner self vis-à-vis external space.

Changing understanding of the self calls for a shift in the literary representations of space. For Japan's modern novelists, this was related to urbanization providing a new and distinct form of external space as well as unprecedented lifestyles. As Maeda Ai and many subsequent researchers have observed, this accentuation of urban space relates to the expression of modern selfhood.[7] The Japanese flaneurs roam about in the cities and commit their encounters and adventures to paper. In their writings, their psyches often correspond with the cityscape. The spaces of Akutagawa Ryūnosuke's Shanghai, Mori Ōgai's Berlin, Natsume Sōseki's Tokyo, and Tanizaki Jun'ichirō's Osaka all stem from the authors' keen observations and lived experiences, and in turn, speak for their minds.

In the postwar period, we see a shift from the naturalism that predominated modern literature to science fiction, surrealism, and magical realism. Equivocal and Kafkaesque spaces emerge in the allegorical narratives by Abe Kōbō, Kanai Mieko, and Kurahashi Yumiko. These writers continue to participate in the tradition, deploying space as a means to delineate the modern self, while making use of fantastical elements to expand the imaginative boundaries of space and identity. These fantastical spaces manifest the experiences and sensations of postmodern Japan—the enduring impact of the collapse of the economic bubble, and the Aum Shinrikyo incident, as well as the anxiety resulting from present-day political and economic circumstances. As John Treat writes, "The dissociation we witnessed in so much of everyday life in Japan at the millennium may be the consequence of the shattering of the integral, solitary self before the onslaught of a post-post-industrial capitalism, its nature is unknown to us and thus traumatic."[8] Japanese writers collectively envision this sociocultural trauma in fantastical landscapes, with Murakami Haruki as the best known exponent.

Murakami emerged in the aftermath of the 1960s–1970s student movement to become one of the most significant figures in contemporary world fiction, thanks in large part to his fantastical approach to space.[9] Against naturalistic representations of urban and suburban spaces, Murakami ventures into abstract worlds to voice his own generation's ambivalence and sense of loss, interrupting otherwise realistic narratives with magical and supernatural elements.[10] In his representations, the everyday world and non-everyday world form an allegorical parallel to one another. Through the creation of what Matthew Strecher terms the "metaphysical realm," Murakami's works create spaces for discussions of war, human nature, memory, and trauma that are excluded from mainstream discourse.[11] Murakami's career has witnessed the economic growth and student movements in the 1960s–1970s, the consumerist fever in the 1980s, the recession in the 1990s, the "age of religion" (Miyadai Shinji's term) around the turn of the century, and the parade of both natural and human-made calamities from the Kōbe earthquake and Aum subway sarin attack of 1995 to the 3/11 triple disaster in 2011 that have shaken Japanese people's faith in narratives of linear progress.[12] His protagonist, often a male narrator "*Boku*" (Japanese male pronoun for "I"), travels to the metaphysical realm for a solitary quest for identity and answers. These motifs of self-discovery amidst contemporary social maladies occurring in fantastical spaces are regarded as a Murakami trademark.[13] It is not, however, his exclusive domain.

Given the long history we have observed of porous boundaries between self and space in Japanese fiction, we see similar techniques are at play in the fiction of contemporaries such as Ogawa Yōko, Murakami Ryū, Murata Sayaka, Tawada Yōko, and Kawakami Hiromi to name just a few. All these writers have crafted narratives with fantastical spaces that are intellectually challenging and culturally significant, forming a profound part of the contemporary Japanese corpus. Contemporary women writers seem to exhibit a particular affinity for fantastic spaces. We observe an emergent feminine sensibility across fantastical works produced across many cultures. Existing scholarships of contemporary Western women's literature, represented by Angela Carter and Margaret Atwood, regard fantasy as a vehicle for transgression.[14] Fantasy is a blunt-force weapon against a canon dominated by naturalism because, as Rosemary Jackson has it, "No breakthrough of cultural structure seems possible until linear narrative (realism, illusionism, transparent representation) is broken or dissolved."[15] Fantasy overturns the social orders "experienced as oppressive and insufficient," according to Jackson, giving rise to its subversive potential.[16]

The fantastic mode challenges reality as a socially and culturally constructed notion.[17] It disrupts the discourses of authority/subject, collective/individual, and masculine/feminine, revealing the patterns of accepted reality as socially and culturally constructed. The fantastic thus threatens to defang the dominant ideologies of everyday life, offering it a particular appeal to writers of marginalized backgrounds.

Susan Napier's *The Fantastic in Modern Japanese Literature* forms the foundation for the theoretical framework of the following collective study.[18] Napier examines the fantastic through a range of formulations, beginning with fantasy as a wish-fulfillment device and an instrument of control, functioning primarily to offer an escape from reality.[19] Adopting Jackson's theorization, she asserts that fantasy is "a literature of subversion."[20] In the context of Japanese modern literature, fantasy serves as a counterdiscourse to narratives of modernity.[21] Tracing the lineage of Meiji and Taishō writers such as Tanizaki and Sōseki through to contemporary authors like Murakami, Napier argues that fantasy is a literary coping mechanism for the fear and anxiety provoked by rapid social change.[22] Furthermore, Napier agrees with Jackson that fantasy sheds light on the aspects marginalized and hidden by the dominant culture: "[T]he fantastic traces the unsaid and the unseen of culture: that which has been silenced, made invisible, covered over and made 'absent.'"[23] Such narratives of un-covering and un-silencing are abundant in Japan's imaginary of the fantastic. For instance, Murakami Haruki and Ogawa Yōko's fictions are united by the presence of entities that are silent, invisible, and absent from the everyday. These common features are neither coincidental nor trivial.

This volume examines a representative selection of contemporary Japanese writers and their use of fantastical spaces. Such spaces grant them access to phenomena occluded from everyday life, including the geographically peripheral, the culturally marginalized, the psychologically liminal, and the physically intangible. Fantastical spaces are by their nature beyond the access of the embodied sensory apparatus: hidden, secluded, guarded, with both ethereal and labyrinthine qualities. They both resemble and yet vary from the everyday world we experience. Such settings resonate with the capacity of the fantastic mode to make visible unseen in culture, but also emphasizes on the boundaries and hence a contrast of two opposing dimensions. Once accessed, the fantastical space both resembles and deviates from the experience of the everyday world. They can be a den in Kanai Mieko's "Usagi" (1972; "Rabbits"), a cave in Murakami Haruki's *Kishi danchō goroshi* (2017; *Killing Commendatore*), an island in Ogawa Yōko's *Hoteru airisu* (1996; *Hotel Iris*), or a made-up town never that existed on any map in Murakami Ryū's *Koinrokkā beibīzu* (1980; *Coin Locker Babies*). In each case, the place is removed from the everyday understanding of *topos*. In many works, the fantastical space appears to be a distorted mirror image of reality, because fantasy is the characters' unfiltered perception of reality unmediated by rationality and consciousness. Plots in the fantastic mode develop as the characters cross the boundaries over to the other world, seeking answers found in between fantasy and reality, the unconscious and the conscious, the spiritual and the physical, the dead and the living, and so on.[24]

Encounters with fantastical space often further involve encounters with the beings, corporeal or otherwise, that inhabit and possess such realms. An otherwise mundane space is sometimes rendered fantastical by mystic beings and happenings. The idea of parallel space or "otherworld" can also be found in Gabriel García Marquez, Jorge Luis Borges, and Umberto Eco. John Carey defines "otherworld" in Irish literature by anomalous patterns in both its inhabitants and itself: "A minimal designation for any place inhabited by supernatural beings and its exhibiting supernatural characteristics."[25] At other times, the enchanted beings engender the otherwise regular space as fantastical. Approaching the fantastical in medieval narratives, Lorraine Daston and Katharine Park center their inquiries on the rare and extraordinary beings, termed as "wonders."[26] "Wonder and wonders," they write, "have risen to prominence on a wave of suspicion and self-doubt concerning the standards and sensibilities that had long excluded them (and much else) from respectable intellectual endeavors."[27] They are oddities and marvels, the deviation of normalcy.[28] They are not only different, but socially, politically, and aesthetically challenging.[29] The corpus and the site they occupy are connected over their singularity, which signifies an attempt to bring into light issues beyond the scope of mundane affairs.

For the purposes of discussion, we exclude the *iyashi-kei* ("healing") genre of fantasy from our definition of the fantastic because its fantastical for escapist purposes, even though extramundane are often reactionary rather than subversive. Whether it be gravity, the flow of time, or spatial distance, *iyashi* narratives of magical spaces defy laws of nature rather than the ones of society, and thereby do not constitute the fantastic in the sense we wish to explore. The last decade has seen some employment of magical space in Japanese narratives for the purpose of "healing." It is a second wave succeeding the 1990s *iyashi* boom, which refers to the popularization of various goods and services to relieve stress and provide emotional support. Both Murakami Haruki and Yoshimoto Banana have produced works that are considered "healing."[30] The 1990s boom is said to be a marketing response to the dual national traumas of 1995 (i.e., Kōbe earthquake and subway sarin attack).[31] The 2010s *iyashi*, by the same token, answers the societal need for solace and comfort after the 3/11 triple disaster. Award-winning examples include Higashino Keigo's *Namiya zakkaten no kiseki* (2012; *The Miracles of the Namiya General Store)* adapted to cinema twice and Kawaguchi Toshikazu's play-turned-fiction *Kōhī ga samenai uchini* (2015; *Before the Coffee Gets Cold*). Both the Namiya general store in *Namiya* and the Café Furikuri Furikura in *Coffee* allow time travel, realizing cosmic ordering for characters to achieve redemption or reconciliation at a second chance. However, unlike the fantastical space, these sites with magical powers are not a stage for characters to interact with, but rather a transport to the past for a revisit. The essential differentiation lies in the development of narratives. The journeys are supernatural, but the protagonists are still largely subjected to the rules of modern society. Absent the heroes' battle with suppressed subconsciousness and reconstruction of identities, such narratives of magical space often unfold under a mainstream framework that poses no threat to conventional values.

For the same reason, we also exclude from our discussion the representations of magical realms in manga-adjacent light novels (LN), typified by series such as Sōdo Āto Onrain (2009; Sword Art Online) by Kawahara Reki. Following the paradigm of LN fiction that teenage protagonists often take a leap into *isekai* (lit. "other world") for adventure, the hero of Sword Art Online crosses into virtual reality and has to clear all the levels in a floating castle in order to return to his life. Yet the story that takes place in a different dimension of reality, reinforces reactionary values only by enacting casual sexism in its patriarchal context.[32] The "lightness" of the genre connotes that it is unlikely to challenge any convention or initiate any discourse. The *isekai* of such fiction, therefore, differs significantly from the *isekai* found in Kanai Mieko and Ogawa Yōko's spaces of alienation and many of the similar *topos* we will see in this volume. The former defangs the subversive power of fantasy, while the latter thrives to destabilize the existing norms.

If extramundane elements do not constitute fantastic spaces in isolation, how are we to distinguish fantastic spaces from their *iyashi-kei* and *isekai* cousins? Tzvetan Todorov locates fantasy in the unresolved tension between the rational and the magical interpretations of the happenings.[33] Once the narratives turn to a magical space, which is "completely separated from 'our' reality," the uncertainty is eliminated, defusing any potential criticism and dissent the work may attempt at.[34] Building on this observation, Rebecca Suter identifies the essence of fantasy as the deliberate void of logical justification, rational explanation, and hence reassurance in the narratives.[35] The "fantastic hesitation," to use Todorov's term, endows "a spirit of critical inquiry, a questioning mindset" unique to the fantastic mode.[36]

In other words, the production of fantastical space must be a cognitive process of resisting the status quo. To quote Marcuse:

> Phantasy plays a most decisive function in the total mental structure: it links the deepest layers of the unconscious with the highest products of consciousness (art), the dream with the reality; it preserves the archetypes of the genus, the perpetual but repressed ideas of the collective and individual memory, the tabooed images of freedom.[37]

Fantastical spaces are landscapes of dreams and memories, manifestations of bodily sensations and mental states, and paths into the deepest layers of self. The authors employ fantastical spaces as portals for their inner voice. Fantastic spaces may act as manifestations of characters' psychological states as well as extensions of their embodied perceptions. They may transgress the material to allow novelty in the literary discussion of the human psyche and conditions in other contexts. This volume will illustrate the ubiquity and interrogate the function of such fantastical spaces in contemporary Japanese literature.

Our study commences with Murakami Haruki, an author celebrated for his literary command of fantastical spaces. In a study spanning Murakami's body of work to date, Matthew Strecher proposes that in such spaces, time, instead of advancing in a linear manner and creating spaces as it advances, piles up on top of its origin point. The layered temporalities are experienced as a unified "Now," generating a multivalent topography that Strecher terms "Everyspace." Murakami's heroes adventure into the labyrinth where the past meets the present, and even the future, and all space becomes Everyspace. The Everyspace collapses not only linear time, but "all things [e.g., the physical and the metaphysical, the real and the hyperreal, the conscious and the unconscious, the magical and the mundane] are merged into a unified singularity, where there can be neither contradiction nor conflict." In the death-rebirth matrix of Murakami's Everyspace, reduction to nonduality offers individuals a chance to reconstitute their identity outside normative systems of meaning. Its temporal dislocation subverts our understanding of historical and personal events because our understandings are previously based on a linear temporal-spatial approach. The technique of displacing fixed spatial identities instigates a philosophical quest for an alternative approach to history, identity, and reality.

Such subversive imaginal spaces created through nonlinear temporalities can also be found in Ogawa Yōko's writing. In her early works, young female protagonists often revisit places connected to their past that are familiar yet strange. Mina Qiao maps these spaces using Barbara Creed's theorization of the female uncanny, exploring the maternal imagery in these narratives. The uncanny is the return of the once repressed, and in this case, the Symbolic Mother, "with which everything begins and ends." Ogawa's characters are under the threat of identity-disturbing motherhood as their past shōjohood (a sociopsychological state that negates the logic of reproduction) will be replaced by the predicted motherhood in the near future. In the light of the politics of nostalgia, the protagonists' wish to prolong their shōjohood is a rebellion against time, history, and social norms. In other words, the uncanny space engages characters' resistance to a dominant discourse of social maturation and identity centered on reproduction. Places of their past—that is, the symbolic childhood home—force them to confront their place in a system of motherhood amid their own ambivalence towards it. The fantastical spatiality also functions as a mirror image of the female body in change, visualizing both the mental and the corporeal. The exploration of such "forbidden" space articulates young women's sociopsychological status in contemporary Japan.

In the subsequent chapter, Anthony Bekirov examines the fantastical space in Kanai Mieko's early fiction, identifying its challenges to traditional perceptions of not only space and time, but also writing, and authorship/readership. Considered one of the crucial voices of Japan's literary avant-garde in the 1960s, Kanai is known for her experimental style and unreliable first-person narrators. The reader is led to shifting, uncertain textual spaces created from fantasies, memories, and distorted realities filtered through unsound minds and limited perspectives. The onus falls upon the reader to navigate the world presented. However, to fixate on placing the events and actions in the story-world into linear systems of cause-and-effect, as one may for a whodunit mystery, would be missing the point. Kanai involves the reader as an active coconspirator in the production of the text. The writing process begins when we turn the pages. Through metanarrative techniques such as her notion of the "corporeal text" (*nikutaiteki na kotoba*), Kanai involves the readers and their bodies in the process of literary meaning-making. Thus, while the fantastic motif of temporal-spatial collapse is a common feature to both Murakami and Ogawa, Kanai's metanarrative textuality represents a far more aggressive challenge to understandings of space and the body vis-à-vis the reader.

In comparison to the above-mentioned authors, the fantastical elements at work in Murata Sayaka and Ono Miyuki's speculative fiction sends a stronger sociopolitical message. Their characters' counterdiscourse of natalism through the celebration of its opposite—resisting reproduction through anthropophagy. Kazue Harada studies how the motif of cannibalism establishes a site of resistance to the conformist heteronormativity of Japanese society in these works. Their socially and spatially alienated characters renounce social norms by relishing in cannibalism as a celebration of what is defined as an uncivilized and primitive use of the body by the natalist mainstream. Whether in the rural spaces of Murata or the futuristic world in Ono, it is the construction of fantastical spaces that overturns the regime. For their marginalized characters, the displacement from the everyday setting provides a means of escaping from social control of bodies, even temporarily.

The body's relationship to space is also pivotal in Hino Keizō's writing on illness. Amanda Seaman walks us through Hino's literary journey of battling with affliction while struggling to make sense of his surroundings. The shadow of death renders the once familiar urban space of Tokyo unrecognizable to the narrator's eyes when he learns about his cancer. As his physical body is in peril, his perception of space is altered and his relationship to space is destabilized. The landmark Tokyo Tower serves as an anchor from his cognition and reality, allowing him to regain himself and reintegrate himself with the world around him. Urban space in Hino's writing is both matter and metaphor: tangible as a concrete physical entity, and intangible as an emergent phenomenon of individual emotions, memories, and consciousness. Hino's writing, again, attests to how spatial are both extension of and incursion into the body and mind.

Taking a turn to the outlandish fantastical space in literature, we have Francesca Bianco examining the illusions of foreign lands in Murakami Ryū's fiction. Murakami configures Tokyo as a site of social malaise, the source of evil and degradation, the source of characters' fury and trauma, and therefore the target of destruction. Their complicated love-hate emotions toward Japan suggest the characters' Kristevian "abjection of self." They turn to form exotic places in their fantasies, which become their salvation, a spiritual mecca to remove their Japanese identities and to constitute alternative ones. However, their attempts end in vain because they have failed to annihilate Tokyo, or the Japanese identity rooted so deeply in themselves, and the abjection of self remains unsolved. The self-imposed exile from the homeland as well as the idealization of the foreign deploys a postmodern cultural critique of the Self and the Other.

The theme of exile is central to Barbara Hartley's understanding of Tawada Yōko's 2011 novel *Yuki no renshūsei* (*Memoirs of a Polar Bear*), a collection of life stories narrated by three generations of bears. Tawada utilizes the motif of exile to expose the modern structure that controls and alienates "outsiders." This spatial practice also has the power of destabilizing the divisions in political, ideological, and linguistic terms, to a point in the narrative a human and a bear can understand each other's words. Through practices of narrating/writing, the narrators (and Tawada) resist hegemonic cultural narratives. The discourse of exile forces us to consider what and who is excluded from systems of language and meaning, and boundaries of the notion of the human. As Hartley notes, "Exile offers opportunities that can never be accessed when enlightenment boundaries remain intact." Like many of the abovementioned writers, Tawada questions the status quo radically through the employment of fantastical space.

We end this magical voyage with Mina Qiao and Matthew Strecher's discussion of Kawakami Hiromi. Kawakami unifies elements of the fantastic mode found in Tawada Yōko, Ogawa Yōko, and Murakami Haruki, but is distinct in her creation of a strange detachment in her characters and a void that haunts the reader. Her use of the fantastic gestures toward the retrieval of a lost or hidden cultural past, but only to find that "We are inexorably being divorced from the historical, mythical, and spiritual roots." In the anthropocentric postmodern society, we find ourselves caught in a gap between the magical and everyday worlds where our beliefs are adrift, our identities interchangeable, our traditions lost, and our connection with nature severed. Especially after 3/11, Kawakami enquires with her stories, where is humanity rushing to?

With this in mind, let us take a break from reality, from the advancement of society, from the rules that ground us to the logic of the postindustrial economy. The characters in these writers' fiction exchange the benefits of modern capitalism for fantastical worlds of instability where meanings and boundaries dissolve. The fantastical allows us to rediscover the true spirit of adventure and rebellion. The studies collected in this volume give voice to this vital role played by fantastical spaces as a locus of resistance in postmodern literature.

## NOTES

1. Ogawa Yōko, "Danjiki katatsumuri," in *Itsumo karera wa dokoka ni* (Tokyo: Shinchōsha, 2013).

2. *Kojiki* (Tokyo: Kadokawa shoten, 1956).

3. *Traditional Japanese Literature: An Anthology, Beginnings to 1600* (New York: Columbia University Press, 2012), Ed. Shirane Haruo, 16.

4. Karatani Kōjin, *Origins of Modern Japanese Literature*, trans. Brett de Bary, (New York: Duke, 1993), 27.

5. Ibid., 115.

6. Massimiliano Tomasi, *Rhetoric in Modern Japan: Western Influences on the Development of Narrative and Oratorical Style* (Honolulu: University of Hawai'i Press, 2004).

7. Maeda Ai, *Genkei no machi: bungaku no toshi wo aruku* (Tokyo: Shōgakukan, 1986). Maeda Ai, *Toshi kūkan no naka no bungaku* (Tokyo: Chikuma shobō, 1982).

8. John Whittier Treat, "Murakami Haruki and the Cultural Materialism of Multiple Personality Disorder," *Japan Forum* 25, no. 1 (2013), 106.

9. Matthew C. Strecher, "Magical Realism and the Search for Identity in the Fiction of Murakami Haruki," *The Journal of Japanese Studies* 25, no. 2 (1999), 263–298.

10. Ibid., 267.

11. Matthew C. Strecher, *The Forbidden Worlds of Haruki Murakami* (Minneapolis: University of Minnesota Press, 2014).

12. Miyadai Shinji, "Transformation of Semantics in the History of Japanese Subcultures since 1992," trans. Kōno Shion, introduction by Thomas Lamarre, in *Mechademia 6: User Enhanced*, eds. Frenchy Lunning et al. (Minneapolis: University of Minnesota Press, 2011), 231–258.

13. Strecher, *The Forbidden Worlds of Haruki Murakami*.

14. Lucie Armitt, *Contemporary Women's Fiction and the Fantastic* (New York: St. Martin's Press, 2000). Danielle Hipkins, *Contemporary Italian Women Writers and Traces of the Fantastic: The Creation of Literary Space* (London: Legenda, 2007), 2.

15. Rosemary Jackson, *Fantasy: The Literature of Subversion* (London: Methuen, 1981), 186.

16. Ibid., 180.

17. Idib., 52.

18. Susan Napier, *The Fantastic in Modern Japanese Literature* (London: Routledge, 1996).

19. Ibid., 6.

20. Ibid., 8.

21. Ibid.

22. Ibid.

23. Jackson, *Fantasy*, 4, quoted in Napier, *The Fantastic in Modern Japanese Literature*, 8.

24. Strecher has explored the fantastical setting in Murakami in a series of works. He first proposes the binaristic characteristics of the two worlds in "Magical Realism and the Search for Identity in the Fiction of Murakami Haruki," 268.

25. John Carey, "Time, Space, and the Otherworld," *Proceeding of the Harvard Celtic Colloquium* 7 (1987), 1.

26. Lorraine Daston and Katharine Park, *Wonders and the Order of Nature, 1150–1750* (Cambridge, MA: MIT Press, 1998).

27. Daston and Park, *Wonders and the Order of Nature*, 10.

28. Ibid.

29. Aisling Byrne, *Otherworlds: Fantasy and History in Medieval Literature* (Oxford: Oxford University Press, 2015).

30. Paul Roquet, "Ambient Literature and the Aesthetics of Calm: Mood Regulation in Contemporary Japanese Fiction," *The Journal of Japanese Studies* 35, no.1, (Winter 2009) 87–111, 90.

31. Roquet, "Ambient Literature and the Aesthetics of Calm," 89.

32. In her academic blog, Japanese studies researcher Kathryn Hemmann reviews the first book of the series and points to the sexism in its representations. For example, the female main character Asuna is portrayed in a supporting role for the hero's adventures and objectified for his romantic fantasies. https://japaneselit.net/tag/young-adult-fiction/ (June 28, 2014).

33. Tzvetan Todorov, *The Fantastic: A Structural Approach to a Literary Genre*, trans. Richard Howard (Ithaca, NY: Cornell University Press, 1975).

34. Rebecca Suter, "Critical Engagement through Fantasy in Hard-boiled Wonderland and The End of the World," *Haruki Murakami: Challenging Authors*, eds. Matthew C. Strecher and Paul Thomas (Rotterdam: Sense, 2016), 61.

35. Ibid.

36. Ibid.

37. Herbert Marcuse, *Eros and Civilization: A Philosophical Inquiry into Freud* (Boston: Beacon 1966 [1955]), 141.

## WORKS CITED

Armitt, Lucie. *Contemporary Women's Fiction and the Fantastic*. New York: St. Martin's Press, 2000.

Byrne, Aisling. *Otherworlds: Fantasy and History in Medieval Literature*. Oxford: Oxford University Press, 2015.

Carey, John. "Time, Space, and the Otherworld." *Proceeding of the Harvard Celtic Colloquium* 7 (1987): 1–27.

Daston, Lorraine and Park, Katharine. *Wonders and the Order of Nature, 1150–1750*. Cambridge, MA: MIT Press, 1998.

Hipkins, Danielle. *Contemporary Italian Women Writers and Traces of the Fantastic: The Creation of Literary Space*. London: Legenda, 2007.

Jackson, Rosemary. *Fantasy: The Literature of Subversion*. London: Methuen, 1981.

Karatani, Kōjin. *Origins of Modern Japanese Literature*. Translated by Brett de Bary. Durham, NC: Duke University Press. 1993.

Maeda, Ai. *Toshi kūkan no naka no bungaku*. Tokyo: Chikuma shobō, 1982.

———. *Genkei no machi: bungaku no toshi wo aruku*. Tokyo: Shōgakukan, 1986.

Marcuse, Herbert. *Eros and Civilization: A Philosophical Inquiry into Freud*. Boston: Beacon 1966 [1955].

Miyadai, Shinji. "Transformation of Semantics in the History of Japanese Subcultures since 1992." Translated by Kōno Shion, introduction by Thomas Lamarre. In *Mechademia 6: User Enhanced*, eds. Frenchy Lunning et al. Minneapolis: University of Minnesota Press, 2011. 231–258.

Napier, Susan. *The Fantastic in Modern Japanese Literature*. London: Routledge, 1996.

No author. *Kojiki*. Tokyo: Kadokawa shoten, 1956.

Roquet, Paul. "Ambient Literature and the Aesthetics of Calm: Mood Regulation in Contemporary Japanese Fiction." *The Journal of Japanese Studies* 35, no.1 (2009): 87–111.

Shirane Haruo. Ed. *Traditional Japanese Literature: An Anthology, Beginnings to 1600*. New York: Columbia University Press, 2012.

Strecher, Matthew C. "Magical Realism and the Search for Identity in the Fiction of Murakami Haruki." *The Journal of Japanese Studies* 25, no. 2 (1999): 263–298.

———. *The Forbidden Worlds of Haruki Murakami*. Minneapolis: University of Minnesota Press, 2014.

Suter, Rebecca. "Critical Engagement through Fantasy in Hard-boiled Wonderland and The End of the World." In *Haruki Murakami: Challenging Authors*, eds. Matthew C. Strecher and Paul Thomas. Rotterdam: Sense, 2016, 59–72.

Todorov, Tzvetan. *The Fantastic: A Structural Approach to a Literary Genre*. Translated by Richard Howard. Ithaca, NY: Cornell University Press, 1975.

Tomasi, Massimiliano. *Rhetoric in Modern Japan: Western Influences on the Development of Narrative and Oratorical Style*. Honolulu: University of Hawai'i Press, 2004.

Treat, John Whittier. "Murakami Haruki and the Cultural Materialism of Multiple Personality Disorder." *Japan Forum* 25, no. 1 (2013): 87–111.

*Chapter One*

# The Layered Everyspace in the Fiction of Murakami Haruki

## Matthew C. Strecher

### INTRODUCTION: WHAT IS THE EVERYSPACE?

Let us begin by imagining a transparent sheet of plastic, upon which is imprinted an image of some kind. Then imagine another, almost the same, and another, until we have accumulated many. Then, let us imagine these transparent sheets, layered one atop another, until we have formed a kind of cube. If we look at the image from the top, with sufficient light to see through them, we should see something like a three-dimensional picture that extends beyond the surface sheet into the depths of the cube. Now, let us imagine that we have also inscribed the image along the edges of the transparent sheets, so that we have a side view of the image as well. It will thus resemble something like an archaeologist's "dig."

This is how we might envision Murakami Haruki's (b. 1949) use of a literary space that we will, here, call the Everyspace. The point of the metaphor is to suggest an alternative to the usual "parallel worlds" or "dual worlds" model that has been propounded by many scholars, including myself, and to suggest something a bit more fluid that allows for both presence and absence, for whether a given scene takes place in the physical or the metaphysical realm, so to speak, it is always connected to the whole structure, which includes both the physical and the metaphysical. The model is also useful in that it allows for interaction between the two modes of consciousness, though one with puzzling chains of causality; it rains in the metaphysical realm, and a butterfly lights up a joint and starts a punk band in Outer Mongolia.

The metaphor is even more useful for the "layering" it offers, if we can think of each transparency sheet as a slice of time, an epoch. The location remains the same, but we see through the layers of time here, like a time-lapse filmstrip in which we watch that same punked-out butterfly emerging from its larval cocoon. This is a handy way of looking at history in Murakami fiction, because it allows us to view history not at the wrong end of an ever lengthening timeline, but from straight above, "the past" situated just beneath the present, like one of those maps that superimposes seventeenth century Edo on top of the present city of Tokyo.

But this is not merely an exercise in perspective; it is an acknowledgment that "past" and "present" (and very likely "future") are not distinct points in the Murakami fictional universe, but simultaneities, coexistent, constantly and endlessly occurring all at once, only on different layers of the four-dimensional grand matrix of time and space. One does not move forward or backward in Murakami's version of time and space, but up, down, sideways, diagonally, virtually any direction at all, to arrive at a point that may be directly beneath another, yet light years away. It is fitting that Murakami's protagonists so frequently change locations not laterally but vertically: down an elevator shaft, or a dry well, or by clambering through a hole in the floor. (Yet we note the predominantly *downward* motion, which seems to be the pathway to the past; Murakami characters seldom climb *upward*.)

They are not simply climbing "down" into past time, but also into another spatial realm, one that grows both larger and smaller as they descend. Okada Tōru, in *Nejimakidori kuronikuru* (1994–1995; *The Wind-Up Bird Chronicle*) climbs down a dry well, and eventually finds himself in an enormous, labyrinthine hotel; the eponymous Tamura Kafka from *Umibe no Kafuka* (2002; *Kafka On the Shore*) passes through a tiny one-room cabin in the mountains of Shikoku and finds himself lost in an ever-expanding forest that shelters fugitives from earlier times, including a pair of Imperial Japanese Army deserters, unchanged since the day they fled into the forest six decades before.

What is this labyrinth into which the Murakami hero descends, confronting themself along the way? It is the "Everyspace," a metaphysical zone in which the temporal and spatial constraints of the physical world are suspended, as noted above, and all space and time are gathered together into a unified singularity. We might imagine this Everyspace to be akin to Plato's *kósmos noetós*, the realm of forms, a state more of mind and consciousness than of space that is posited in the *Politeia*. We ought not think of a place—this is not heaven—so much as of a mental or intellectual connection with what Archimedes called the *archē*, origins. The Everyspace is a memory, or rather, *all* memories, of the origins of what we see and know in the physical world. The objects and persons and events that surround us in the physical, everyday world have their singular origins—their *archē*—in this metaphysical realm, archetypal forms that give meaning and sense to those physical objects. We could liken it to the way that paper money derives its value and meaning from a vast store of gold. We imagine the paper dollars we carry to have value, and they do within the exchange economy in which we function, but really, they represent something else that is believed to have an intrinsic value that a scrap of paper, finally, does not. The paper is a symbol, a copy, or an imitation, of the gold on which it is grounded.

Yet this is an imperfect metaphor, because the gold from which paper money derives its value is itself valuable only because value has been imposed upon it. Gold itself (or diamonds, or coal) is grounded in a less arbitrary archetype of "exchange value." And it is in the realm of thought that the concept—the *eidos*—of exchange value exists and has always existed, since primitive man first exchanged a flint axe head for a cut of meat. That conceptual realm is the Everyspace, and this is where Murakami's protagonists carry out their quests.

Plato's *kósmos noetós* has taken on a modern twist in C. G. Jung's idea of the collective unconscious (*das kollektive Unbewusste*), wherein live numberless archetypes: unchanging figures (mother, wise man, God, trickster), events (birth, initiation, graduation, death), and motifs (the big bang, the apocalypse) that ground and give meaning to all that we encounter in the everyday world. Jung argued that we activate these archetypes as we move through life, understanding intuitively what we encounter through the experiences of our primordial ancestors.[1]

Murakami's Everyspace shares the qualities of both the collective unconscious and the *kósmos noetós*; his heroes and heroines travel through layerings of experience, of unbound time and space, to locate in this four-dimensional space the entities they require to answer the central questions in their lives, from specifics like "why did my best friend commit suicide?" to questions more common to us all: "why am I here?" and "what does my life mean?"

It is, generally, not a comfortable journey; the protagonist of *1973-nen no pinbōru* and *Hitsuji o meguru bōken* passes through unnerving, surrealistic landscapes to reach a world that is cold, dark, and solitary. The narrator of the "end of the world" sequences in *Sekai no owari to hādo-boirudo wandārando* has his shadow sliced away from his body as a condition to entry. Okada Tōru, as noted above, must sit for hours or even days in the pitch darkness at the bottom of a dry well in *Nejimakidori kuronikuru*. Tamura Kafka forces his way through a forest that seems to be watching him with disapproval and hostility in *Umibe no Kafuka*. Aomame Masami makes a precarious descent (sensibly removing her heels!) down an escape stairway from one of Tokyo's elevated expressways to find herself in the strange world of "1Q84." Tazaki Tsukuru journeys through a labyrinth of roads and paths to find an old friend in a secluded cabin in rural Finland in *Shikisai o motanai Tazaki Tsukuru to, kare no junrei no toshi*. And the nameless narrator of *Kishidanchō-goroshi* enters what appears to be Hades itself. All of these journeys are harrowing, signaling the symbolic death of the traveler, his transference from the world of the living to that of the dead. Once there, his companions, when he has them, are friends and loved ones who have died or disappeared; but they are also archetypal figures who represent events belonging both to the hero's past, and to the collective past of his society.

We note, for instance, the narrator's final meeting with his friend, known only as Nezumi ("Rat"), who has already committed suicide, at the end of *Hitsuji o meguru bōken*. What does Nezumi's death mean to the hero? Obviously, the loss of the friends of his youth, and by extension, his own youth. Collectively, Nezumi symbolizes the death of youthful idealism in the generation that came of age in the late 1960s. We might also consider the aforementioned meeting between the fifteen-year-old Tamura Kafka and two Imperial Army deserters in the magical Shikoku forest in *Umibe no Kafuka*. To Kafka they are a reminder of the recurring violence he seeks to escape in his own life; to his collective society they represent the suppressed voice of resistance against a world war that most Japanese dared not oppose.

What we see, then, is a realm, or a mode of consciousness, in which temporal and spatial distinctions are suspended, allowing past and present to coexist, the dead to mingle with the living. For this reason, the Everyspace is also a setting where the collective or universal merges with the individual and unique. As a peculiar by-product, its deployment also seems to diminish the gap between reader and narrative, which may be one reason so many readers feel as though Murakami's stories were written about themselves.

## THE EVERYSPACE AS UNCONSCIOUS SPACE

Naturally, the Everyspace allows for the intermingling of separate characters as well as spaces and times, meaning that one character may use the Everyspace to exchange places with another. The implications of such a mechanism are considerable, for it calls into question the connectivity of body and soul, or rather, it lays those two concepts before us in much the same way that the physical and metaphysical are laid before us: as symbiotic entities that complement one another, but which may also separate as the demands of the narrative require. Obviously, it also raises serious questions about the nature of identity itself, for if our body and soul—or more practically our body and mind—may be divorced from one another, then where does our core identity reside?

We first see this mechanism in action, arguably, in *Nejimakidori kuronikuru*, during one of the sexy dreams for which Murakami's texts are justifiably known. In this scene, Okada Tōru dreams that he is making love to his wife, Kumiko, who wears a blue dress. As she writhes atop him, he suddenly realizes that she is no longer Kumiko, but the self-described "prostitute of the mind" Kanō Creta, still wearing the same blue dress. And while this all takes place in a dream, Kanō Creta surprises Tōru by referring to their metaphysical lovemaking when they next meet in the waking world.

The same mechanism works to effect a switch between an individual's inner and outer (or conscious and unconscious) selves. Later in the same novel a young man called Cinnamon, son of Nutmeg, describes in a computer file how he came to be a mute: One night he dreamed that he saw someone out of his bedroom window burying a cloth bag—probably filled with the internal organs of his murdered father—and when he returned to his bed he found another Cinnamon already there. He forced his way into the bed alongside his doppelgänger, and upon waking the next morning—alone—discovered that he was mute. His body had remained the same vessel, but its contents had been exchanged, conscious self (which can speak) for unconscious self (which cannot speak).

At issue here is not merely the switching of the contents of the container, but the act of separating mind and body itself. As Tōru sits at the bottom of his dry well, "I try to separate from myself. Crouched in the darkness, I try to escape from this awkward body of mine. I am nothing but an empty house now, nothing more than a cast off well."[2] At length, his mind slips through the wall of the well and enters the Everyspace, here taking the form of a labyrinthine hotel.

Something very similar occurs in *Umibe no Kafuka*, in which the title character has fled from his father's home in Nakano Ward, Tokyo, in part to avoid fulfilling an Oedipal prophecy that he will murder his father and then reunite with his long-lost mother and sister and have sexual relations with them. On the night when his father actually is stabbed to death in Tokyo, Kafka, now hiding out in Takamatsu City on the island of Shikoku, awakens behind a Shintō shrine and is covered in fresh blood. The actual murder is accomplished by a mild-mannered, mentally impaired geriatric named Nakata, but by novel's end it is clear that Kafka's inner self, leaving his body behind in Shikoku, has passed through the Everyspace to inhabit Nakata's body, using it to hack Kafka's father to death.

The idea of mind-body separation receives it clearest expression, however, in the 2013 novel *Shikisai o motanai Tazaki Tsukuru to, kare no junrei no toshi*, expressed here by a young philosopher named Haida, who explains to the title character Tsukuru that in such separations lies the height of purity and thought. Without mentioning Plato, Haida is really extolling the virtue of the *kósmos noetós*:

To think freely about things is also to separate ourselves from the flesh we are crammed into. To escape from that limiting cage that is our flesh, to break free of our chains and take flight into pure reason. In reason lies the natural life. That's what is at the core of freedom of thought.[3]

Later that same night, Tsukuru has an erotic dream in which he is having sex with two girls who were his closest friends in high school. At the moment of ejaculation, however, the girls are suddenly replaced by Haida, who takes Tsukuru's penis into his mouth and accepts his semen. Afterward, Tsukuru cannot quite decide whether the last part was a dream, or if Haida had, perhaps in an astral form, actually fellated him.

Clearly, separation of mind from body is one key to joining with the Everyspace; it is also true, however, that while one appears to retain a sense of individual identity in the Everyspace, by its nature the Everyspace also absorbs that identity, merging the individual with itself until one is, finally, one with that space. The protagonist of the "End of the World" sequences in *Sekai no owari to hādo-boirudo wandārando* gradually forgets who he is, ultimately recognizing that the End of the World is himself: "'The wall is a wall that surrounds me, the river is a river running through me, the smoke is me burning.'"[4] The world he inhabits is not only of his own making, but actually *is* him. The same thing is revealed to Tamura Kafka, who is told by one resident at the heart of the metaphysical forest, "'Here we are all, every one of us, merging our selves together with this place.'"[5] This appears to be a process; the longer one spends in the Everyspace, the more completely "merged" one is likely to become. Perhaps this is why that same character urges Kafka to get out of this place as soon as possible; at fifteen, he is too young to give himself entirely to the Everyspace.

This is no easy feat, however, for the Everyspace has a powerful attraction about it. It is a realm in which differences are gradually erased, where all things are merged into a unified singularity, where there can be neither contradiction nor conflict. The narrator of the "End of the World" is told in warning tones by his now-severed shadow that the town in which they find themselves is "perfect," and indeed it appears to be so; yet such perfection, whether "natural" (in Haida's terms) or not, is the antithesis of the imperfections that make us all unique, and thereby meaningful. That is to say, we become who we are, as individuals, through our responses to conflict, through the things that cause us to stop and ask questions, to seek answers. We become who we are through our mistakes more than anything else. Pure thought is an ideal state, but our own imperfections make us incompatible with such ideals. Even Haida, we might surmise, eventually must return from his flights of pure thought back into the physical space of *actual living*. The alternative may be eternal life as part of the Everyspace, but it may not be actual living.

## HISTORY IN THE EVERYSPACE

One of the by-products of the temporal suspension of the Everyspace is that distinctions between "past," "present," and "future" are eliminated, leaving only what St. Augustine calls *aeternitas* in Book XI of his *Confessions*, and what I call "metaphysical Time" (differentiated using an uppercase "T"). Such a vision of Time is difficult to grasp in the physical world, for it lies beyond the convenient, but artificial, divisions of time that govern daily life. This is a Time that has neither beginning nor end, the very archetype of Time. Yet this is not to say that nothing ever happens in the Everyspace; rather, *everything* happens, simultaneously, yet distinctly, too. Stephen Hawking usefully ascribes to physical time the "increase of disorder or entropy,"[6] thus giving it a discernible direction, but this is not evident in metaphysical Time, wherein the simultaneity of all events means that nothing decays, for in a mode of existence that eliminates all contradiction, nothing needs to change.

What this means, in brief, is that "history" as we understand it, as a description of discrete events or conditions, cannot exist in the Everyspace; yet the archetypal groundings of history, too, are found in the Murakami Everyspace, which we usually come to know not from examining those archetypes themselves, but by the bursts of energy they release into our physical world, in the form of the peculiar figures that I have elsewhere called "nostalgic images."[7] That is to say, when the individual or psychic pressure of a particular archetypal event builds up beyond critical mass, it forces its way into the physical world in the form of a figure that has no business existing in our everyday world.

Such figures are unmistakable in their oddity: a pinball machine that talks; an angry, staccato-speaking, chain-smoking little man dressed in a sheep's costume, but with real horns and tail; a diminutive, archaic-speaking gentleman roughly the size of a garden gnome, who appears literally to have stepped out of a painting that depicts his murder; life-sized figures of "Colonel Sanders" and "Johnny Walker"; the pale image of a "poor aunt" perched on the back of a man, shape-shifting into whatever form will bring the most pathos to each individual viewer. On their own these figures, while playing significant roles in their narratives, make very little sense; in archetypal terms, however, they speak volumes.

The pinball machine, for instance, which turns up in *1973-nen no pinbōru*, is individually a surrogate for the lost love of the narrator, while on a wider scale she evokes the idea of "loss" or more specifically, "lost love." The Sheepman (*Hitsuji-otoko*) that turns up in both *Hitsuji o meguru bōken* and *Dansu dansu dansu*, represents for the narrator the object of his quest—his missing best friend—and more generally, the tension between power and self-control, and may be the cause of war since time immemorial. In *Umibe no Kafuka*, Johnny Walker (a "spirit" of chaos) precipitates the death of the title character's father, while in the same novel Colonel Sanders peddles a different kind of flesh—sex—in the streets of Takamatsu for one character, while more broadly evoking "excess" and "pleasure." Taken together, these two figures might be understood as the endless fluctuations, throughout time, of war and peace.

Within the Murakami text, then, the immense complexity, and the complex immensity, of historical events is frequently reduced in the most radical fashion to individual figures. From an historical perspective this can feel frustrating; are the major events of history—wars, revolutions, genocides—really reducible to these often absurd, even comical figures? In terms of the specific aspects of those events, the effect may be less than satisfying; from the readerly perspective, however, it can also be liberating. As the Everyspace lends its archetypal grounding to fictitious events occurring within the narrative, spewing out such archetypal figures, the reader is free to build upon that very generality—the universality—of the archetype, and to imagine freely whatever they wish. As the narrator weeps for his lost pinball machine/girlfriend, the reader is invited—almost required—to adapt the archetype into something more personal and thus meaningful. This is, admittedly, a reading strategy applicable to any text, a form of Reader Response, but deployment of the Everyspace, upon which is layered a series of specific narratives, effectively creates a third space in which readers are encouraged, through imaginative play with the aforementioned archetypal figures, to construct their own parallel narratives, specific and meaningful to themselves.

A simple example of this process will illustrate this point. In *Hitsuji o meguru bōken*, Murakami provides us with a shadowy right-wing figure known as Sensei (trans. as "the Boss"), a pair of free thinkers (the narrator and his best friend, Nezumi), and an open symbol in the form of an all-empowering magical sheep. Within the novel's world the sheep inhabits its host like a parasite, replacing that individual's consciousness with its own in order to exert its controlling influence over the entire political structure of society. The sheep is "perfect" in the sense that it allows for neither doubt nor internal conflict; it has a single will, and acceptance of that will as absolute is the condition imposed upon the host. But what does any of this mean? For critic Katō Norihiro the "Sensei" character was an obvious reference to Kodama Yoshio, a notorious right-wing figure whose fortune, amassed during Japan's wartime years of plunder in China, was used in part to found the postwar Liberal

Democratic Party (LDP).[8] For journalist Kawamoto Saburō, a contemporary of Katō's, the overall plot was an equally clear reference to the Japanese government's bringing to heel of the student movements of the late 1960s.[9] For me, the story spoke to the power that governments exert over individuals in any society, in any age, ostensibly to maintain order and tranquility.

The point, clearly, is that open symbols employed by Murakami such as the sheep, and the narrative structures they inhabit, may be read from a specific or generalist perspective, taking on radically different forms in each case, yet all are linked through the archetypal meanings that ground them. By centering his historical narratives in the Everyspace, Murakami arguably forfeits the prerogative of the text to convey a specific historical narrative; in its place he establishes the dominancy of the reader to supply multiple—indeed, numberless—historical narratives, in perpetuity, that will resonate with the archetypal grounding he evokes in his text. This is made possible, in part, by the use of the Everyspace as an historical setting wherein, ironically, linear time has no place, but where the unified singularity of metaphysical Time remains constant.

## THE EVERYSPACE AND THE MYTHIC JOURNEY

We have now considered the Everyspace as a space that requires separation of mind and body, a repository for memory and other contents of the unconscious that enables innovative ways of exploring the archetypal constants of history. But the most critical and obvious use for the Everyspace is the mythic journey, which enables Murakami's heroes (and his readers) to access these archetypal elements. And while one of the narrative goals of Murakami fiction is to explore Japan's recent historic past, these stories are also about the development of the individual in a perpetually homogenizing social structure throughout that history. In other words, as I have suggested above, alongside the broader social-historical narrative we always find an equally important personal one, dealing with the struggles of the lone man (or, occasionally, lone woman) who prefers not to give in to the pressures of those homogenizing forces. One path to this that we see over and over in Murakami fiction is the symbolic "death" of the hero, enacted by his descent into the Everyspace, followed by his rebirth. Such a process corresponds to Campbell's "belly of the whale," in which "the passage of the magical threshold is a transit into the sphere of rebirth . . . symbolized in the worldwise womb image of the belly of the whale."[10] In other words, mythically speaking, in order to be reborn, better and stronger, the hero must first undertake an initiatory journey which, if it does not *actually* kill him, at any rate entails his *symbolic* death.[11]

Such initiatory journeys are a staple in Murakami fiction; his protagonists regularly make their way into the forbidding realm of the Everyspace, initially to confront themselves, but also to face more archetypal threats to humankind itself. The narrator of *Hitsuji o meguru bōken* makes an arduous trek to the wilds of Hokkaido to discover his friend Nezumi, in the process thwarting the plans of the all-empowering sheep to continue its conquest of human society. Okada Tōru traverses the labyrinth of a metaphysical hotel to locate his imprisoned wife Kumiko, and finally batters her evil brother to death with a baseball bat, ending the latter's widespread political ambitions. Tamura Kafka confronts the woman who might be his mother in the forested Underworld, while short-circuiting Johnny Walker's plans for violent conflict. The hero of *Sekai no owari to hādo-boirudo wandārando* chooses eternal imprisonment in the Everyspace rather than participate further in the ultramodern information wars raging in a slightly futuristic Japan.

Whether the heroes of these stories emerge from the Everyspace triumphant, they return *different* men from the ones who went in. For the Murakami hero this does not mean an actual transformation, however; instead, we see a process by which the hero casts away the various impedimenta of his life, like a snake shedding its skin, until he stands defenseless, ready to begin the reconstitutive process. The narrator of *Hitsuji o meguru bōken*, having been divorced by his wife, next gives up his job, and eventually his girlfriend. Tamura Kafka is more explicit; as he moves through his Everyspace forest he drops, one by one, the bits and pieces of his survival gear: spray paint (for marking trees), hatchet, knife, compass, and the bag that holds them. Tazaki Tsukuru's abandonment of his former self takes place more than a decade prior to the novel's present; rejected and expelled by his best friends at the age of twenty, he deliberately mortifies his own flesh through near-starvation, and after five months can no longer recognize his own face in the mirror. This is, quite simply, because his old self is gone:

> Looking at himself in the mirror, no traces remained of the soft face of that mediocre, unfocused youth.... Look at it how you may, the youth who had been Tazaki Tsukuru was dead. He had gasped out his last breath in desolate darkness, and was buried in some tiny forest clearing.[12]

The quest for Tazaki Tsukuru, then, is not to regain this "soft youth," but rather to understand the circumstances and necessity of his destruction. This he discovers in a secluded lakeside cabin near Haemeenlinn, a sleepy town in rural Finland. Yet, we have the distinct sense that Tazaki Tsukuru is about to undergo yet another transfigurative rebirth; now that he has discovered the "cause of death" of his boyhood self, he has also unblocked his own path forward to yet another life. If a character goes into the Underworld in order to be reconstituted and reborn, one might say that Tazaki Tsukuru's gestation has lasted for sixteen years, unusually long even for a Murakami character.

The notion of death and rebirth is given its most explicitly mythic depiction in *Kishidanchō-goroshi*, wherein the protagonist travels into a recognizable Underworld, complete with a subterranean river and a faceless boatman (Charon) who demands a token in exchange for ferrying him across the river. In this instance the hero traverses a vast, rocky space to connect with a light-bearing girl who encourages him, later in the voice of his deceased sister—despite severe claustrophobia—to push himself through increasingly narrow tunnels, until at length he emerges from the other end.

> Suddenly the narrow hole came to an end. Like a clump of grass forced out of a pipe by the pressure of the water, my flesh was released out into empty space. Before I had time to think about what was happening, I dropped, utterly defenseless, into space.[13]

One could search in vain through countless volumes to find a more clearly-written description of symbolic childbirth—and from the infant's point of view!

The point here is that the Everyspace in Murakami fiction, from beginning to end, is a realm not only of death and memory, but of reconstitution. The hero finds there not merely answers, but a path to his own reconstitution as an individual. As such, it formulates a nexus between Campbell's mythic Zone of Magnified Power, the mythic Underworld, and Jung's collective unconscious with its grounding archetypes. All of these modes of consciousness have their own origins in the Platonic realm of forms, alternately imagined by Murakami's characters as a state of "pure thought" (Haida), a space housing the soul (Kafka), or merely a space underground, to which we return, and from which we reemerge, *ad infinitum*.

## CONCLUSION: FINDING OUR WAY HOME

What makes these apparently disparate renditions of reality—perhaps reality and a kind of metareality—function so well together in the Murakami text is the fact that they are always linked within the same "layered" structure, the spatial and temporal latticework that makes up the four-dimensional Everyspace. For the Everyspace is not separate from our physical space, but contains and suffuses it. Murakami's narrative structure is superficially dualistic (real versus hyperreal, conscious versus unconscious, urban versus rural, and so forth), but really the physical and metaphysical are always woven together in an inseparable and symbiotic relationship in which each penetrates and permeates the other. And herein may lie, ironically, the most realistic aspect of Murakami fiction: that encounters with the Everyspace come as naturally as falling asleep and dreaming, as easily (but unconsciously) as letting our imaginations roam freely. For the layered latticework in which Murakami's protagonists move and act is really no different from the layered latticework of our own reality; rather, it is (or at least it may be) our very modern biases that lead us firmly to divide the "real" from the "unreal," or "waking" from "dreaming," privileging the former as "rational" or "empirical," and the latter as mere "fantasy."

Jung warns against this bias: "Rationalism and doctrinairism are the disease of our time," he writes. "They pretend to have all the answers. But a great deal will yet be discovered which our present limited view would have ruled out as impossible."[14] To what might this refer? Perhaps he means the existence of the soul, or that soul and mind are one and the same, as the ancient Greeks believed. Or he may be defending his oft-maligned belief in the collective unconscious, that collection of archetypes—of narrative—that connects us all. Possibly he merely defends Plato.

Murakami, too, defends Plato, though he may not realize it, for in his development of the Everyspace as a realm in which answers are sought and found, time and space suspended, we discover the real key to grasping this author's *modus operandi* as a novelist.[15] The central points to be drawn from his fictional works—and perhaps a few of his nonfictional works as well—is that the narrative by which each of us lives is grounded in and given meaning by the archetypal figures and narratives that occupy the Everyspace depicted in so many of his stories. Readers are guided by the Murakami text to imagine themselves connected to that very same Everyspace, which might here simply be called the imagination, a "space" that admits to no boundaries, in order to explore their own relationship to the archetypal realm, to view their own experience from that context.

In so elevating what I am calling the Everyspace to its primary literary trope, the Murakami text walks a path well trodden by both Jung and Campbell, one that reinscribes the critical importance of such connections, and is itself a gesture of resistance against modernity, for, as Campbell notes:

> [T]he psychological dangers through which earlier generations were guided by the symbols and spiritual exercises of their mythological and religious inheritance, we today ... must face alone, or at best, with only tentative, impromptu, and not often very effective guidance. This is our problem as modern, "enlightened" individuals, for whom all gods and devils have been rationalized out of existence.[16]

But the Everyspace is more than a mere coping mechanism for life's conundrums; it is also a return to our origins, a reconnection with our forgotten (but not lost) past, one that we share with all humanity, from our beginnings down to the last person who will walk this earth. It is a rejoining with the narratives of ancient people who looked upon the rising sun and the waning moon, the myriad stars and bright planets, and saw in them the gods, and in those gods saw also a reflection of themselves. It is through "remembering" all this, even if only in our dreams, fantasies, and stories that we gain an inkling of our own place in the grand narrative of humanity and, perhaps, a glimpse of the lines we ourselves write in that shared story.

Murakami's deployment of the Everyspace grants readers access to these mythic and psychological groundings, in fictional, even parable form, as we have seen. And what is gained by this experience? For some, perhaps, nothing more than a good story. For others, the narrative experience may unlock what Aldus Huxley called the "doors of perception," inviting and exciting in those readers both the desire and the means to awaken to the narratives that live within their own consciousness, personal and collective.[17] For while we are all connected by the contents of the Everyspace, each individual reader brings a unique set of experiences to the process, and thus those contents, though perfect and unchanging, must appear differently to all. For those who open their "doors of perception" wide, the experience can be both psychologically and spiritually rewarding. For in allowing ourselves to be drawn into the Everyspace, albeit through the imagination (but after all, the Everyspace *is* imagination), we discover our origins, our present, and even our future. We learn, as Eliade would say, how we came to be as we are, or as Jung and Campbell might have said, why we need to know that.

As we go through this process within the Murakami narrative, we discover that the key to finding ourselves, paradoxically, is to let go of ourselves and merge with the Everyspace. To yield ourselves to the Everyspace, though it suggests the death of the individual, also means the potential for rebirth of the individual back into this world, as occurs so regularly in these texts. For death and transfiguration is as old as myth itself, a recurring narrative that finds contemporary expression through Murakami's Everyspace.

## NOTES

1. For more on archetypes and the collective unconscious, see C. G. Jung, "The Archetypes and the Collective Unconscious" in *The Collected Works of C. G. Jung*, translated by R. F. C. Hull (Princeton, NJ: Bollingen Series XX, Princeton University Press, 1980), vol. 9, part 1.

2. Murakami Haruki, *Nejimakidori kuronikuru* (Tokyo: Shinchōsha,1994–95), 3:100. All translations from the Japanese are by the author unless otherwise noted.

3. Murakami Haruki, *Shikisai o motanai Tazaki Tsukuru to, kare no junrei no toshi* (2013; Colorless Tazaki Tsukuru and his year of pilgrimage), 66.

4. Murakami Haruki, *Sekai no owari to hādo-boirudo wandārando*, in *Murakami Haruki zensakuhin 1979–1989* (Tokyo: Kōdansha, 1990–91), 4:590.

5. Murakami Haruki, *Umibe no Kafuka* (Tokyo: Shinchōsha, 2002), 2:374.

6. Stephen Hawking, *A Brief History of Time: From the Big Bang to Black Holes* (New York: Bantam Dell, 1988), 149.

7. See Matthew Strecher, *Dances With Sheep: The Quest for Identity in the Fiction of Murakami Haruki* (Ann Arbor: University of Michigan Press, 2002).

8. Katō Norihiro, *Murakami Haruki wa, muzukashii* (Tokyo: Iwanami Shinsho No. 1575, 2015), 129.

9. Kawamoto Saburō, "Murakami Haruki o meguru kaidoku," in *Shiiku & fuaindo Murakami Haruki*, edited by Murakami Ryū (Tokyo: Seidōsha 1986), 45.

10. Joseph Campbell, *The Hero with a Thousand Faces* (Princeton, NJ: Bollingen Series XVII, Princeton University Press, 1973; orig. pub. 1949), 90.

11. Mythic structures of death and rebirth are not merely fiction; in societies primitive and developed alike, initiatory rituals are an important aspect of passage from one life stage to another. From circumcision and fasting to baptism and confirmation, such changes are marked and celebrated as the "death" of the former person (for instance, a child) and his or her "rebirth" as a new person (an adult). This is why many such rituals, including baptism, include the bestowing of a new name and new spiritual parents. For more on such rituals, see Mircea Eliade, *Myth and Reality*, translated and edited by Willard Trask (New York: Harper and Row, 1963); for a detailed discussion of this in Murakami fiction, see Matthew Strecher, "Out of the (B)earth Canal: The Mythic Journey in Murakami Haruki" in *Japan Forum* 32.3 (2020).

12. Murakami, *Shikisai o motanai Tazaki Tsukuru to, kare no junrei no toshi*, 50–51.

13. Murakami Haruki, *Kishidanchō-goroshi* (Tokyo: Shinchōsha, 2017), 2:382.

14. C. G. Jung, *Memories, Dreams, Reflections*, translated by Richard and Clara Winston (New York: Pantheon Books, 1961), 300.

15. In his long interview with Kawakami Mieko, Murakami denies having read Plato, to which Kawakami responds with appropriate skepticism. See Kawakami Mieko and Murakami Haruki, *Mimizuku wa tasogare ni tobitatsu* (Tokyo: Shinchōsha, 2017), 157–158.

16. Campbell, *The Hero with a Thousand Faces*, 96.

17. See Aldous Huxley, *The Doors of Perception and Heaven and Hell* (New York: Harper and Row, 1990[1954]).

# WORKS CITED

Campbell, Joseph. 1949. *The Hero with a Thousand Faces*. Princeton, NJ: Bollingen Series XVII, Princeton University Press.

Eliade, Mircea. 1963. *Myth and Reality*. Trans. and ed. by Willard Trask. New York: Harper and Row.
Hawking, Stephen. 1988. *A Brief History of Time: From the Big Bang to Black Holes*. New York: Bantam Dell, 1988
Huxley, Aldous. 1990 [1954]. *The Doors of Perception and Heaven and Hell*. New York: Harper and Row.
Jung, Carl Gustav. 1961. *Memories, Dreams, Reflections*. Translated by Richard and Clara Winston. New York: Pantheon Books.
———. 1980. "The Archetypes and the Collective Unconscious." Translated by R. F. C. Hull. In *The Collected Works of C.G. Jung*. 20 vols., vol. 9, part 1. Edited by Sir Herbert Read, Michael Fordham and Gerhard Adler. Princeton, NJ: Bollingen Series XX, Princeton University Press.
Katō Norihiro. 2015. *Murakami Haruki wa, muzukashii*. Tokyo: Iwanami Shinsho no. 1575.
Kawamoto Saburō. 1986. "Murakami Haruki o meguru kaidoku." In *Shiiku & fuaindo Murakami Haruki*, edited by Murakami Ryū. Tokyo: Seidōsha.
Murakami Haruki. 1990a. *1973-nen no pinbōru*. In *Murakami Haruki zensakuhin 1979–1989*. 8 vols. Tokyo: Kōdansha. volume 1.
———. 1990b. *Hitsuji o meguru bōken*. In *Murakami Haruki zensakuhin 1979–1989*. 8 vols. Tokyo: Kōdansha. volume 2.
———. 1990c. *Sekai no owari to hādo-boirudo wandārando*. In *Murakami Haruki zensakuhin 1979–1989*. 8 vols. Tokyo: Kōdansha. Volume 4.
———. 1994. *Nejimakidori kuronikuru*. vols. 1 and 2. Tokyo: Shinchōsha.
———. 1995. *Nejimakidori kuronikuru*. vol. 3. Tokyo: Shinchōsha.
———. 2002. *Umibe no Kafuka*. 2 vols. Tokyo: Shinchōsha.
———. 2009–2010. *1Q84*. 3 vols. Tokyo: Shinchōsha.
———. 2017. *Kishidanchō-goroshi*. 2 vols. Tokyo: Shinchōsha.
Strecher, Matthew. 2002. *Dances With Sheep: The Quest for Identity in the Fiction of Murakami Haruki*. Ann Arbor: University of Michigan Press.
———. 2014. *The Forbidden Worlds of Haruki Murakami*. Minneapolis: University of Minnesota Press.
———. 2020. "Out of the (B)earth Canal: The Mythic Journey in Murakami Haruki." *Japan Forum* 32, no.3: 338–360.

*Chapter Two*

# Shōjo, Mother, and the Uncanny Space in Ogawa Yōko's Writings

## Mina Qiao

Driven by nostalgia, young women returning to their spiritual homes is the literary trope of Ogawa Yōko's writings in the early 1990s. Distorted in these other-worldly spaces, time seems to be on the side of shōjos—young women who are in the sociopsychological status that reject maturation and advancement embodied in reproduction and motherhood. In order to extricate the crux from the enigmatic narratives, we need to approach the representations of space as a vital forum for channeling a romanticized yet eerie past and the uncanny effects such representation creates. Space is critical to these tales, which are premised upon the characters' literal as well as a symbolic revisitation of their pasts. Lurking beneath these spaces is the symbolic mother, threating to end the shōjohood the characters are desperate to prolong.

Ogawa Yōko (b.1962) began her writing career with stories bordering on psychological horror: "Samenai kōcha" (1990; "Tea That Never Cools"), "Ninshin karendā" (1991; "Pregnancy Diary"), and "Domitorī" (1991; "Dormitory").[1] Young women in the stories are haunted by a phantasmic past in one way or another. As is a paradigm of the horror genre, the narratives turn mysterious as the protagonists come to reconnect with their past via a site of their childhood or adolescence, a space that is uncanny in a Freudian sense. The nostalgic sentiment saturating the characters' dreamlike journeys exhibits their strong connection with the past as well as their anxiety concerning the present and the future. In these narratives, the uncanny space manifests the women's fear of identity-shifting and is the remaining link to their bygone shōjohood.

Ogawa has a strong tendency of engaging with shōjo discourses in her writing. John Treat asserts that shōjo is not defined by age or gender, but primarily by its detachment from "the productive economy of heterosexual reproduction."² Deborah Shamoon adds that the shōjo status is marked by social convention rather than physical age.³ Shōjohood creates, in Shamoon's words, "the liminal adolescent space between childhood and adulthood."⁴ It is thus fragile and instable as it is "between the social roles of child and wife or mother."⁵ Shōjohood, which is central to the uncanny space in this discussion, refers to the past time when the female protagonists are younger in Ogawa's narratives, the literal "*shōjo jidai*," and more significantly, what it carries in cultural studies, a state divorced from social reality and a strategy to elude production and reproduction.⁶ Many researchers, including Takahara Eri, Eve Zimmerman, Nakamura Miharu, and Suzuki Tomoyuki, attribute Ogawa's writing to her perpetual source of inspiration, *Anne Frank: The Diary of a Young Girl*.⁷ Ogawa summarizes Anne's Diary's depiction of a young girl's psyche as "resistance to mother, yearning for boys, anxiety towards maturation," which resonates with her own adolescent experience and greatly impacts her writing.⁸ Zimmerman especially points out that Anne Frank as the eternal shōjo evokes Ogawa's fascination with shōjohood in her own creations.⁹ Studying Ogawa's novel *Mīna no kōshin* (2006; Mina's March), Zimmerman suggests the opening with the protagonist and narrator Tomoko gazing at an old photo, which is a token of the past, demonstrates her "illusion of stasis."¹⁰ The entire story is told in retrospect. Tomoko's psychic state combined with her denial of the present and continuity with the past in her internal landscape aligns with what Zimmerman describes as the "liminal period of girlhood" in Ogawa's early writings.¹¹

The wistful return to shōjohood is related to "moratorium," a prolonging of the transition from childhood to adulthood, proposed by Japanese psychiatrist Okonogi Keigo in *Moratoriamu ningen no jidai* (1978; The Age of Moratorium People). Lisette Gebhardt argues that moratorium is a sociocultural diagnosis of 1970s Japan, which translates into various literary expressions.¹² Showa-retro is a national sentiment in postmodern Japan and can be seen in many Heisei literary works. Chūjō Shōhei sees Murakami Haruki's protagonists who are reluctant to enter adulthood as typical "moratorium guys (*moratoriamu yarō*)."¹³ Susan Napier argues that Murakami's narratives channel ghosts and memories to dwell on the past, and John Treat identifies a nostalgic search of characters' shōjo past in Yoshimoto Banana's novels.¹⁴ Gebhardt suggests that both Murakami and Yoshimoto's protagonists are sensitive shōjo characters searching for soulmates and identities in late capitalist Japan.¹⁵ Against "a joyless and malignant banal everyday reality in late capitalism," the shōjo character, long for "a moment of 'longing to be back' (*natsukashisa*)."¹⁶

Moreover, Gebhardt approaches Ogawa's nostalgic narratives as a part of this larger body of "moratorium literature."¹⁷ Ogawa Yōko and Kawakami

Hiromi (b.1958) are the next generation authors who follow the paradigm of shōjo longing to go back in time.[18] Gebhardt examines Kawakami's *Sensei no kaban* (2001; Teacher's Briefcase) and "Dormitory" by Ogawa and argues both revolve around a "retro-erotic" relationship between the female protagonists and older men, through which they seek refuge in a different world.[19] The protagonists try to run away from their reality, which is social maturity and the implied obligations to participate in labor and reproduction. The works are hence constructed upon a nostalgic lifestyle and regressive psychological model.[20] Amanda Seaman also recognizes the important role the shōjo element plays in Ogawa's "Pregnancy Diary."[21] The young and unmarried female protagonist perceives her sister's pregnancy as "an impending future at once repulsive and contradictory to her 'girlish' self-identity" and therefore is intent on sabotaging it.[22] Echoing the concept of the moratorium in Gebhardt's study, Seaman proposes that the protagonist's actions are motivated by a desire to prolong her shōjo status.[23] Both Gebhardt and Seaman link Ogawa's narratives to an ambivalence towards adulthood as well as the gender-specific adulthood, motherhood.[24]

## THE UNCANNY SPACE AND THE SHADOW OF MOTHERHOOD

Ōtsuka Eiji proposes that shōjo literature usually presents fictional worlds that captivate the characters (and the readers) in a space defined by emotions rather than physical boundaries.[25] In other words, the shōjo experience is discussed through dreams, memories, and fantasies free from spatial-temporal conventions, which we see in Ogawa's narratives. The characters often search for shōjohood in spaces that exist outside a chronological timeline. Ogawa has commented on her nostalgia complex and constitution of literary space for shōjo narratives. "When I write novels, I often find myself lingering in the past. [. . .] Stories flourish in the forest somewhere in a distant time, a place I once have been but which has almost disappeared by now."[26] Literary critic Svetlana Boym argues that nostalgia is more of "a yearning for a different time" than "a longing for a place," and is by extension, "rebellion against the modern idea of time, the time of history and progress."[27] Rebellion against temporal progression supports Ogawa's construction of nostalgia. The author's shōjo narratives largely adopt an antidevelopment pattern where the protagonists strive to revisit phantom places and set time counterclockwise.

The locations in the selected narratives all feature disturbing imageries, puzzling developments, and unsettling endings, which fit a dictionary definition of "uncanny." Ogawa also borrows psychological traits embedded in the term "nostalgia" while constructing uncanny spaces. Formed by the Greek words "homecoming" (nóstos) and "pain" (álgos), nostalgia suggests a separation anxiety due to being away from home. The uncanny locations are symbolic homes to the protagonists, providing sanctuary for their memories and identities. In "Tea That Never Cools," the uncanny space is the home of the female protagonist's high school classmate. In "Pregnancy Diary," M Clinic, an obstetrics clinic near the protagonist's home where she and her sister go to play in their childhood, is the source of the uncanny. So is the protagonist's university dormitory in "Dormitory." We can see that all three are connected to the protagonists' early days, innocent childhood and carefree student life, prior to any contact with heterosexual economy or domestic structure. These places are uncanny not only because they host mystifying persons and unexplainable events, but because they offer a chance to relive the past.

The experiences the protagonists encounter are therefore familiar and yet estranged by repression of adulthood, as Sigmund Freud writes in "The Uncanny" (1919).[28] According to Freud, the uncanny is nothing new or foreign, but something old and familiar with a frightening twist.[29] "[A]n uncanny experience occurs either when repressed infantile complexes have been revived by some impression, or when the primitive beliefs we have surmounted seem once more to be confirmed."[30] In other words, the uncanny is the return of the repressed and the primitive.[31] In Ogawa's narratives, the repressed and the primitive are the Mother (capitalized as a sociocultural archetype), with which everything begins and ends. Commenting on Freud's association of death with Mother Earth in "The Theme of the Three Caskets" (1913), Barbara Creed underpins the cultural tropes of the female uncanny in *Phallic Panic* (2005): "The mother herself absorbs the infant's body in her own yet also confers independence; she gives life and takes life away insofar as life contains within itself its own end."[32] The Mother results in anxiety for its capability of blurring boundaries—between life and death, origin and end, and Self and Other. Furthermore, for the female protagonists, the Mother is both their origin and their inescapable destiny. They see themselves in the identity-disturbing maternal, a past shōjo self and a possible future self that adopts a maternal identity.

In Ogawa's characterization of the uncanny, we also see maternal allusions such as suction, dark void, and abyss.[33] The intersecting of the uncanny and the maternal is in line with a long tradition of works. It echoes with the Freudian interpretation of a common fear toward the female genital organs.[34] "This *unheimlich* place, however, is the entrance to the former *Heim* [home] of all human beings, to the place where each one of us lived once upon a time and in the beginning."[35] The place in a man's dream which he finds familiar can be interpreted as "being his mother's genitals or her body."[36] We thus trace the uncanny back to the maternal body where Freud allocates the primal fear. Similarly, Creed discusses the uncanny of uterine imagery being largely employed in horror films in *The Monstrous Feminine* (1993).[37] The uncanny are visualized as womb-like spaces that disturb boundaries and consume humans.[38] The haunted houses in this genre are former homes, the literal *unheimlich* bearing the token of repression in the prefix *un*, homes that are no longer homey.[39] Instead, "[t]he house is haunted by the ghost or trace of a memory which takes the individual back to the early, perhaps fetal, relation with mother."[40] The spectral presence is the symbolic mother taking the form of usually the husband's former wife, as in *Rebecca* (1940) and *Secret Beyond the Door* (1947). In more violent representations such as *Poltergeist* (1982), the ghost can also be "a huge sucking uterus."[41] In Japanese cinema, Obayashi Nobuhiko's *Hausu* (1977; House) is an instance of the uncanny space of the symbolic mother. A group of young girls goes to visit the protagonist's aunt, a substitute to the protagonist's deceased mother, in her house. The haunted house represents the threatening yet alluring Mother and her calling for a return to her womb. Both the room flooded with blood and the gigantic engulfing lips that materialize out of the wall indicate the house's allusion to female reproductive organs. We see the shōjo's resistance to motherhood and its inevitable transformation as the protagonist is possessed by her aunt in the end. The following sections will examine such conflicts between the maternal and the shōjo represented in Ogawa's narratives as well.

The space for such struggles, like a haunted house in a horror film, is associated with the individual's quest for his or her origins.[42] Ogawa creates a dysfunctional mother-child dyad by making many of her protagonists orphans, so as to intensify such a pursuit.[43] Creed suggests that a haunted house, as a symbolic womb, entices characters to explore, because it serves as the stage where all three primal scenes linked to origin—"conception, sexual difference, desire"—are played out.[44] "Behind the quest for identity [. . .] lies the body of the mother represented through intra-uterine symbols and devices. Here the body/house is literally the body of horror, the place of the uncanny where desire is always marked by the shadowy presence of the mother."[45] The protagonists in the discussed narratives step into the uncanny, embarking on a nostalgic journey to the past for their lost shōjohood. When the past becomes alive again, they confront the symbolic mother as well as their own ambivalence toward mothering.

Motherhood functions as an obstruction to the prolonging of shōjohood in Ogawa's writings. The narratives are often centered around a clash between girlhood/youth/stagnation/the past/the fantasy and motherhood/maturity/advancement/the present/the reality, while the shōjo protagonists embrace the former and resist the latter. Since the start of her career, Ogawa has had her female characters confront this carnal reality foremost linked to women's social maturity. Let's not forget her literary debut "Agehachō ga kowareru toki" (1989; "When the swallowtail butterfly is broken"), which is about a young woman, Nanako, dealing with an unexpected (and unwanted) pregnancy while mulling over the maternal lineage in her family. Pregnancy is depicted as a terrifying process of bodily and mental destruction in "Pregnancy Diary."[46] On the other hand, "Daiweingu pūru" (1990; "The Diving Pool") is an instance of condemned symbolic motherhood where the threefold kernel of shōjohood—"resistance to mother, yearning for boys, anxiety towards maturation"—are illuminated.[47] Teenage girl Aya, whose home is turned into an orphanage by her parents, is deprived of her shōjo identity and imposed with a maternal role for the foster children. She is tormented by her parents' negligence of her feelings and her increasing erotic desire for her foster brother Jun. Aya's suppressed emotional and erotic needs are channeled through the imagery of a warm and moist pool that resembles "the inside of a gigantic animal's body."[48] This central imagery is a metaphor for the womb and represents Aya's wish to return to an infantile state and to be relieved of all responsibilities. "Dormitory" can also be read as a veiled portrayal of maternal anxiety and disapproval of motherhood, which I will scrutinize in a later section.

## TEA THAT NEVER COOLS: FREEDOM BY DEATH

We begin with the origin of Ogawa's mixture of fantastical elements with shōjo and nostalgia, "Tea That Never Cools." This novella was shortlisted for the 1990 Akutagawa Prize, the third time for Ogawa, but lost to Tsujihara Noboru's (b.1945) "Mura no namae" (1990) by a narrow margin. We see in it an archetype for many of Ogawa's succeeding narratives. The unnamed narrator of "Tea That Never Cools" is in her twenties and lives with her boyfriend Satō, whom she has been dating for three years. After she is reunited with K. at the vigil of a classmate, she frequents K.'s place to enjoy the company of him and his lady and grows increasingly discontent with her own relationship in comparison. Toward the end of the narrative, the narrator suspects that K. and his lady may have died in a fire several years ago. She leaves K.'s house and steps into a different dimension. It ends with the narrator coming to a sea and wondering where the water comes from. The whole narrative seems to depict the narrator's near-death experience, which includes a review of her life from childhood to the present (*sōmatō* in Japanese) and a "tunnel experience" of her moving down an endless slope and entering darkness.

"Tea That Never Cools" is Ogawa's first work that experiments with such fantastical elements as temporally suspended space and encounters with the dead. The Akutagawa Prize committee's perception of the fantasy in "Tea That Never Cools" is pulled toward one of two extremes: splendid delicacy

(Ōba Minako, Kuroi Seiji, Yoshiyuki Jun'nosuke) and implausible ambiguity (Ōe Kenzaburō, Miura Tetsuro, Kōno Taeko).[49] The key to understanding the fantasy in this story is to acknowledge death as the ultimate fortification of shōjohood. Death suspends time and frames everything and everyone in stagnation, hence the tea never cools. The narrative aims at removing fear and romanticizing death by associating death with subjects of the narrator's desires—K. and his lady.

The narrator's nostalgic journey to shōjohood begins with K.'s place. The narrative implies that this primary stage of the story belongs to the other world. The narrator has lost her sense of time after her first visit. Their gatherings never take place outside the premises of K.'s house. Nonetheless, K.'s house is much more welcoming, nurturing, and appealing to the narrator than the home she shares with Satō. K., their alma mater, and K.'s beautiful and elegant girlfriend, who turns out to be the school librarian, form a trinity of nostalgia that enchants the narrator. K.'s home is uncanny in the perfect Freudian sense. The narrator finds it strangely familiar although she has never even been to this neighborhood before. "I had the strangest sense of nostalgia, like I'd seen this place before. It drew out memories of picture books I'd read as a child, of the dreams of jungles I'd always had when feverish. I searched my mind for the source of this nostalgia, but in vain."[50] We will see the symbolic homecoming to a nostalgic place in "Pregnancy Diary" and "Dormitory" as well. The narrative explicitly nominates nostalgia as a prime drive for the narrator's actions. It also states through K. that "everyone likes that sense of nostalgia."[51] Sociologist Fred Davis suggests that nostalgia is "the search for continuity amid threats of discontinuity."[52] The narrator seeks continuity in bonding with a classmate and metaphorical studenthood, in other words, a shōjo identity, amid the threats of adulthood represented by Satō.

The narrator's rejection of social maturity is denoted in her contempt toward Satō, who signifies production and reproduction as a heterosexual partner. His practical lifestyle, monotonous character, and emotional insensitivity are crimes of adulthood. His physicality is thus nothing but an abomination to the narrator as it portends impregnation. Satō, more than once, evokes the imagery of a hole (*ana*). In a scene where Satō complains to the narrator about his toothache, we see from the narrator's point of view into Satō's grotesque mouth. "Looking down that throat, as he exhaled his stinking smoker's breath at me, I would realize that all those organs were hanging down at the bottom of that hole. It made me sick to my stomach."[53] Her visual perception highlights terror of the hole, dark and moist, which represents motherhood. In another scene in which the narrator explains her relationship with Satō to K. and the librarian, she stresses the fact that they are not a married couple but merely two people who live together. "We just live together . . . once I'd uttered these words, a gaping hole seemed to open in my head."[54]

According to Creed, "The voracious maw, the mysterious black hole [. . .] signifies female genitalia that threatens to [. . .] incorporate everything in its path."[55] Despite being a male/neutral dark hole in "Tea That Never Cools," this imagery is linked with heterosexual marriage and the danger of being consumed. Oyamada Hiroko (b.1983), in her Akutagawa Prize-winning fiction "Ana" (2013; "The Hole"), also employs the imagery of a hole to represent the female protagonist's anxiety about losing her identity over her marriage. We see in the narrator's revulsion her fear of being assimilated into Satō, the social body, adulthood, and ultimately, motherhood. Simply put, the narrator's heterosexual relationship with Satō jeopardizes the continuity of her shōjo identity.

In stark contrast to Satō's corrupted and carnal existence stand K. and the librarian's purity and ethereality. Anna Felicia Sanchez argues that the absence of explicit physical contact is critical to the construction of shōjohood.[56] Therefore, we often see a substitute emphasis on sensuality in shōjo manga, in "the unintentional meeting of gaze, finger brushing accidentally, an impulsive embrace."[57] The sensuality through gazing and innocent touches are ubiquitous in the representation of the relationship between K. and the librarian. The narrator praises their spirituality by noting a "pure water flowing between [them]."[58] As Sanchez summarizes: "[T]here is never explicit sex, and anything sexual is bleached and disembodied, cleansed of malice and bodily filth, and thus the 'sexless' shōjo."[59] The sensuality is critical to the structure of shōjohood because it is nonreproductive. As the narrator reconnects with K., she salvages her memories of her school years and regresses to a wide-eyed girl who craves platonic romance. The shōjo eventually finds the prolonging of innocence in death.

## "PREGNANCY DIARY": SEPARATE PATHS

Ogawa continues the discussion of shōjo against advancement in her Akutagawa Prize-winning novella "Pregnancy Diary." Out of all her stories, "Pregnancy Diary" most explicitly engages with the motherhood discourse. The story takes the form of a young woman's diary that records her older sister's pregnancy. The narrative begins and ends with the older sister's visit to M Clinic, an obstetrics clinic near the protagonist's home. The first time is for a confirmation of conception, and the last for childbirth. M Clinic gives rise to all conflicts and oppositions.

Firstly, M Clinic symbolizes the bond between the sisters and announces their divergence. The narrator introduces us to M Clinic in her diary. It used to be a playground for the sisters when they were only schoolchildren. They liked to roll around on the grass in its yard. The narrator recalls that "I loved the moment when the sky, the wind, and the ground all pulled away from my body, leaving it to float in space."[60] For the young sisters, M Clinic is pure bliss. The sensation of her body floating in space is the taste of freedom exclusive to children whose bodies are not yet fully controlled by society. The rooms hold alien objects such as chemicals, medical equipment, and posters of maternal positioning, which are beyond the sisters' comprehension. They find these exotic and fascinating. Through the innocence of a child, the narrator cannot understand the blank expression on the new mothers' faces. She thinks that they ought to be thrilled with all those interesting gadgets up there.

The discourse of spectatorship shows in an important scene from the narrator's memories in which the sisters peer through the window to look inside. "'We're gonna get yelled at if anyone catches us.' I was more skittish than my older sister. 'Don't worry. We're just kids. We can get away with anything,' she replied casually while wiping the fogged-up window glass with her sleeve."[61] This is significant because the older sister during her childhood is portrayed as disobedient and even more daring than the narrator, in contrary to her fragile characterization in the present time. In this scene, the older sister exploits the advantages of being children. It implies again that as children, they are safe from the threat of motherhood represented by the clinic. In the scene from the narrator's remembrance, both sisters are spectators of pregnancy. This dynamic in spectatorship changes when the older sister becomes pregnant herself. The older sister is now subjected to the narrator's indifferent observation and recording of her bodily vicissitudes. The baby drives a wedge between the sisters who were once close. The narrator feels edged out as the older sister is growing her own family. On the other hand, the older sister is the one who is expelled from the world of shōjo due to her pregnancy. M Clinic, which holds their happy memories, now witnesses them taking separate paths.

After a return to M Clinic, we begin to see its uncanny sides. The older sister chooses M Clinic as her maternity hospital over better-equipped hospitals for sentimental reasons. When the narrator asks about M Clinic, the older sister responds, "It hasn't changed at all. [. . .] It seems in there time is suspended from flowing and just collects to pile up."[62] However, as the older sister returns to the place as a registered pregnant woman, the clinic threatens the loss of innocence and an end to shōjohood. One example of this loss is that she finds everything inside the exam room exactly the same, except for "one thing that is brand new and doesn't belong," the ultrasound device.[63] The high-tech device is the twist given to the familiar setting of M Clinic and hence a source of the uncanny. Ironically, to both sisters, the fetus is also something that is "brand new and doesn't belong."[64] The narrator describes her sister's body in the second trimester as "a big tumor that keeps multiplying."[65] The fetus is a terrifying twist added to the older sister's body, which was once familiar, intimate, and private, and turns that pregnant body into an uncanny existence. M Clinic parallels the pregnant body itself in this context. The mirroring is also verified by the intrauterine metaphor the older sister proposes: "[W]hen I approached [M Clinic], I put my hand on the knob, and turned, I felt as if I was being sucked into a bottomless abyss."[66]

The uncanny functions to voice the older sister's anxiety due to a lack of control over her own body and self. Pregnancy renders the character passive and powerless. Not only is she subject to the narrator's spectating, but also to the symbolic male gaze projected from the medical profession, which monitors and reprimands her. For instance, approaching the end of the story, the older sister comes home from a check-up agitated and frustrated, because the doctor has warned her about being overweight. "Weight management" is written in red on her maternal and child health Handbook.[67] She is required to lose weight before giving birth. Yet, she responds with "but what can *I* do?" which expresses her pessimistic view of her diminished agency.[68] In another scene, the older sister claims that it is the "preg-nan-cy (*ni-n-shi-n*)" in her, rather than herself (*watashi jishin*), that wants loquat sorbet in the middle of the night.[69] Her way of pronouncing "pregnancy" as "the name of a grotesque worm" speaks to her increased hostility toward the changes in her body.[70] Her pregnant body becomes an uncanny space that has turned strange and spun out of control. She only wishes to segregate the pregnancy from her being in such verbal terms to sustain a sense of self-identity.

Despite being the subject of pregnancy, women are subjected to masculine control over the course of pregnancy, which further alienates the female body and adds to the uncanny effects. For this discussion, we return to the ultrasound that governs the pregnancy. Interestingly, the older sister compares the experience of ultrasound imaging to getting a dental impression done by her husband, a dentist. Both transgress bodily boundaries, reveal the innermost secrets of the body, prepare the body for a foreign object (baby/dental cap or crown), and are performed by and through a masculine symbol. Rosalind Pollack Petcheskyargues that fetal imaging places the fetus at the center as autonomous while rendering the woman as "absent and peripheral" and reducing the pregnant body to an "empty space" for the hero (fetus)'s adventure.[71] The woman's self-identity is suppressed and her reproductive freedom undermined in such practices.[72] Cristina Mazzoni suggests that imaging technology challenges the pregnant woman's reliability by making pregnancy public knowledge assessed by scientific means.[73] Seaman cites Mazzoni and writes: "A woman's knowledge of her own body and of her pregnancy has been overshadowed by the insistence of the medical world to look inside the body through the use of ultrasound, and by the authoritative gaze of the (masculine) medical establishment."[74] As a result, the older sister's fear of birth and the baby is intensified, and so is the narrator's desire to prolong her shōjohood after witnessing this.

The opposition between the shōjo and the mother is more evident in the ending. On the narrator's way to M Clinic for her sister's childbirth, the surroundings are depicted as if in a dreamscape—blindingly bright and hauntingly vacant, except for two children running past in this bizarre scenery. M Clinic appears as exactly the same, which seems incredible. "My sister was right. Only in here has time been suspended. The M Clinic that was sealed in my memories now stood in front of my eyes. [. . .] No one was around but my vivid shadow on the road."[75] The narrator is lonesome and isolated as the last standing shōjo while her sister has lost her innocence. Instead of going in through the front door, the narrator sneaks in through the back like she and her sister used to. The nervous feelings she got from childhood adventures are revived. This detail gives away the narrator's psychological antidevelopment. Seaman sees the story as a "stunted Bildungsroman" because the shōjo protagonist stubbornly refuses to mature.[76] We know that she is still in denial of her sister becoming a mother when she fails to recognize the face of the melancholy woman she sees in the hallway. It gives the reader another taste of the uncanny by rendering the sister someone familiar yet strange. Takanezawa Noriko suggests that here the image of the sister in the present overlaps with the new mother(s) they have seen in the past, thus closing the loop by ending the story where it began.[77] We may even interpret the two children flashing before the narrator's eyes as a reminiscence of her and her sister. She is reluctant to let go of her sister. Unlike the sister who has been "turned," the narrator manages to escape but is doomed to loneliness. The phrase in the very last line "*hakaisareta* (ruined) *ane no* (my sister's) *akachan* (baby)" hints at both the baby's potential deformity and the irreversible damage the sister has suffered due to pregnancy.[78] What is also beyond repair is the crack in their sisterhood as one remains a shōjo and the other becomes a mother.

## "DORMITORY": BODY IN CHANGE

Different from the head-on engagement with motherhood in "Pregnancy Diary," "Dormitory" is more reticent to discuss the shōjo's fear of social maturity. Ogawa highlights the representations of nostalgia and the uncanny in "Dormitory." The story begins with a phone call the unnamed narrator receives from her long-estranged cousin. She returns to her old student dormitory for her cousin's admission, where she reunites with the manager, a disabled man. The dormitory that holds her dear memories has become unusually dilapidated and deserted. Its operation is endangered by the mysterious disappearance of a student and horrifying rumors. After her cousin moves in, the narrator never sees him around. She therefore takes her visits to the dormitory as opportunities to mother the increasingly feeble manager. It ends with a bewildering scene, in which the narrator discovers a beehive behind an air vent that is dripping blood-like honey.

The dormitory, being both home and a haunted house, without a doubt serves as the uncanny space in this novella. Like the school the protagonist had formerly attended in "Tea That Never Cools," the dormitory for students is also an emblem of youth and preadult experiences, and the home to the shōjo who evades the heterosexual economy. Ogawa's construction of space as the embodiment of the characters' psyche is a paradigm in her writings.[79] The dormitory reappears out of the narrator's apprehension about poststudent life at a critical turning point of her life—moving to Sweden to join her husband there. The keyword "*hen-*" (the kanji implies change) is emphasized throughout the text. The deformation (*henkei*) of the manager's rib cage, the changes (*henka*) in the dormitory, and its degeneration (*hensei*) all suggest an interconnection between the collapsing dormitory and the decrepit manager, as well as the narrator, who faces relocation.[80] In other words, the dormitory's deterioration embodies the psychological challenges the narrator undergoes as she struggles to adapt to her role as a wife and potentially a mother. Her commitment to her marriage is symbolized by the expected move to Sweden. Although her husband eagerly awaits her reply, she chooses to ignore his letters, neglect all preparations for relocating, and focus her mind solely on taking care of the manager. Like K.'s place in "Tea That Never Cools," the dormitory is portrayed as a refuge for the narrator to elude her disagreeable spouse, to break away from her current relationship, so as to prolong her shōjohood.

The narrative resembles an anxiety dream for its incorporation of elusive atmosphere and surreal elements such as the color-changing tulips, residents vanishing, the dormitory and the manager surviving under extreme conditions, and the giant beehive that appears from nowhere. The technique of employing dreamlike fantasy to realize a psychoanalytical description of young women's uneasiness concerning marriage can also be found in Ogawa's "Yūgure no kyūshoku-shitsu to ame no pūru" (1991; "The Cafeteria in the Evening and a Pool in the Rain") and works by her contemporaries, such as Murakami Haruki's (b.1949) "Nemuri" (1989; "Sleep"), Tawada Yōko's (b.1960) "Kakato o ushinakute" (1992; "Missing Heels"), and the abovementioned "The Hole" by Oyamada. The eerie occurrences beyond everyday experience result from the romantically committed female protagonists' fear of their social transformation and the annihilation of subjectivity. The uncanny arises from their doubts about marriage repressed by their consciousness.

Gebhardt astutely points out that "Dormitory" is centered on the shōjo's attempt at moratorium; however, our opinions diverge on understanding the key imageries. Gebhardt associates the dormitory with an educational institute, the manager a symbolic teacher, and the beehive the sweetness of knowledge, which are a series of positive metaphors.[81] I would like to offer my alternative interpretation based on reading the narrative as a negative experience dominated by angst and a sense of loss. The dormitory thus is a visualization of the narrator's maternal anxiety, the manager a symbolic baby, and the beehive a uterine emblem. In addition, the young cousin who provokes maternal instinct in the narrator is also a symbol for the baby. The dormitory, as discussed above, functions as a double of the protagonist, and the narrative is structured upon its transformation. The manager says to the narrator, "The dorm is advancing toward an inevitable degeneration. It'll take time, not as simple as flipping a switch. [. . .] When you finally realize you're somewhere else, it'd be too late. You've reached the point of no return."[82] The defining point which marks the end of shōjohood is motherhood rather than leaving school. The shōjo's purity and innocence are renounced through reproduction like nothing else. The gradual degeneration in the dormitory implies the physical changes during pregnancy. Towards the end of the narrative, the manager becomes bedridden and completely dependent on the narrator. The narrator comes to the dormitory every day to hand feed sweets to the infantilized manager, as a mother devoted to her deformed baby. In the meanwhile, the manager describes in disturbing details the missing math student's perfect physique, which symbolizes a desirable healthy alternative. The representations of desires, in both the narrator's attachment to the manager's impaired body and the manager's longing for the math student's vigorous body, strongly resemble a maternal erotic transference, the initial sensual contact between mother and baby.[83] It adds to the dreamlike quality of the narrative and emphasizes the narrator's lack of fulfillment, in both emotional and sexual terms, in her marriage.

In the final scene, the narrator discovers the enormous beehive hidden inside the dorm building. Her description of it corresponds to a gestating uterus: "It looked like an outlandish fruit that had multiplied in an unguarded moment. [. . .] It was so big that I could no longer make out its shape, and it was cracked in several places."[84] Furthermore, her view of the overflown honey, stinky as blood and dripping restlessly, mimics a miscarriage. The last sentences depict the manager, the math student, and the cousin all falling into the depths of the dormitory while her attempt to reach out to them ends in vain. The failed attempt at rescue renders her powerless as a maternal protector. The story ends with the narrator's agitation for motherhood peaking and unsolved.

## CONCLUSION

From "Tea That Never Cools" to "Pregnancy Diary" and to "Dormitory," the female protagonists' attitudes toward social maturity transform from total rejection to increased ambivalence. In "Tea That Never Cools," the protagonist dreads any development in her relationship with Satō that will commit her to marriage and motherhood. She would rather turn to death. The protagonist in "Pregnancy Diary" does not completely reject the idea of marriage and pregnancy, which is evident in her fantasizing how she would want her future husband to act during her pregnancy. She disapproves of her sister's pregnancy out of concerns such as the well-being of her sister and the marginalization of her in the household, rather than the narrator's unsubstantiated abhorrence of commitment in "Tea That Never Cools." Unlike the first two protagonists, the protagonist in "Dormitory" is married and never directly voices any complaint about her relationship or committed relationships in general. Her boredom and anxiety about moving overseas are the only clues to her discontent. In her interactions with her cousin and the manager, she displays maternal qualities, which is unprecedented and continues to be sporadic in Ogawa's writings. Motherhood is depicted as daunting in "Dormitory" nevertheless, even with expressions of vague desire. The absence of the husband figure throughout the narrative also testifies to women's lack of security and confidence in marriage and motherhood.

The uncanny breaks the rule that "you can't go home *again*." This symbolic home is a self-contained place that eludes the passing of time, defying the laws of nature, and thus forbidden and treacherous. The uncanny space is the preserved land for the homecoming shōjo. They are coming home and also returning to their old selves. Ogawa gives us an antagonist—the semiotic mother—as an obstructive force to the prolonging of shōjohood. In other words, the hegemonic heterosexual script that demands the female to mother imperils the shōjo. The shōjo is fighting against assimilation with the mother possessed by a patriarchal specter. As in *Hoteru airisu* (1996; *Hotel Iris*), which also adopts the framework of daughter-against-mother, these narratives do not "offer any clear-cut feminist solution."[85] What Ogawa offers us is a distinctive interpretation of the shōjo theme, "the homecoming of the shōjo," by representing female psychodynamics in a temporal-spatial nexus.

In exploring female experiences, Ogawa constructs spaces as tangible emblems of female protagonists' corporeal and mental states. Female body finds its mirror image in the space that shifts, transmutes, and metamorphoses. The fantastical spatiality launches discussions of gender-specific experiences within a psychoanalytic framework. Setting the narratives in the present sociocultural environment, the elements of fantasy prevent patriarchal denunciation of the woman's lack of domesticity and allow her to express hesitation about maternal norms, even though provisional and veiled. The new expression of the shōjo discovers the equivocal nature of the woman's domesticity. Her journey begins with home and ends with it, the difference being the role she plays—from a shōjo to a mother. So into the fantastical space she goes, for dreams of never-ending innocence and youth.

## NOTES

1. Ogawa Yōko, "Samenai kōcha," in *Kanpeki na byōshitsu* (Tokyo: Chūō kōronshinsha, 2004). Ogawa Yōko, "Ninshin karendā," in *Ninshin karendā* (Tokyo: Bungei shunjū, 1991). Ogawa Yōko, "Domitorī," in *Ninshin karendā* (Tokyo: Bungei shunjū, 1991). When the book *Kanpeki na byōshitsu* was published by Fukutake shoten in 1989 for the first time, it includes two novellas only, "Kanpeki na byōshitsu" and "Agehachō ga kowareru toki." It was later republished with the addition of "Samenai kōcha" and "Daiweingu pūru."

2. John Whittier Treat, "Yoshimoto Banana Writes Home: Shōjo Culture and the Nostalgic Subject," *Journal of Japanese Studies* 19, no.2 (1993): 364.

3. Deborah Shamoon, *Passionate Friendship: The Aesthetics of Girls' Culture in Japan* (Honolulu: University of Hawai'i Press, 2012), 2.

4. Shamoon, *Passionate Friendship*, 2.

5. Ibid., 9.

6. Examples of the cultural studies of shōjo are *Shōjo minzokugaku: sekimatsu shinwa wo tsumugu miko no matsuei* (Tokyo: Kōbunsha, 1991) by Ōtsuka Eiji and *Shōjoron* (Tokyo: Aoyumisha, 1991) edited by Honda Masuko et al.

7. Takahara Eri, "Ogawa Yōko no kioku," *Yurīka* (February 2004), 104. Eve Zimmerman, "Angels and Elephants: Historical Allegories in Ogawa Yōko's 2006 Mīna no kōshin (Mena's Procession)," *U.S.-Japan Women's Journal* 49 (2016): 68–96. Nakamura Miharu, "Ogawa Yōko to Anne no nikki: kusuriyubi no hyōhon, hoteru airisu, neko o idaite, zō to oyogu nado," *Hokkaido daigaku bungaku kenkyū-ka kiyō* 149 (2016): 87–126. Suzuki Tomoyuki, "Anne furanku o sōki/ sōzō suru: Ogawa yōko "mitsu ya kana kesshō," aruiwa shōshitsu ni sarasa reru nama," *Shakai Shirin* 64 (2018): 37–58.

8. Ogawa Yōko, *Anne furanku no kioku* (Tokyo: Kadokawa shoten, 1995), 9–12.

9. Zimmerman, "Angels and Elephants," 73.

10. Zimmerman, "Angels and Elephants," 69. Ogawa Yōko, *Mīna no kōshin* (Tokyo: Chūō Kōronsha, 2006).

11. Ibid.

12. Lisette Gerhardt, "Lifestyle und Psychodesign in der Japanischen 'Moratoriumsliteratur'—Kawakami Hiromi und Ogawa Yōko. [Lifestyle and psychological design in Japanese 'moratorium literature'-Kawakami Hiromi and Ogawa Yōko]," *Johann Wolfgang Goethe-Universität Frankfurt am Main Fachbereich 9: Sprach und Kulturwissenschaften Japanologie Literaturschwerpunkt* 1 (2009), 1.

13. Chūjō Shōhei, "Moratoriamu yarō kara puroretaria bungaku e. Kyūjū-nendai Nihon bungaku no henshitsu," in *'90 nendai J-bungaku mappu. Bungei Bessatsu* (magazine). Tokyo: Kawade shobō shinsha, 1998, 76.

14. Susan Napier, *The Fantastic in Modern Japanese Literature* (London: Routledge, 1996), 207. Treat, "Yoshimoto Banana Writes Home."

15. Gerhardt, "Lifestyle und Psychodesign in der Japanischen 'Moratoriumsliteratur,'" 2.

16. Ibid.

17. Ibid., 3.

18. Ibid.

19. Gerhardt, "Lifestyle und Psychodesign in der Japanischen 'Moratoriumsliteratur,'" 3.

20. Ibid.

21. Amanda Seaman, *Writing Pregnancy in Low-Fertility Japan* (University of Hawai'i Press, 2017), 2016, 46.

22. Seaman, *Writing Pregnancy in Low-Fertility Japan*, 46.

23. Ibid.

24. Gerhardt, "Lifestyle und Psychodesign in der Japanischen 'Moratoriumsliteratur.'" Seaman, *Writing Pregnancy in Low-Fertility Japan*.

25. Ōtsuka Eiji, *Sabukaruchaa bungakuron* (Tokyo: Asahi Bunko, 2004), 184–189.

26. Ogawa Yōko, *Fukai kokoro no soko yori* (Kyoto: PHP bunko, 2006), 89.

27. Svetlana Boym, *The Future of Nostalgia* (New York: Basic Books, 2001), xv.

28. Sigmund Freud, "The Uncanny," in *The Standard Edition of the Complete Psychological Works of Sigmund Freud, volume XVII (London: Hogarth, 1953)*.

29. Ibid., 241.

30. Ibid., 249.

31. Ibid.

32. Sigmund Freud, "The Theme of the Three Caskets," in *The Standard Edition of the Complete Psychological Works of Sigmund Freud, volume XII (London: Hogarth, 1958)*. Barbara Creed, *Phallic Panic: Film, Horror and the Primal Uncanny* (Melbourne: Melbourne University Press, 2005), 21.

33. I will discuss the maternal allusions in later sections.

34. Ibid., 245.

35. Ibid.

36. Ibid.

37. Barbara Creed, *The Monstrous Feminine: Film, Feminism, and Psychoanalysis* (London: Routledge, 1993), 54.

38. Ibid., 54–55.

39. Ibid., 54.

40. Ibid.

41. Creed, *The Monstrous Feminine*, 55.

42. Ibid.

43. In *Mīna no kōshin* (2006), the protagonist Tomoko has lost her father and is separated from her mother and thus symbolically orphaned. Aya in "Daiweingu pūru" (1990) is also symbolically orphaned as her parents turn her home into an orphanage

and ignores her emotional needs. The young protagonists in "Kanpeki na byōshitsu" (1989) and *Neko o idaite, zō to oyogu* (2009) have lost both parents. In some other cases such as *Hoteru airisu* (1996) and *Kōritsuita kaori* (1998), the mother appears as a tyrant, authoritarian and abusive, while the father has died prematurely. Mayako Murai suggests that mother in *Hoteru airisu* can be regarded as "a fairy-tale stepmother" who represents the destructive side of the mother (*From Dog Bridegroom to Wolf Girl: Contemporary Japanese Fairy-Tale Adaptations in Conversation with the West* (Detroit: Wayne State University Press, 2015), 75). In all, Ogawa's young protagonists are often deprived of maternal love.

44. Creed, *The Monstrous Feminine*, 55.
45. Ibid.
46. Ogawa, "Ninshin karendā."
47. Ogawa Yōko, *Anne franku no kioku* (Tokyo: Kadokawa shoten, 1995), 9–12.
48. Ogawa, "Daiweingu pūru," 191.
49. Prize world, https://prizesworld.com/akutagawa/jugun/jugun104OY.htm#novel103 (Accessed October 7, 2020).
50. Ogawa, "Samenai kōcha," 155. All citations of "Samenai kōcha" are from the unpublished translation by Mina Qiao and Matthew C. Strecher (2020).
51. Ibid., 183.
52. Fred Davis, *Yearning for Yesterday: A Sociology of Nostalgia* (New York: Free, 1979), 35.
53. Ogawa, "Samenai kōcha," 166–167.
54. Ibid., 158.
55. Creed, *The Monstrous Feminine*, 27.
56. Anna Felicia Sanchez, "Romantic Love in the Early Fiction of Banana Yoshimoto," *Journal of English Studies and Comparative Literature* 9, no.1 (2006), 64–76.
57. Ibid., 67.
58. Ogawa, "Samenai kōcha," 177.
59. Sanchez, "Romantic Love in the Early Fiction of Banana Yoshimoto," 67.
60. Ogawa, "Ninshin karendā," 12.
61. Ibid.
62. Ibid., 26.
63. Ibid., 26–27.
64. Ibid., 26.
65. Ibid., 63–64.
66. Ibid., 26.
67. Ibid., 66.
68. Ibid., 67.
69. Ibid., 54.
70. Ibid.
71. Rosalind Pollack Petchesky, "Fetal Images: The Power of Visual Culture in the Politics of Reproduction," *Feminist Studies* 13, no. 2 (1987), 268–270.
72. Ibid.

73. Cristina Mazzoni, *Maternal Impressions: Pregnancy and Childbirth in Literature and Theory* (Ithaca and London: Cornell University Press, 2002), 62.

74. Seaman, *Writing Pregnancy in Low-Fertility Japan*, 41.

75. Ogawa, "Ninshin karendā," 72.

76. Seaman, *Writing Pregnancy in Low-Fertility Japan*, 46.

77. Takanezawa Noriko, "On Ogawa Yoko 'Pregnancy Calendar,'" *Bulletin of Faculty of Management Information Sciences, Jobu University* 26 (2003), 158.

78. Ogawa, "Ninshin karendā," 74.

79. Mina Qiao, "Escaping the Physical: Liminal Body and Liminal Space in Ogawa Yōko's Hotel Iris," *U.S.-Japan Women's Journal* 55/56 (2019), 156.

80. *Henkei* appears on page 129 of Ogawa, "Domitorī." *Henka* also appears several times, the first time on page 86. *Hensei* is emphasized on page 87 and 133.

81. Gerhardt, "Lifestyle und Psychodesign in der Japanischen 'Moratoriumsliteratur,'" 7–11.

82. Ogawa, "Domitorī," 133–134.

83. For more on maternal erotic transference (MET), please see Harriet K. Wrye and Judith K. Welles, *The Narration of Desire: Erotic Transferences and Countertransferences* (Hillsdale, NJ and London: The Analytic Press, 1994).

84. Ibid., 148.

85. Murai, *From Dog Bridegroom to Wolf Girl*, 80.

# WORKS CITED

Boym, Svetlana. *The Future of Nostalgia*. New York: Basic Books, 2001.

Chūjō Shōhei. "Moratoriamu yarō kara puroretaria bungaku e. Kyūjū-nendai Nihon bungaku no henshitsu." In '90 nendai J-bungaku mappu. Bungei Bessatsu (magazine). Tokyo: Kawade shobō shinsha, 1998.

Creed, Barbara. *The Monstrous Feminine: Film, Feminism, and Psychoanalysis*. London: Routledge, 1993.

———. *Phallic Panic: Film, Horror and the Primal Uncanny*. Melbourne: Melbourne University Press, 2005.

Davis, Fred. *Yearning for Yesterday: A Sociology of Nostalgia*. New York: Free, 1979.

Frank, Anne. *Anne Frank: The Diary of a Young Girl*. New York: Bantam, 1993 [1947].

Freud, Sigmund. "The Uncanny." In *The Standard Edition of the Complete Psychological Works of Sigmund Freud*, volume XVII. London: Hogarth, 1953 [1919].

———. "The Theme of the Three Caskets." In The Standard Edition of the Complete Psychological Works of Sigmund Freud, volume XII. London: Hogarth, 1958 [1913].

Gerhardt, Lisette. "Lifestyle und Psychodesign in der Japanischen 'Moratoriumsliteratur'—Kawakami Hiromi und Ogawa Yōko." Johann Wolfgang Goethe-Universität Frankfurt am Main Fachbereich 9: Sprach und Kulturwissenschaften Japanologie Literaturschwerpunkt 1 (2009): 1–41.

Mazzoni, Cristina. *Maternal Impressions: Pregnancy and Childbirth in Literature and Theory.* Ithaca and London: Cornell University Press, 2002.
Murai, Mayako. *From Dog Bridegroom to Wolf Girl: Contemporary Japanese Fairy-Tale Adaptations in Conversation with the West.* Detroit: Wayne State University Press, 2015.
Nakamura Miharu. "Ogawa Yōko to Anne no nikki: kusuriyubi no hyōhon, hoteru airisu, neko o idaite, zō to oyogu nado." Hokkaido daigaku bungaku kenkyū-ka kiyō. 149 (2016): 87–126.
Napier, Susan. *The Fantastic in Modern Japanese Literature.* London: Routledge, 1996.
Ogawa Yōko. "Ninshin karendā." In *Ninshin karendā.* Tokyo: Bungei shunjū, 1991.
———. "Domitorī." In *Ninshin karendā.* Tokyo: Bungei shunjū, 1991.
———. *Anne franku no kioku.* Tokyo: Kadokawa shoten, 1995.
———. "Samenai kōcha." In *Kanpeki na byōshitsu.* Tokyo: Chūō kōronshinsha, 2004 [1990].
———. "Daiweingu pūru." In *Kanpeki na byōshitsu.* Tokyo: Chūō kōronshinsha, 2004 [1990].
———. *Fukai kokoro no soko yori.* Kyoto: PHP bunko, 2006 [1999].
Ōtsuka Eiji. *Sabukaruchaa bungakuron.* Tokyo: Asahi Bunko, 2004.
Petchesky, Rosalind Pollack. "Fetal Images: The Power of Visual Culture in the Politics of Reproduction." *Feminist Studies* 13, no.2 (1987): 263–292.
Qiao, Mina. "Escaping the Physical: Liminal Body and Liminal Space in Ogawa Yōko's Hotel Iris." *U.S.-Japan Women's Journal 55/56* (2019): 153–173.
Sanchez, Anna Felicia. "Romantic Love in the Early Fiction of Banana Yoshimoto." *Journal of English Studies and Comparative Literature* 9, no.1 (2006): 64–76.
Seaman, Amanda. *Writing Pregnancy in Low-Fertility Japan.* Honolulu: University of Hawai'i Press, 2016.
Shamoon, Deborah M. *Passionate Friendship: The Aesthetics of Girl's Culture in Japan.* University of Hawaii Press, 2012.
Suzuki Tomoyuki. "Anne furanku o sōki/ sōzō suru: Ogawa Yōko 'mitsu ya kana kesshō,' aruiwa 'shōshitsu' ni sarasa reru nama." *Shakai Shirin* 64 (2018): 37–58.
Takahara, Eri. "Ogawa Yōko no kioku." *Yurīka* (2004), 104.
Takanezawa, Noriko. "On Ogawa Yoko 'Pregnancy Calendar.'" *Bulletin of Faculty of Management Information Sciences*, Jobu University 26 (2003): 148–162.
Treat, John Whittier. "Yoshimoto Banana Writes Home: Shōjo Culture and the Nostalgic Subject." *Journal of Japanese Studies* 19, no.2 (1993): 353–387.
Wrye, Harriet K., and Welles, Judith K. *The Narration of Desire: Erotic Transferences and Countertransferences.* Hillsdale, NJ and London: The Analytic Press, 1994.
Zimmerman, Eve. "Angels and Elephants: Historical Allegories in Ogawa Yōko's 2006 Mīna no kōshin (Mena's Procession)," *U.S.-Japan Women's Journal* 49 (2016): 68–96.

*Chapter Three*

# Textual, Liminal, Fantastical Spaces in Kanai Mieko's Early Writings

## Anthony Bekirov

Since her first short story "Ai no seikatsu" (1967, "The Life of Love"), Kanai Mieko (b. 1947) has demonstrated her keenness for metafictional storytelling through spatially and temporally ambiguous narratives. Even with tried rhetorical devices—a story with a beginning, a middle, and an end, a consistent narrator throughout, and long descriptions of places and ambiances, she progressively strips the narratives from these conventional literary tropes as they unfold. We often see reality and fantasy melt into each other in her writings, as the fictional worlds effectively spill out into reality. Kitada Sachie observes that "ever since she debuted, Kanai unwaveringly asserted her place among literary circles. She would 'fight' against the *status quo* of modern literature and question the 'starting point of writing.' From this day forward, she has been consistently seeking to write experimental meta-fiction, to "write about writing."[1] I thereby identify this metanarrative strategy as a composition *en abyme*, where the topological spaces in which the novels[2] characters "exist" are recursive images of the text itself being written.

Critics refer to Kanai's style as "post-modern," "experimental," situated within the "1960's avant-garde."[2] Three factors in all personal, sociohistorical, and literary aspects, in her upbringing are significant in shaping her writings. Kanai was born in 1947, in the town of Takasaki in Gunma Prefecture, to parents who were avid readers and cinephiles. Her father passed away in 1953, the same year the American occupation ended. Losing her father at the age of six had a lasting impact on Kanai, who wrote: "The death of my father was definitely what pushed me to write. As we shared the same blood, his death left a blank, a hole in my flesh (*nikutaiteki na kūhaku to ketsujo*). I was living under this nightmarish veil of darkness, and in order to escape its thralls, the best I could do was lose myself in reading books."[3] Kitada Sachie has argued that the recurrent male characters named either "P" or "F" in Kanai's early fiction refer to "Papa" and "Father," cementing the idea her passion for literature served as a way to fill in this "hole."[4] Secondly, Hannah Osborne and Sharalyn Orbough suggest that being a young girl in a Japan occupied by the Allied Forces and moving out thereafter to a megapolis still in the process of mending scars from war has heightened Kanai's sensibility to liminal spaces, that is, thresholds between discrete realities.[5] The last element that influences her writings is her exposure to Lewis Carroll's (1832–1898) Alice series, which has been examined in particular by Yoshikawa Yasuhisa (1997) and Mary Knighton (2011).[6] Throughout her early works we see Carrollian references, be it a direct quote used as an epigraph, names borrowed from the books, or allusions to elements of the plot. This textual dialogue with Carroll is not anecdotical, considering the Alice series is known for its playful use of language as a mean to obfuscate the distinction between reality and fantasy. Undoubtedly, this technique must have appealed to Kanai, whose notoriously obscure early novels argue with space, time, and the reader in order to create a unique kind of *textual* space. Thus, we will try our best to untangle the narratives of some of her most well-known early writings, in order to offer an analysis of the literary processes behind Kanai's deconstruction of "traditional" storytelling. Her debut novella, "The Life of Love," is an ideal starting point, as it already displays several features of her style, and contains others in ovo, which are more fleshed out in her subsequent novels, as we will see.

## "THE LIFE OF LOVE"—A PRELUDE TO DECONSTRUCTING NARRATIVE SPACE

"The Life of Love" in many ways lays the foundation of Kanai's peculiar treatment of spatiality and textuality. The story opens on a female protagonist battling with memory loss. Although she keeps a diary, she feels that her recollections contradict her records. The tension between her own writings and what she perceives as reality in her mind leads her to musings about the fleeting and ultimately void notion of love ("Ai" in Japanese), and especially in regard to her husband F. The tension escalates when F seems to divert from his daily routine, as he is uncharacteristically absent from work when the protagonist calls his secretary. She then embarks on a journey through an unnamed town to look for him, as her various encounters make her reminisce of past events, and cogitations about his whereabouts start to make reality and fantasy coalesce.

During the nameless protagonist's journey, random events or objects keep triggering her memories, and the two temporalities would segue into each other without any clear textual indication. These transitions are well exemplified in an episode near the end where the protagonist sits down at a restaurant, tired from looking for her husband. In front of her, a man orders a bowl of spaghetti. As he starts eating, the white, tubular appearance of the pasta reminds her of a time at her primary school, when she was looking at a box-frame in the infirmary displaying roundworms. Realizing she has been staring at the man the whole time, she feels the need to exchange a few words, but still enthralled by her vision of "the creamy, white elongated roundworms, spread across rosy (*momo-iro*) bits," she can only comment about the likeness of the spaghetti with worms. Visibly upset by her remark, the man gets up and leaves behind his half-eaten food. The protagonist then recalls visiting her aunt at a maternity and leering at the genetic monstrosities kept in formalin in a nearby ward. This passage is striking in how seamless the transitions are from what the protagonist is seeing and what she is remembering. Let us take a look at some of these "hinges" where her mind retreats into fantasy:

[After my comments, the man] left two or three mouthfuls of spaghetti and stood up without saying a word. Was I being too rude?

On the wall facing the one with the box-frames, there was a stadiometer, a scale and, of course, another frame. This one was displaying models of stools from new-borns. [. . .] Stools of five different colours!

The stew is slowly getting cold. The waitress brings me my coffee.

The old OB-GYN clinic my aunt was admitted in was constructing a new aisle on the adjacent site, so the medical resources building was in the midst of being dismantled.[7]

Finally, she remembers a corridor full of formalin jars and her husband holding her by the hand, to help her pass without having to look at the freaks inside the jars. We can see how the protagonist goes back and forth between the diner and memories. Though she stated at the beginning of the story that her memory is failing her, and often clashes with even the simplest data from her diary, there she is, vividly reliving moments from the past, thanks to a bowl of pasta. The reader can piece together the main thread weaving together these events: the appearance of the spaghetti reminds her of medical models showing tenias at her school, which in turn evoke the sickness, hospitals, and eventually her bed-ridden aunt. These relationships however are left unspoken, and instead the protagonist jumps from one thought to another, crossing the gap between different times, different spaces. In quite a Proustian manner, Kanai writes of memories not like building blocks stacked upon each other chronologically, but as indented, shapeless forms on a horizontal plane, waiting for an event of the present to "latch" onto it and be relived anew. Memories, unlike calendars, exist in a state between past and present, as they can only reflect what is already gone and yet are only to be experienced now. The spaghetti is, *at the same time*, pasta and vermin, meal and maternity ward. Even the most trivial of items can be catalysts of the deepest memories.

"The Life of Love" is written from the perspective of the protagonist and thus written from the perspective of a character whose reality is a mesh of fact and fantasy. This means space and time within the story become convoluted as well, as the protagonist seems to create her own solipsist world. In fact, the only world where she feels at ease. We can now better understand why the accounts in the protagonist's diary are irrelevant to her, if not unreliable altogether. For the diary keeps a chronological, vertical record of events: the data is a dead relic, as it holds validity only for the infinitesimal moment at which it was written and cannot assert anything else. But as soon as this moment passes, memory will write its own account, endlessy reshaping it to fit the ever-changing flow of subjective experiences. In other words, memory is protean, and its objects have no clear identities: they can change at will and assume several forms simultaneously. This becomes evident right after the aforementioned scene at the restaurant: as she prepares to leave the restaurant, she goes over various theories she has made up during the day regarding her husband's unusual absence; she then concludes these are all just "hypotheses," and thus do not matter, as all hypotheses are by nature equivocal.

> However, trying to rationalize F's actions today with examples from his past, is nothing but meaningless hypotheses (*katei*). Whether he skipped work and meeting with his friends to run away with a lover, whether he's died already or gone on a long trip, whether he's back to our apartment or having an affair, this should not matter. For this is all just hypotheses, and hypotheses are nothing definitive (*aimai da*). I stand up, and head for the rosy (*momo-iro*) telephone near the entrance. I turn the dial [. . .]. It rings three times before the wife of a friend of F's picks up the phone. I check whether F has come over their place. I can't hear properly, as the volume is low.
> 
> —Yes, he's here. A moment please, I'll call him over.
> 
> F was there. I'm so mad I'm about to hang up the phone. He's there. He's neither died nor fled: he was at a friend's house. All my theories seem so pale now (*iroasete shimau*). They were just meant to end up stale, it seems.[8]

In this scene, the description of the telephone being "rosy" (*momo-iro*, literally "peach-colored") is significant. For this is the same color as the unidentified bits in the anatomical chart where the protagonist saw the roundworms in the previous scene. Up to this very moment, the protagonist is still in her *space* where elements from her memories and from the material world she is in echo each other, a space where different times overlap, a space where entities are in intermediary states, where only probabilities exist. But as soon as she calls her husband's friend and learns he is indeed there, she becomes distraught. She shows none of the relief one would expect from such a situation. Instead, she is taken over by rage (*hara ga tatte*) as the theories that shaped her reality are now obsolete, stripped of any appeal. Until that point, she had "found" her missing husband a few times, locked away in memories. Throughout the story however, she never encounters him in the flesh. The idea that he has not truly disappeared and is even within reach is unbearable to her, for she has constructed her reality around probabilities, states of existential fluidity, and her husband's factual reappearance would annihilate this very reality. She feels endangered—not for her life, but *as a fictional character*, as I will attempt to demonstrate in the following.

Let us look back once again on the beginning of the novel. The diary she keeps seems alien to her, as if it were written by someone else. This "someone else" is none other than herself, but a self from the past. Today, she is already someone different from the day before. What this version of herself wrote yesterday needs not hold true for any other version. It is as if the protagonist had come to the stark realization that she had no life "before" the actual book we, the readers, are reading her story in. Indeed, a character does not exist outside of the pages of a book, and its every movement is strictly bound by what the author is writing. It would be naïve to assume fictional characters are bound by the same spatio-temporal rules as the reader's, just as it is absurd to presume a divide between what the characters think and what they do, because everything takes place in the same space—the textual space.

The end of the story expands on this idea. After the phone call, the protagonist goes out in the street and witnesses a young couple, a boy and a girl, arguing, before throwing themselves under the wheels of a car in an apparent lovers' suicide; she then picks up a nondescript book the deceased girl was carrying, and turns it over to the policemen; she finally recalls she thought that F had died today in a car accident too. This last scene mirrors the whole plot of "The Life of Love," as the protagonist not only identifies the deceased man with her husband, but also herself with the girl and her own story with the book of which the cover has been torn off. Osborne argues that the book the protagonist is holding in the unfinished chronicle of her life, which in turn is the novella the reader is reading; and as we do not know what book it is, she argues it may very well be the young girl's epitaph. But I would argue even further and say it can be the protagonist's epitaph.[9] If we look at the accident scene, we will see it is described in gruesome details: the young man's limbs are convulsing, the girl's head has been reduced to mush. More than mere sensationalism, this description highlights the literally faceless-anonymous nature of the young girl, and the now-nameless book. They are thus perfect vessels for projection: these lovers' death could have been one possible outcome of the protagonist's story. As is reminded by the presence of this book, that is to say, a place that can conjure contradictory possibilities, like being alive and dead at the same time, bystander and casualty. Moreover, the protagonist is bewildered at how "easy" or "casual" (*muzōsa*) her death was. This remark can refer to the death itself (casual because it was thrown away) but also to the the way it is written: death comes in a single word, by the author's hand. Osborne suggests that the demise of the young woman is, so to speak, written by the book the protagonist is holding in her hand: this book has produced a story.[10] I even argue it produced the story of "The Life of Love." If the protagonist is so fascinated by this young woman's death, it is likely because she contemplates how such a death would liberate her from the constraints of a factual biography, such as a diary. Once dead, her existence becomes the material of stories, thus timeless, which further explains why Kanai insists on this nameless book.

This specific metanarrative strategy has precedents in literature, most nostably, Miguel de Cervantes' *The Ingenious Gentleman Don Quixote of La Mancha* (1605–1615). After the first part of the book was published, an anonymous author published a spurious sequel titled *Second Volume of the Ingenious Gentleman Don Quixote of La Mancha: by the Licenciado Alonso Fernández de Avellaneda of Tordesillas* in 1614. When Cervantes was made aware of this, he incorporated the existence of this "other" Don Quixote in the second part of his book: the "real" Don Quixote discovers there are legends of exploits he never accomplished, and even encounters the fictitious writer Avellaneda. Afterward, Don Quixote decides to retire and let himself die, as he/Cervantes knows that only death can stop the spurious accounts of his life and be granted eternity through literature.[11] Kanai is aware of this and has made a reference to it in "*Akashia Kishidan*" (1974, "The Knights of Acacia"), referring to Don Quixote as a work/character that foregoes the distinction between fantasy and reality: "*don-kihōte wa kūsō to genjitsu no kubetsu wo mushi shita kara deshō* (Don Quixote ignored the divide between fantasy and reality)," which is a technique she incorporates in "The Life of Love."[12]

"The Life of Love" is constructed around connected planes of diverging states of reality. The places visited by the protagonist in her memories and her fantasies sway the factual world in which she experiences her husband's disappearance. A locked door holds mysteries that can produce theories and songs, but once opened, the reality might be made too clear and the equivocal beauty of poems might become irrelevant. Kanai Mieko involves the reader by playing with their expectations through a mise en abyme of the act of reading, as the reader's posture is mirrored in the protagonist's posture towards her own alien diary. That is, the contents of her diary is as novel to us, the readers, as it is to her, the character. It is as if her intradiegetic "life" began with her "life" as a fictional character in a book. The reader creates the character by the mere act of reading. As I stated earlier, within Kanai's textual space, there is no distinction between a character's actions and their motives: they simply *are* because they are *read by us*.

Moreover, the phrase "*Ai no seikatsu*" can mean many things. The translation of the title poses several difficulties as it is a multilayered play on words. "Ai" in the original is written with the Chinese character for love "愛" and "seikatsu" means something in the lines of "daily life." For this reason, the expression "Ai no seikatsu" does not translate to the English phrase "love life"—which implies sentimental and sexual behavior. Moreover, "Ai" can be a female surname, and in her subsequent short stories, Kanai often named her protagonists "Ai" written in phonetics. She wrote an essay on the polysemy of "Ai" in her works, *Watashi no "Ai"* (1970, "My 'Ai'"): "eye," "I," the first entries of the classical Japanese phoneme-ordering system *gojūon* (thus akin to Latin alphabet), etc. On an interesting note, though Kanai never seemed to address it, Ai is also the nickname for Alice in one of the earliest Japanese translations/adaptations of *Alice's Adventures in Wonderland* titled *Ai-chan no yume-monogatari* (1909, "The dreamy tales of little Ai") by Maruyama Eikan.[13] "Ai" can be taken for "love"—but it can also be taken for a phonetic transcription of the English pronoun "I," a reading Kanai acknowledges herself. Thus, one meaning possible is "the daily life of I." But as we know, the Japanese language has no marker for plural. Therefore, the title could also be understood as "The daily life of I's," making this short story a statement on the fluidity of identity, as "I," or the Self, is not a fixed entity with a unique, linear life.[14] The fantastical can be found in the most mundane of items: a bowl of spaghetti in "The Life of Love" leads the protagonist down a hole where memories and reality melt into one another. Alice's reality, too, becomes intertwined with fantasy through books and language. In other words, Kanai likes to write about liminal spaces, spaces in-between where notions are reversed, specifically "Subject" and "Object," "the Self" and "the Other," "Body" and "Mind," and ultimately, "the Writer" and "the Reader." She addresses these ideas in a more theoretical way in her essay "Kotoba/Genjitsu/Nikutai" (1984, Text/Reality/Body), which provides invaluable insight about her *modus scribendi*, and how she incorporates this blending of identities and spaces into her books.[15]

## THE BODY AS THRESHOLD

Kanai has always been preoccupied with *nikutai*, a rather difficult notion to render in English. Hannah Osborne, among other researchers, has used Kanai's own *nikutai* theories to approach her writings.[16] A lot of energy has been put by commentators, Western and Japanese alike, into drawing parallels between Kanai's corporeal text and French essayist Roland Barthes' theories about readerly and writerly texts. I disagree with the assumption that Kanai has "anticipated" Barthes's theories, as the two only look similar on a superficial level, and a closer analysis of Kanai reveals how specific are her theories to the Japanese language, and that they owe more to her own ingenuity than to some other Western thinker. Her idea of *nikutai* also differs from, say, the *nikutai-ha*, "literature of the flesh" that was quite popular in the immediate years after the end of the Second World War in Japan, especially for it depicted, in a blunt fashion more often than not, sexual acts, physical violence, and squalid bodily functions.[17] Kanai's "*nikutai*" refers to the body/flesh, as opposed to the idea of one's own body as a vessel for a soul, for example, and thus is not a synonym of *karada*, the more common word for "body." She writes in the essay "Nikutairon e josetsu dai'ippo" (1969, "Towards a Theory of *Nikutai*"), "When it is said that the self discovers everything in the body, it goes without saying that 'everything' includes language and sexuality. When I use words and when I behave, my body is always already there; thus I cannot conceive of splitting the consciousness from the body."[18] To be sure, Kanai too often portrays raw *flesh* in her stories as we saw in "The Life of Love." Where there is exposed flesh, there is more importantly a discourse about language and writing. But how do the two interact?

The body is a threshold in and of itself, a threshold between the external and the internal, the world and an "inner Self." For this reason, Kanai subsumes all gainable knowledge under corporeal experiences: if we can know anything, it is through our body (*nikutai*), a theme that she develops in "Towards a Theory of *Nikutai*." In this essay, Kanai focuses on explaining how physical pain enables new ways to gain knowledge because it makes one aware of how the "exterior" interacts with one's "interiors." She illustrates this theory by discussing *butō*, a type of choreography invented by Hijikata Tatsumi and Ōno Kazuo in 1959, which demands excruciating feats of agility from the dancer; as well as Hans Christian Andersen's fairy tales, which often make little girls go through painful endeavors.

In other words, bodily experiences are our only way to access reality. The bloody scenes are therefore meant to explore the limits of the human body, and thus, our relation to reality. This is not surprising that her early writings demonstrate a tendency for the transgression of this threshold through images of butchered bodies and exposed flesh. We saw it with the gruesome death of the young girl in "The Life of Love"; "Usagi" (1972, "Rabbits") has several scenes of gory violence, such as a young girl bathing naked in the blood of rabbits she slaughters, or getting one of her eyes gauged out by her father; the title of "Funiku" (1972, "Rotting Meat") refers to the rotting cadaver of a butcher the protagonist discovers under the bed of a prostitute; "Boshizō" (1972, "Mother-Child Portrait") shows a young girl losing one leg and becoming disfigured in a car accident with her father. Traumatic as these events can be, they often serve as catalysts for epiphany for the characters. Through the bodily sacrifices, they have all discovered a hidden truth or desire within themselves or realized a tabooed sexual fantasy, put another way, transgressed the threshold.

Through language, Kanai, too, tries to express this transgression of corporeal limits. She coins the term *nikutaiteki na kotoba* ("corporeal text") in her essay, to give a proper name to this characteristic of literature. Corporeal text demands the reader, you and I, to do their part in the writing, for these texts do not pretend to be monolithic written monuments that the readers should revere as "completed works," but are endowing the reader with a "*nikutaiteki*" (physical) presence.[19] However, noncorporeal texts are, according to Kanai, lost in their own internal world, and only treat the reader as an abstract entity, whose unique role is to ensure the internal coherence of the story.[20] To rephrase it accordingly, those authors write "naïvely" as if their characters had an intradiegetic life of their own, and readers could only peep at them: the limit between writer and reader seems insurmountable. Therefore, the internal coherence becomes loose, and it is up to the person who reads it to "connect the dots," to make it work—just like the protagonist of "The Life of Love" confers meaning to her surroundings by connecting them to her inner "readings," her memories.

To be clear, any text can be corporeal, just at different intensities that vary according to a factor of intangibility or ambiguity. Hence, Kanai's common usage of anonymous characters of difficult-to-assert genders, nondescript places, seemingly *nonsequitur* transitions, porosity between reality and fantasy, double entendres, and narrative inconsistencies. The reader has no choice but to fill in the gaps, suspends their disbelief and accept that literature needs not abide by common logic. These visible "gaps" in Kanai's writings have spurred a number of observations about the "presence of absence" in the stories, most notably from translator and critic Shibusawa Tatsuhiko who writes:

> In Kanai Mieko's abstract compositions, "absence" can be considered as a form of presence; our perspective is reversed, and positive becomes negative. It could be argued that the literary worlds that she orchestrates all similarly

invert presence, and are negative worlds. Which is to say that the writer makes it look as if she is, throughout the narrative, on the side of "absence," operating language. Or rather, perhaps it is closer to the truth to say that, in simply making the decision to operate language, the writer is compelled to stand on the side of "absence."[21]

Indeed, we see many "absences" in "The Life of Love": the absence of the husband, the absence of memories, and the absence of names both for characters and places. Shibusawa identified this absence with the overarching figure of the "eternal lover" (*ei'en no koibito*, a term he borrows from Kanai's story of the same name).[22] What is "eternal" about this lover is the quest thereto, because said lover is out of time and out of space. However, there are not always absent lovers in her fiction, and this out-of-spacetime quality can assume many forms. This applies to bodies as well: the heavily injured body of the young girl is of course missing parts, the anatomical models having holes with parasites in them, the sudden hunger of the protagonist. Such bodily conditions as deformities, disfigurement, injuries from accidents, mutilations, and amputations are legion in Kanai's writings, as they are all figures of absence, in corporeal and carnal terms, much like the "hole in the flesh" she described at the loss of her father.

One striking example can be found in her story "Kūki-otoko no hanashi" (1974, "Story of the Inflated Man"), which combines both carnal and spatial absence in the same figure. The story was originally published in 1974 in a special edition of the literary magazine *Shingeki* (Attack) about a circus.[23] The story tells the apropos fascination of a painter for a circus of freaks, somewhere deep in his childhood memories. By the painter's own admission, the circus is less of a memory, and more of a "vast expense of grey misty sea within [themselves]," situated out of reality where time and memory are indistinct.[24] The protagonist recalls being especially captivated by an "inflated" man, whose main gig consisted of him eating prodigious amounts of food before a disgusted audience.[25] He was not eating out of hunger, but because he wanted to attain the spherical perfection of celestial bodies. When he meets the painter again thirty years later, still working at a circus and still aiming at perfect rotundity, he goes on a tirade about the void inside of him:

> Perhaps you've noticed even when you were just a small child (or should I say, *because* you were a child), but I am an inflated ball or a balloon of sort—for I have this cavern inside of me. You see, food *should* become part of my flesh and blood, but inside of me, it keeps expanding, like some kind of air, a void out of this world (*genjitsu no nai kūkyo*).[26]

Why would the protagonist have noticed this void precisely because he was a child? This is answered by the opening remark of the narrator, which we quoted above, that is, as a child they did not know the difference between time and memory, and subjective experiences were akin to a vague sea, "in a world that did not exist." Of course, the inflated man, as an intradiegetic character, would have had no way to know this is how the painted has described his childhood memories. But, he states, his body acts like some kind of alchemical contraption: food does not disappear, but creates an ever-expanding void inside of him.[27] His own body defies time and space and exists in a space in-between. Now the phrase Kanai uses, *genjitsu no nai kūkyo*, a void without reality, calls to mind the Japanese word for literary fiction, *kyokō*, literally an "empty structure"—much like the inflated man is a structure "full" of void. The inflated man has found a way to transcend his status as *fictional character* and become *fiction* itself. He has become self-aware as a figment of fiction, and hence knows what the painter said about his memories because the painter is part of the fiction. In a narrative tour de force, Kanai created a character whose body conjures the structure of her own novel. Bodies are, as we discussed earlier, fantastical spaces after all, as they are the ultimate expression of the threshold between reality and fantasy, presence and absence.

## THE TEXT AS LIMINAL SPACE

Agreeing with Victor Turner, I define liminal spaces as places where subjects are stripped bare of their identities, where the Self is neither this nor that, eager to become some Other.[28] The inflated man symbolizes how textual space is liminal, in the way it nullifies the preexisting qualities of what enters it, in order to transform it into something new, something that has no connection with what preceded it. Kanai more often than not has materialized liminal spaces in her stories, as a narrative device *en abyme*.

For instance, the house in "Rabbits" where the writer protagonist, also the frame narrator, encounters the Alice-like young girl phasing in and of reality. The frame narrator first discovers the house after following a human-sized white rabbit through shrubberies and falling into a hole. The rabbit turns out to be the young girl, Sayuri, wearing the pelts of the rabbits she slaughtered back when she was cooking them for her incestuous father. Sayuri, the internal narrator, then proceeds to tell the frame narrator her whole life up to this point, which takes up the majority of the novella. As soon as she concludes her story, we seemingly jump forward in time, without any textual indication whatsoever from Kanai's part. The frame narrator now tells us about the second time they meet with Sayuri—however this time around, they are only able to find the house because they have a sudden *recollection* of it, as the house seems to have vanished and no one else has any knowledge of its existence.

Sayuri is now dead, but not before having brutally enucleated the eyes of her pet rabbits. The frame narrator undresses Sayuri wears her rabbit costume, and lies down next to her body and the blind rabbits, forever immobile.

The house, where the main events of the story take place, offers the frame narrator a chance to overcome their writer's block (mentioned at the beginning of the story), it is a place for them to retreat into and experience liminality, and transcend their own limited self. The house is no ordinary house, as it does not exist in the physical plane, but once again in a space in-between. As Nakamura Miharu terms it, the house is an "eternal machine of fiction."[29] That is, the house is a device that enables the frame narrator to write again—since the frame narrator is a writer, whatever narratives, even within the frame, is de facto what they write, thus Sayuri's own account of the story cannot be anything else than one written by the narrator. In the end, much like the protagonist of "The Life of Love," the narrator attains (literary) eternity by metamorphosing into their literary creation (the rabbits and Sayuri), effectively dying with them, both intradiegetically and extradiegetically, as this is the last line of the novella. This "eternal machine" is none other than the text itself.

Let us consider lastly "The Knights of Acacia" (1974), for it is a paragon of when the liminal space becomes the text itself, a testament to Kanai's bold experimentations with language. Kanai epigraphed the work with a quote from *Through the Looking-Glass and What Alice Found There* (1871), in English: "*He was part of my dream, of course—but then I was part of his dream, too!*"[30] It is Alice, back from the looking glass, speaking to her cat about the Red King. This quote is particularly relevant as it challenges the common idea that our dreams are our own—but perhaps, Carroll and Kanai are asking, we may confuse our dreams with another's, where we are being dreamt of. It hints that this is yet another story that plays with the interchangeability of Subject/Object and Writer/Reader.

The narrator in this story is, as in "Rabbits," an uninspired writer, idling his time away at a local carpentry where one of his friends work, to escape the confines of his study. One day, however, his friend has a confession to make: he too was once a writer, albeit an unsuccessful one. Fifteen years ago, he wrote a book called *The Knights of Acacia*, named after an anonymous engraving who bore the same name. He recently recalled the book after receiving a letter from an unknown and unnamed sender, telling him the events in *The Knights of Acacia* did actually take place, and the murder described in the novel happened in real life. The friend insists he made up the whole plot, and has never heard of any crime in relation to a group called "The Knights of Acacia." Nonetheless, intrigued by this letter, the narrator's friend decides to write his novel again. Not to "copy" it from his original manuscript—of which he is no longer in possession anyway—but to write the *exact same text* a second time over. The narrator, albeit deeming his friend's idea a folly, decides to write the story down—both the confession and the new story of *The Knights of Acacia*, which we, the readers of Kanai, are reading. Once his friend's rewriting is over, the narrator invalidates it saying "somewhere out there, a book called *The Knights of Acacia* already exists."[31] The narrator tries to locate the original version, but has only found one mention in an obscure literary magazine, cited among other new publications at the time—it is unrevealed to us readers whether the author's name is the same as their friend's. Finally, the narrator decide to stop spending time at the carpentry, as there is already one writer too many over there—indeed, it would be the same as staying in his room.

The idea that the narrator's friend is rewriting his lost and forgotten book *identically*, although fifteen years have passed, ties in well with Kanai's comments about the work of the writer as Penelope: the passage of time alone makes the identical into the dissimilar. That said, what we, the readers, are actually reading is not so much the friend's book as what the narrator is writing from what his friend told him. Moreover, with the narrator being a writer looking for inspiration, the whole story we are reading could be his doing. When he says "I'm going to write his story," it may very well be that he is already writing it. In fact, the whole situation (the friend, the letter, the forgotten book) might have never happened in the first place. And indeed, the mysterious letter would point us in that direction: the only way the events imagined by his friend in his fictional story could have happened "for real" is if this entire conundrum was made up by the narrator-writer, for only textual space can conjure such impossibilities. Therefore, the narrator-writer's "novelist friend" is nothing more than an alter-ego, a projection of himself into a fiction in order to overcome their creative block. Having achieved this goal, the "friend" is discarded at the end, as it was only another, transitional Self for the narrator. Conversely, the narrator-writer is Kanai's alter-ego as well, as her *The Knights of Acacia* is the story of a writer writing *The Knights of Acacia* as told by his ex-writer friend rewriting his first book *The Knights of Acacia*. The experimental nature is particularly visible in *The Knights of Acacia* but even more so in her subsequent short story "Puratonteki na ai" (Platonic Love)—which revives the *Ai* figure in some kind of send-off to "The Life of Love"—where the "story" consists entirely of a writer writing about the letters he receives, in which an anonymous sender writes word for word the same story as the one he is writing, that is, the story, *we readers*, are reading.

Here we see the textual space acting as liminal, that is, allowing the writer to become the Other in order to create fiction.[32] And rather than signifying the presence of liminality through fictional places and narrative devices, like the house in "Rabbits" for example, Kanai writes about the process of writing by writing a text that acts as a writing process, thus reducing to a minimum, if not zero, the distinction between author and reader, intradiegetic and extradiegetic levels, fantasy and reality.

## CONCLUSION

Kanai's experimental forrays into corporeal text lead her to compose stories in which the characters' identities are transitional, changing over the course of the "intrigue" (to be sure, a word to use loosely in Kanai's case). These characters go through liminal spaces where reality and fantasy collapse into one another: they can be an old hospital ward, enchanted woods, a hidden house, or a circus. Ultimately, these spaces become one with the text of the novella itself, as Kanai aimed to push her experiments to the extreme. In summary, the spaces where the blending of identities, the blending of reality and fiction happens has gradually moved from being intradiegetic to being the body of the text.

The "body" of the text, of the corporeal text encompasses the reader's body as well—as per Kanai's essays on literature, reality, and body. Faced with these complex metanarratives where reading habits are barely relevant anymore, the reader is forced to act as the author in order to internalize the story and make it into their own narrative. The body is after all, according to Kanai, our sole medium to know the world; as well as language is learned through our bodies and used by our bodies to create literature. Kanai's early writings are especially corporeal for they engage the reader as a physical presence in the process of writing: the reader's body becomes part of the fiction. If we are to look for fantastical space in Kanai's story, we might just need to look at our own bodies.

## NOTES

1. Kitada Sachie, "Kanai Mieko ni okeru 'shōjo' to 'boken'" ("'Girlhood' and 'Matriarchy' in Kanai Mieko"), in *Haha to musume no feminizumu* ("The Feminism of Mothers and Daughters"), eds. Kitada Sachie, Mizuta Noriko, & Hasegawa Hiroshi, (Tokyo: Tahata Shoten, 1996), 140–156, 140.

2. Mary Knighton, "Kanai Mieko," in *The Columbia Companion to Modern East Asian Literature*, ed. Joshua Mostow (New York: Columbia University Press, 2003), 242–245; Yoshikawa Yasuhisa, "Arisu Shōkan" ("Summoning Alice"), in *Ai no seikatsu—Mori no Meryujīnu* ("The Life of Love—Melusine of the Forest"), Kanai Mieko (Tokyo: Kōdansha, 1997) 257–272; Kitada, "Kanai Mieko ni okeru 'shōjo'

to 'boken'"; Hannah Osborne, *Gender, Love and Text in the Early Writings of Kanai Mieko* (doctoral thesis, University of Leeds, 2015), 134; Watanabe Naomi, *Kakumo sensai naru yokobō: Nihon 'roku hachi nen' shōsetsuron* ("Such an intricate hyphen: a Theory of the '1968 Novel' in Japan") (Tokyo: Kōdansha, 2003).

3. Quoted in Kitada Sachie, "Usagi: Hito to bungaku" ("Rabbits: Kanai's Life and Work"), in *Tanpen josei bungaku: Gendai* ("Contemporary Short Stories by Women"), eds. Yabu Teiko, Watanabe Sumiko, & Imai Yasuko, (Tokyo: Ōfū, 1993), 153–160; 153.

4. Kitada, "'Girlhood' and 'Matriarchy,'," 149–150; Kitada, "Kanai's Life and Work," 153.

5. Osborne correlates the depiction of derelict hospital wards in Kanai's *The Life of Love* to the Japanese government's rebuilding initiative throughout the country, in particular Tokyo's Shinjuku district, where old crumbling structures were gradually replaced by skyscrapers. See Osborne, *Gender, Love and Text*, 135–137. Although Sharalyn Orbaugh acknowledges there is little to nonpolitical allusion in Kanai's early fiction, she does argue that the radical questioning of society fundamental values after the war helped shape her style. See Sharalyn Orbaugh, "Arguing with the Real: Kanai Mieko," in *Ōe and Beyond*, eds. Stephen Snyder & Philip Gabriel (Hawai'i: University of Hawai'i Press, 1999), 145–277, 247–248.

6. Yoshikawa, "Summoning Alice"; Mary Knighton, "Down the Rabbit Hole: In Pursuit of Shōjo Alices, from Lewis Carroll to Kanai Mieko," *U.S.-Japan Women's Journal*, 2011, no. 40 (2011): 49–89.

7. Kanai Mieko, *Ai no seikatsu—Mori no Meryujīnu* ("The Life of Love—Melusine of the Forest") (Tokyo: Kōdansha, 1997), 49–50. All quotations from the Japanese original are translated by this author, unless otherwise indicated.

8. Ibid., 52–53.

9. Hannah Osborne, "The *Ai*-Novel: *Ai no seikatsu* and Its Challenge to the Japanese Literary Establishment," *Japanese Language and Literature* 53, no. 1 (2001): 95–121.

10. Ibid., 114–115.

11. Daniel Eisenberg, "Cervantes, Lopes and Avellaneda," in *Estudios cervantinos*, ed. Daniel Eisenberg (Barcelona: Sirmio, 1991), 119–141.

12. Kanai Mieko, "Akashia Kishidan" ("The Knights of Acacia"), in *Ai no seikatsu*, 217–240, 231.

13. Kawato Michiaki, "Meiji no Ruisu Kyaroru" ("Meiji and Lewis Carroll"), *Honyaku to Rekishi*, no. 2, (2000), https://www.ozorasha.co.jp/nada/page040.html.

14. I am certainly not alone on this reading. See for example Yoshikawa Yasuhisa, *Kanai Mieko no sōzōteki sekai* ("Kanai Mieko's Fantastical World") (Tokyo: Suiseisha, 2011); Watanabe Naomi, "Kanai Mieko no kyōkai sen" ("Kanai Mieko's Borderline"), in *Nihon 'roku hachi nen' shōsetsuron ("Such an intricate hyphen: A Theory of the "1968 Novel' in Japan')* (Tokyo: Kōdansha, 2003), 201–253; Tomoko Aoyama, 'Transgendering Shōsetsu: Girls" Intertext/Sexuality," in *Genders, Transgenders and Sexualities in Japan*, eds. McLelland Mark & Romit Dasgupta (New York: Routledge, 2005), 49–64; Takeuchi Kayō, "Kanai Mieko: 'Usagi' o meguru kuia, 'shōjo' no monogatari kara 'watashi' no monogatari e" (Kanai Mieko:

The Queer in 'Rabbits,' from a 'Girl' Novel to an 'I-novel'"), *Shōwa bungaku kenkyū*, no. 56 (2008): 163–84; Knighton, "Kanai Mieko"; Obsorne, "The *Ai*-Novel."

15. Kanai Mieko, "Kotoba/genjitsu/nikutai" ("Words/Reality/Flesh"), in *Obasan no disukūru* Kanai Mieko (Tokyo: Chikuma shobō, 1984), 62–68.

16. See Osborne, *Gender, Love and Text*, 165–231 for a discussion of Kanai's idea of *nikutai*.

17. Douglas Slaymaker provides a useful summary of the different meanings of the word "*nikutai*" before and after the war in Japan in *The Body in Postwar Japanese Fiction* (London: Routledge, 2004), 8–10.

18. Kanai Mieko, "Nikutairon e josetsu dai'ippo" ("Towards a Theory of *Nikutai*"), *Gendai shi techō*, no. 12 (1969): 20–26, 22. Translated in part in Osborne, *Gender, Love and Text*, 166–178.

19. For a discussion on the topic, see Atsuko Sakaki, "Breezes through Rooms with Light: Kanai Mieko by Roland Barthes by Kanai Mieko," *Proceedings of the Association for Japanese Literary Studies*, no. 10 (2009), 204–219.

20. Kanai, "Words/Reality/Flesh," 67–68.

21. Shibusawa Tatsuhiko in Kanai Mieko, *Zentanpenshū* ("Complete Short Works") (Tokyo: Nihon bungeisha, 1992), vol. 1, 625, quoted in Osborne, *Gender, Love and Text*, 148–149, from which we humbly borrow the translation.

22. Kanai Mieko, "Ei'en no koibito" ("The Eternal Lovers"), in Kanai Mieko, *Ai no seikatsu—Mori no Meryujīnu* ("The Life of Love—Melusine of the Forest") (Tokyo: Kōdansha, 1997), 153–158.

23. Kanai Mieko, "Kūki otoko no hanashi," *Shingeki*, no. 21 (1974), 138–144. This version differs slightly from the subsequent one published in the anthology *Akashia kishidan* ("The Knights of Acacia") in 1976, as it features an introduction and a conclusion written from an external narrator, who relates what the painter (the main protagonist of the story) has told him. The latter version only has the painter as the narrator and has become the canon for ulterior reprints. For a discussion on these changes, see Hannah Osborne, "Structuring the Void: Kanai Mieko's 'Inflated Man' and Pictorial Allusion," *Proceedings of the Association for Japanese Literary Studies*, no. 18 (2017), 134–153.

24. Kanai, "Kūki otoko no hanashi," 207.

25. It is my theory that this *kūki otoko*, as he is named in the original title, is a reference to a short story by the most proeminent figure or *erotique-grotesque*, Edogawa Ranpo, published in 1959 with the title "Petenshi to kūki otoko" ("The Charlatan and The Vaporous Man"). Though this particular story is not set in a circus (the protagonist is said to be like "air" (*kūki*) because his character is particularly bland), Kanai and Edogawa's shared interest for freaks, paraphilia, and compositions *en abyme* makes me believe she has been influenced by his writings, if only in an indirect way. Let us also note that the expression *kūki otoko* can be traced back to the father of Japanese science fiction, Unno Jūza, who penned an identically named short story in 1937 about a man who dissolves into thin air.

26. Kanai, "Kūki otoko no hanashi," 215.

27. I am using this metaphor *apropos*, as Kanai has mentionned alchemistry in other fiction, most notably "Boshizō" ("Portrait of a Mother and Child"), in which

the internal narrative is told by a disembodied voice described by the narrator as an alchemist (*renkinjutsushi*). For Kanai, "fiction," or literature in general, seems to be akin to alchemistry in its ability to turn anything into something entirely different, as I discussed for the way memories worked in "Ai no seikatsu."

28. Liminality has been defined first by Dutch-German-French ethnographer Arnold van Gennep in his book "Les Rites de Passage" (*Rites of Passage*, 1909) for his field anthropological field work in Africa. Victor Turner is however responsible for much of the conceptual backbone of liminal spaces and their meaning in postindustrial societies. See in particular Victor Turner, *The Ritual Process: Structure and Anti-Structure* (New-York: Cornell Paperbacks, 1969).

29. Nakamura Miharu, "Kyokō no ei'en kikai: Kanai Mieko 'Usagi' to *gensō* no ronri" ("An Eternal Machine of Fiction: Kanai Mieko's 'Rabbits' and the Logic of Fantasy"), *Japanese Literature Association* 41, no. 2 (1992): 33–42.

30. Carroll Lewis, *Through the Looking-Glass and What Alice Found There* (London: MacMilland and Co., 1872), 222.

31. Kanai, "Akashia Kishidan," 240.

32. It is only fitting that the so-called real Knights of Acacia, according to the letter received by the narrator's friend, is the name of a fraternity of teenagers at a school, whose rites of passages resulted in a murder—as liminality is the essence of rites of passage.

# WORKS CITED

Aoyama, Tomoko. "Transgendering Shōsetsu: Girls' Intertext/Sexuality." In *Genders, Transgenders and Sexualities in Japan*, edited by Mark McLelland & Romit Dasgupta, 49–64. New York: Routledge, 2005.

Carroll, Lewis. *Alice's Adventures in Wonderland*. London: MacMilland and Co., 1866.

———. *Through the Looking-Glass and What Alice Found There*. London: MacMilland and Co., 1872.

Eisenberg, Daniel. "Cervantes, Lopes and Avellaneda." In *Estudios cervantinos*, edited by Daniel Eisenberg, 119–141. Barcelona: Sirmio, 1991.

Kanai Mieko. "Nikutairon e josetsu dai'ippo," *Gendai shi techō*, no. 12 (1969): 20–26.

———. "Kūki otoko no hanashi," *Shingeki*, no. 21 (1974), 138–144.

———. "Kotoba/genjitsu/nikutai." In *Obasan no disukūru*, Kanai Mieko, 62–68. Tokyo: Chikuma shobō, 1984.

———. "Ai no seikatsu." In Mieko Kanai, *Ai no seikatsu—Mori no Meryujīnu*, 7–57. Tokyo: Kōdansha, 1997.

———. "Mori no Meryujīnu." In Mieko Kanai, *Ai no seikatsu—Mori no Meryujīnu*, 143–152. Tokyo: Kōdansha, 1997.

———. "Ei'en no koibito." In Mieko Kanai, *Ai no seikatsu—Mori no Meryujīnu*, 153–158. Tokyo: Kōdansha, 1997.

———. "Boshizō." In Mieko Kanai, *Ai no seikatsu—Mori no Meryujīnu*, 181–188. Tokyo: Kōdansha, 1997.

———. "Usagi." In Mieko Kanai, *Ai no seikatsu—Mori no Meryujīnu*, 159–180. Tokyo: Kōdansha, 1997.

———. "Kūki-otoko no hanashi." In Mieko Kanai, *Ai no seikatsu—Mori no Meryujīnu*, 207–216. Tokyo: Kōdansha, 1997.

———. "Akashia kishidan." In Mieko Kanai, *Ai no seikatsu—Mori no Meryujīnu*, 217–240. Tokyo: Kōdansha, 1997.

———. "Puratonteki na ai." In Mieko Kanai, *Ai no seikatsu—Mori no Meryujīnu*, 241–252. Tokyo: Kōdansha, 1997.

Kawato Michiaki. "Meiji no Ruisu Kyaroru," *Honyaku to Rekishi*, no. 2, 2000. https://www.ozorasha.co.jp/nada/page040.html.

Kitada Sachie. "*Kanai Mieko ni okeru 'shōjo' to 'boken.'*" In *Haha to musume no feminizumu*, edited by Sachie Kitada, Noriko Mizuta & Hiroshi Hasegawa, 140–156. Tokyo: Tahata Shoten, 1996.

———. "*Usagi: Hito to bungaku.*" In *Tanpen josei bungaku: Gendai*, edited by Teiko Yabu, Sumiko Watanabe, & Yasuko Imai, 153–160. Tokyo: Ōfū, 1993.

Knighton, Mary. "Down the Rabbit Hole: In Pursuit of Shōjo Alices, from Lewis Carroll to Kanai Mieko." *U.S.-Japan Women's Journal*, no. 40 (2011): 49–89.

———. "Kanai Mieko." In *The Columbia Companion to Modern East Asian Literature*, edited by Joshua Mostow, 242–245. New York: Columbia University Press, 2003.

Mutō Yasushi, "Nenpu—Kanai Mieko." In *Ai no seikatsu—Mori no Meryujīnu*, Mieko Kanai, 273–282. Tokyo: Kōdansha, 1997.

Nakamura Miharu, "Kyokō no ei'en kikai: Kanai Mieko 'Usagi' to *gensō* no ronri." *Nihon bungaku* 41, no. 2 (1992): 33–42.

Orbaugh, Sharalyn, "The Body in Contemporary Japanese Women's Fiction." In *The Woman's Hand. Gender and Theory in Japanese Women's Writing*, edited by Paul Gordon Schalow & Janet A. Walker, 119–164. Stanford: Stanford UP, 1996.

———. "Arguing with the Real: Kanai Mieko." In *Ōe and Beyond*, edited by Stephen Snyder & Philip Gabriel, 145–277. Honolulu: University of Hawai'i Press, 1999.

Osborne, Hannah, "Gender, Love and Text in the Early Writings of Kanai Mieko." Doctoral thesis, University of Leeds, 2015.

———. "Structuring the Void: Kanai Mieko's 'Inflated Man' and Pictorial Allusion," *Proceedings of the Association for Japanese Literary Studies*, no.18 (2017): 134–153.

———. "The *Ai*-Novel: *Ai no seikatsu* and Its Challenge to the Japanese Literary Establishment," *Japanese Language and Literature* 53, no. 1 (2019): 95–121.

Sakaki, Atsuko, "Breezes through Rooms with Light: Kanai Mieko by Roland Barthes by Kanai Mieko," *Proceedings of the Association for Japanese Literary Studies*, no. 10 (2009), 204–219.

Slaymaker, Douglas N. *The Body in Postwar Japanese Fiction*. London: RoutledgeCurzon, 2004.

Takeuchi Kayō, "Kanai Mieko: 'Usagi' o meguru kuia, 'shōjo' no monogatari kara 'watashi' no monogatari e," *Shōwa bungaku kenkyū*, no. 56 (2008): 163–84.

Turner, Victor. *The Ritual Process: Structure and Anti-Structure*. New York: Cornell Paperbacks, 1969.
Watanabe Naomi. "Kanai Mieko no kyōkai sen." In *Kakumo sensai naru yokobō: Nihon 'roku hachi nen' shōsetsuron*, Naomi Watanabe, 201–253. Tokyo: Kōdansha, 2003.
Yoshikawa Yasuhisa. "*Arisu Shōkan*." In *Ai no seikatsu—Mori no Meryujīnu*, Mieko Kanai. 257–272. Tokyo: Kōdansha, 1997.
———. *Kanai Mieko no sōzōteki sekai*. Tokyo: Suiseisha, 2011.

*Chapter Four*

# Cannibalistic Space and Reproduction in Japanese Speculative Fiction

## Kazue Harada

The Brazilian poet, Oswald de Andrade (1890–1954) in "Manifesto Antropófago," wrote, "Only anthropophagy [i.e., cannibalism] unites us. Socially. Economically. Philosophically."[1] His manifesto is a call for challenging European colonizers and hegemonic power. His idea of cultural cannibalism "permits the Brazilian subject to forge his specular colonial identity into an autonomous and original (as opposed to dependent, derivative) national culture."[2] Andrade's manifesto for cultural cannibalism illustrates a powerful resistance to the colonizers since it opposes the Western colonial myth of anthropophagy or cannibalism as an uncivilized, primitive, and evil practice. In recent Japanese female speculative fiction works, cannibalism is employed not only as a form of resistance to the hegemonic power of the institutionalized reproductive ideology but also as a means of survival and a coping strategy for alienated individuals living in coercive, reproductive-centered, futuristic worlds. Cannibalism is presented as a way to reveal hegemonic and normative power.

Japanese modern literary scholar Tomoko Aoyama argues that Japanese modern "texts that have cannibalism as a theme involve [. . .] a notion of "displacement.' . . . In its literal representations, anthropophagy, in these Japanese texts, does not simply pop up of its own accord, [. . .] out of the everyday, like a long-repressed element in what is domestic and familiar. On the contrary, to encounter it, we have to move out of the everyday, and beyond any notion of the familiar."[3] The idea of "displacement" is key for these female authors' depictions of anthropophagy in relation to geographical and physical space and time. In their works, the practice of human cannibalism directly connects to the domestic and public spheres, especially the success of fertility and pregnancy, as cannibalism is normalized and institutionalized in most of their stories.

In the speculative fiction of Murata Sayaka and Ono Miyuki, cannibalism challenges the norms of reproductive-oriented, heteronormative, and patriarchal societies. Paradoxically, alienated individuals in these stories may also use cannibalism as a path to temporarily fit into society, though they find unique ways to practice it. Many recent Japanese speculative stories depict reproductive-centered futuristic societies as a social critique of the governmental, pronatal policies that are prevalent in contemporary Japan due to the country's low birth rates. The practice of and beliefs surrounding cannibalism that are depicted in Murata's two works and Ono's work differ from each other, yet all of these stories are centered around alienated protagonists who do not fit into the home or the reproductive-centered society. Because of this, the alienated individuals try to find a space to fit in or try to survive the normative pressures of the society through cannibalistic practice. In this chapter, I will explore how cannibalism is presented in Murata's novella "Seimei-shiki" ("Ceremony of Life"), her novel *Chikyū seijin* (*Earthlings*), and Ono's novella "Pyua" ("Pure").[4]

## CANNIBALISM IN LITERARY REPRESENTATIONS

In contrast to the Western colonial myth of cannibalism tropes, there is a strong resonance with Andrade's manifesto in Brazilian speculative fiction in the first half of the twentieth century. According to Elizabeth M. Ginway, cannibalism presented in the protozombie narratives in Brazil is a critique of how the texts "parody foreign models [the colonizers' civilization and technology] and consume bodies to question hegemonic power."[5] Literally or metaphorically, cultural cannibalism is used in the narratives. Ginway describes this as "eating the past": how the protozombie narratives reflect the displacement of population due to socioeconomic change in the early twentieth century.[6] She concludes that the tropes describe "inarticulate anxiety accompanying the incursion of social and technological change that erodes cultural traditions or institutions, provoking the return of the living dead who refuse to remain buried."[7] Murata and Ono's cannibalistic tropes are not directly connected to the colonizers' hegemonic power, but they certainly illustrate anxiety over the socioeconomic change in the Japanese population, reproductive technology, and the state's use of coercive and highly conforming hegemonic power.

There is not much existing scholarship on cannibalism in literary representations in Japanese literature, as Aoyama observes. Tomoko Aoyama traces a wide range of cannibalism presented in various genres of modern Japanese literature from the 1890s to the 1980s. In contrast to these Japanese texts, as she notes, in modern Western literature, the cannibalism trope is often dichotomized between the colonizers/colonized, the civilized/savage, and culture/nature. Borrowing from William Arens' idea, she states, "Anthropophagy acts as a mystic justification for the dominance of colonizer over colonized. In the Japanese imagination, the world of the Other is more ambiguous."[8] Although Japan was unmistakably positioned as a colonizer of other Asian countries during the late nineteenth and the half of the twentieth centuries, it has not been quite colonized. In the Japanese texts, Japan has not quite become "the colonizing Westerners."[9] I primarily concur with Aoyama's assessment regarding cannibalism representations in modern Japanese literature.

As mentioned above, cannibalism presented in Japanese imaginations encompasses a notion of displacement. As Aoyama further summarizes cannibalism in Japanese texts, cannibalism appears in various themes to be an extension of displacement: "ritual, mortuary, institutional, and pathological, all of both the 'aggressive' and the 'affectionate' varieties."[10] Cannibalism is used both literally and metaphorically and is employed as "a feminist rebellion against social or sexual victimization," whereas some other texts employ cannibalism as "a satirical device for attacking bourgeois smugness and hypocrisy."[11] In addition, some texts depict cannibalism based on actual wartime experiences. Particularly, in Aoyama's discussion of Kurahashi Yumiko's (1939–2007) *Sumiyakisuto Q no bōken* (The Adventures of Sumiyakist Q, 1969), cannibalism is presented as a parody of Marxism or any ideology—Q as a Sumiyakist (Kurahashi's made-up term) understands "everything, cannibalism included, as a product of class conflict."[12] Kurahashi's concepts of antinovel and nowhere as a utopia are relevant to Murata's and Ono's social critiques of reproduction.[13] In Kurahashi's novel, the institutionalized practice of cannibalism in the reformatory does not end with a solution while Q does not do anything.[14] Although Murata's and Ono's works provide resistance in the end, the societal norms in their worlds do not change.

Additionally, it is important to note that the man-eating woman tropes like *yamamba* or *yamauba* (a mountain witch) are abundant in folktales from medieval Japan. Particularly, the *yamamba* trope is relevant to Ono's story, "Pure," of the man-eating women, although the author does not specifically state its influence or its relevance.[15] Noriko Reider argues that the cannibalistic side of women is primarily associated with the image of *oni*-woman ("female demons, ogres, or monsters").[16] However, Noh plays, such as *Kurozuka*, depict two conflicting images of the "evil and cannibalistic side" (*oni*-woman) and "helping, giving fortune and fertility" (*yamamba*) intertwined together.[17] As Reider also points out, "The interchangeability of *yamauba* and *oni*-woman in the proactive behavior of *yamauba* indicates the influence of patriarchy, where men tried to confine women to the private sector."[18] It is intriguing how cannibalistic images of the man-eating woman can be associated with fertility as are presented in Murata's and Ono's works. Ono's story can even be read as the reversal of the trope of confinement, as it depicts women who exert dominance and control over men.

Murata's and Ono's works include the themes that have been discussed in previous classical and modern literature, but in a similar vein as Aoyama's argument, the stories of cannibalism in their works do not simply align with the dichotomized story between the colonizer and the colonized that is prominent in modern Western literature. In Murata's and Ono's stories, while cannibalism can be a means of resisting the highly conforming reproductive society, it also paradoxically offers a way for alienated individuals to fit in or cope with society with only minor resistance.

## CANNIBALISM AS A WAY TO FIT IN AND INTIMACY WITHOUT SEX

Murata Sayaka (b.1979), winner of the prestigious Akutagawa Prize, has consistently written about the themes of reproduction to create alternative reproductive futures. As Anna Specchio argues, Murata Sayaka's works such as "Birth Murder" prioritize reproduction over bodies.[19] Murata's recent works are not an exception to this idea. Many of her works also focus on a reproductive society that uses means other than sexual intercourse, namely a sexless reproductive system. Murata's 2014 novella, "Satsujin shussan" ("Birth Murder"), received the 2014 Special Award for a Counter Measure to the Low Birthrate by The Japanese Association for Gender Science Fiction and Fantasy. The story depicts a childbirth system in a near-future world where, to solve the problem of low birth rate, *umibito* (child-bearers) must give birth to ten children and then are allowed to kill one person. In this world, both men and women are able to become child-bearers, similar to the fictional worlds of Murata's 2015 novel, *Shōmetsu sekai* (*World Vanishing*).[20] *World Vanishing* presents worlds that are sexually sanitized yet reproductive through the use of reproductive technology. In the story, Eden is portrayed as the ideal reproductive city, where everyone participates in reproductive efforts for the future of children and where sexual desire and reproductive activities are entirely separate practices. Specchio also claims that Murata's works often represent the combination of utopia and dystopia to achieve her feminist agenda.[21] Similarly, *Earthlings* and "Ceremony of Life" also depict reproductive-centered societies with an element of cannibalism and the combination of utopia and dystopia in service to a feminist argument. While cannibalism only appears toward the end of *Earthlings,* funerary cannibalism is depicted as a normative practice to enhance fertility in "Ceremony of Life." Both stories offer a social critique of the reproductive-centered world and are simultaneously survival stories of alienated individuals.

In "Ceremony of Life," people are encouraged to have a "ceremony of life" [*seimei-shiki*], which is subsidized by the government, instead of having a funeral. In the ceremony, guests eat the flesh of the deceased person prepared by the family as a ceremonial banquet, which is depicted as an economical method of food production and consumption. This funerary cannibalism is presented as a path to fertility, as afterward, reproductive aged attendees are encouraged to engage in a fertility ceremony [*jusei-shiki*]—namely, sexual intercourse for a reproductive purpose—as a response to the dramatic decrease in population. The belief "life is born from death" is adapted as a ritual in the society.[22] Both funerary anthropophagy and sexual intercourse are treated as sacred practices. The protagonist, Miho, does not feel at ease with the ceremony of life or the fertility ceremony, although she is not opposed to anthropophagy. She feels strange about how the social taboo has become a sacred ritual over the course of only three decades. However, Miho is eager to help cook and eat the human flesh when her colleague and good friend, Yamamoto, dies. This is a turning point of Miho's attitude toward the ritual, yet she does not fully conform in the exact same way in regard to the fertility ceremony. The change in Miho's attitude provides her with an alternative, momentary way to fit into the societal practice without fully adopting it. To contrast Miho's change, I will first discuss a regular ceremony of life.

As we can see from the descriptions of Miho's attendance to her former retired colleague's ceremony of life, anthropophagy is a normalized practice in this society. As mentioned above, cannibalism presented in this story is treated as both a common, everyday practice and something that is beyond or outside of everyday practice.[23] This technique is employed here: the uncommon practice of anthropophagy is transformed into familiar and common practice.[24] Set in contemporary Japan, the story integrates the alien practice of anthropophagy into the everyday life of cooking culturally familiar food, food consumption, funeral customs, and sexual activities. In literal representations of cannibalism, the combination of the familiar and the unfamiliar creates a visceral feeling for many readers. For example, the descriptions of the recipe and cooking methods for human flesh enable the reader to visualize the food and to engage emotionally with anthropophagy. In the story, since human flesh is not suited for a simple cooking method and seasoning (e.g., grilling with salt) due to the distinctive smell of the meat, the common recipe used for preparing and eating human flesh is a hot pot with a rich miso-based soup.[25] As the miso-based soup is a daily dietary consumption for many

Japanese readers, imagining a familiar dish made with human flesh might make the readers experience the story in a more visceral way.

Murata's descriptions of the ceremony and the conversation between the wife of the deceased (Nakao) and an old male attendee further emphasize anthropophagy as a normalized practice and evoke a visceral feeling and the strangeness of the custom:

> The wife said, "Well then, I will now begin Nakao's ceremony of life. Everyone, please eat a lot of lives (Nakao's flesh) and create new lives."
>
> While saying that, she opens the lids of the hot pots. Nakao-san is in the pots boiled together with napa cabbages and *enoki* mushrooms.
>
> Everyone, putting their hands together, says, "Itadakimasu" [Thank you for the meal] and starts eating Nakao-san. Everyone brings beautifully sliced meat of Nakao-san to their mouths and gives high praise for the quality of the meat.
>
> "Mm, delicious! Mrs. Nakao, Nakao-san tastes rather nice." The white-haired old man nods with approval while eating the meat.
>
> He continues, "This is really a good custom. Eat a life, and create a life . . ."
>
> Mrs. Nakao gently wipes her tears with her handkerchief.
>
> "Thank you. My husband is pleased."[26]

Except for the addition of human flesh, the description of the hot pot with the sliced meat and vegetables portrays a normal hot pot banquet or the meal after the funeral and gives a sense of realism. However, praise for the deceased's flesh highlights just how out of the ordinary the meal is. This ritual is presented as the act of mourning and celebration and gives meaning to the deceased's life to the family. For example, Nakao's wife, weeping after hearing the compliments on the deceased flesh, offers a dark sense of humor. Simultaneously, the funerary cannibalism brings the domestic and public spaces together. The house of the deceased is opened to the public. Sharing a hot pot also emphasizes a communal and collective eating of the dead. This collective value of anthropophagy is striking, as the story notes that the practice was a taboo only thirty years prior.

The quick adaptation of the collective value of anthropophagy and the following public sexual intercourse by the mass population underscores the strangeness of the normalcy. After eating, a couple stand up and tell Mrs. Nakano, "'Well, we are going to fertilize.' She responds, 'Oh, dear. That's nice. Congratulations.' Everyone starts clapping their hands. The two respond, 'Gochisoosama deshita. [Thank you for the meal.] We will try our best to create a new life.'"[27] This collective funeral anthropophagy is directly connected to sexual intercourse solely for reproductive purposes and thus to participate in a collective reproductive system. The combination of these two practices together illustrates the constructed and contingent nature of current social values. Miho, particularly, is concerned that people do not question the collective value of the practices as norms but adopt them without critical thinking.

Miho's discomfort regarding the collective social value of the practices manifests in her decision not to eat the human flesh. Although they are not against the practice of anthropophagy per se, Miho and Yamamoto are not willing to eat at Nakao's ceremony. Miho recalls an incident in preschool thirty years earlier. When other children were listing what they wanted to eat (clouds, water striders,[28] elephants, giraffes, monkeys) on a school bus, Miho jokingly said a "human." Everyone else was freaked out by what Miho said. The teacher scolded her with a scary face the next day. Anthropophagy was a taboo in her preschool years.[29] Thirty years later, funeral anthropophagy is normalized and considered sacred. Miho cannot shake off the strange feeling of how people have adapted the customs.[30] At her workplace, a female colleague who had participated in the funeral anthropophagy and a fertilization ceremony returns from maternity leave and childbirth, and everyone thanks her.[31] The female colleague says that she got pregnant after a ceremony of life, and other colleagues respond, "how mysterious" or "anthropophagy is human instinct."[32] Miho quietly says in her mind: "I wanted to say, 'You guys were saying that another thing was human instinct before.' No instinct exists in this world. No ethics exist. This is a fake sense (of value) given by the constantly transforming world."[33]

Murata's story is a critique of the prevalence of reproductive futurism in contemporary Japan's pronatal policies. Since 1995, the Japanese government has instituted countermeasures to combat the low birth rate by promoting childbirth. The Basic Act for Measures to Cope with a Society of Declining Birth Rate (Shōshika shakai taisaku kihon hō, enacted in 2003) recently was reinforced by programs such as the Three Children and Childrearing Related Acts (Kodomo/kosodate bijon 2010, enacted in 2012). These programs operate under the concept of reproductive futurism: "A child is a hope for the society and a power force for the future. Children filled with smiles make a society that embraces hopes and dreams."[34] This program's main goals are "to support the environment for childrearing as an entire society" ["the Dynamic Engagement of All Citizens"] and "to achieve everyone's dream."[35] This program, thus, aims at establishing societal, regional, and community support systems for childrearing for the betterment of everyone's life as well as improving the lives of youths. Although the government recognizes that having children is ultimately a personal choice and that single parents are in need, the implementation of pronatal policies endorses heterosexual marriage and the assumption that having children will solve the problems of the low birth rate and secure the future of Japan.[36]

In contrast to Nakao's ceremony, Miho's reaction to her colleague Yamamoto's ceremony of life and anthropophagy is quite different. She prepares several dishes with his mother and younger sister and enjoys tasting the flavor of his flesh. The detailed recipe is left by Yamamoto himself: Yamamoto Meatballs in a Grated Radish Pot, Stir-fry Yamamoto with Cashew Nuts, and Braised Cubed Yamamoto. In contrast to the common recipe, his recipes bring out the flavor of the meat through light seasoning. Again, the combination of the familiar dishes and the human flesh gives a sense of normalcy yet a visceral feeling. Although she treats the meat with affection, the description of his flesh and cooking process illustrates that her affection for Yamamoto is neither romantic nor erotic. She looks at his flesh and describes it as "the mixture of vivid red and white meat" and "beautiful."[37] While she is slicing the meat from the bones, she recalls Yamamoto's hairy arms as she describes in her mind: "That's right. On Monday, this arm tapped my back as if he were encouraging me. Now I see his big and gentle arm as the meat with the bones on the top of the cutting board."[38] Miho's recollection of Yamamoto through the flesh is the part of her process of mourning, yet how she cuts, slices, and grates his flesh without hesitation makes the reader cringe. To exemplify further, the detailed descriptions of Miho eating Yamamoto's meat dishes offer the paradoxical feeling of the familiar and the unfamiliar. The taste of his flesh seems correlated to Miho's understanding of Yamamoto. Miho describes Yamamoto Meatballs in a Grated Radish Pot and Braised Cubed Yamamoto:

A whole meatball fills in my mouth, and I bite it gently.

The juice gradually comes out from the meat. With the mixture of *yuzu*'s acidity and texture of grated radishes, the meatball begins to melt in my mouth. The meatball tastes stronger than beef or pork, yet less pungent in smell than wild boar's meat. The flavor is smooth yet rich.

[. . .]

*Umami* (good) flavor is condensed in the cubed meat. *Yuzu koshō* (*yuzu* pepper seasoning) matches well with the rich flavor of the human flesh. A hint of animalistic flavor is refined by the condiments. [. . .] The more I chew, I feel both the firmness of the meat with a bit of tendon parts and the tenderness of jiggly fatty parts, the more depth of his flavor I can taste.[39]

As we can see, the flavor, scent, and texture of Yamamoto's flesh highlight the complexity and depth of the meat flavor, which is associated with Yamamoto's gentle personality. Yamamoto's dishes emphasize the natural flavor of the flesh itself rather than a strong-flavored sauce, spice, or condiment. His personality is characterized as rich yet smooth without having a strong quirk (*kuse no nai*). The description of the process of chewing the meat can be interpreted as understanding Yamamoto's personality: the more Miho gets to know him, the more depth she discovers. Miho's process of eating can be understood as affective expressions toward Yamamoto and emotional closeness to him. Because of her close friend, she has felt for the first time that a ceremony of life is wonderful.[40]

In the end of the story, Miho participates in a fertilization ceremony without having sexual intercourse yet achieves emotional intimacy with Yamamoto. Miho goes on a picnic to the sea in Kamakura at night, with leftovers from Yamamoto's ceremony. When she tries to eat rice balls along with Yamamoto's braised meat in it and the stir fry with cashew nuts, a young gay man approaches her and explains that he is worried she might commit suicide. After talking to him, she shares the food of Yamamoto with him. He cannot participate in a fertilization ceremony, but he later brings his sperm in a sealed container for use in the ceremony. While other people are practicing a fertility ceremony by the sea, Miho goes in the sea, scoops the sperm she received, puts them inside of her body, and thinks about how Yamamoto liked the sea. Miho describes the moment:

> I've conformed with the normalcy in this world for the first time since I was born. I've taken on the value of this ever-changing world and become a momentary part of the value.
>
> The night progresses, and both the sky and the sea become pitch black. Yamamoto's life is slowly absorbed into my body.
>
> Yamamoto and I merge into one life. I close my eyes while soaking my feet into the feel of the water that I've long forgotten. The sound of waves keeps echoing in my ears that we are fertilizing.[41]

Miho finally feels that she has successfully participated in the reproductive-centered society, although the passage notes that her adaptation may be fleeting since the social values keep changing. She enjoys consuming and digesting Yamamoto's flesh, and the practice converges into her fertilizing process without sexual intercourse. The act of anthropophagy of Yamamoto allows Miho to have an intimate moment with Yamamoto and to adapt to the society temporarily. The location of the sea is also used as a symbolic image of the process of fertilization. However, Miho is not so completely changed that she can practice a traditional fertility ceremony, and she does so without sexual intercourse. A sexless reproductive method is a recurring theme in many of Murata's works. Perhaps, this temporary adaption to cannibalism is Miho's way of surviving and coping with the reproductive-centered society; however, the imperfect adaptation to the practice is Miho's small resistance to its compulsory heterosexual reproductivity.

## CANNIBALISM AS SOCIAL SURVIVAL AND RECOVERY FROM TRAUMA

Unlike "Ceremony of Life," Murata's *Earthlings* does not focus on the theme of cannibalism but tells the life story of the protagonist's, Natsuki's, sexual abuse in her childhood and isolation from family and the society, which is centered around reproduction. Natsuki sees this world as an Earthling's "baby factory" and begins to believe that she is an alien from the imaginary Planet Popinpobopia. She feels that she does not fit into any society, but especially a reproductive-centered world where all humans are social tools for the baby factory. As Murata herself mentioned in an interview at 2020's Cheltenham Literature Festival, "People in Japan are living in a sort of hell. Politicians see people as child-bearing machines."[42] The low fertility rate in contemporary Japan overlaps with the world of *Earthlings*. Reproduction becomes an important force for labor and economic production. In *Earthlings*, the cannibalism that takes place at the end of the story functions as a recovery from trauma as well as resistance to a highly conforming reproductive capitalistic society that only permits a uniform ideal and neglects those who do not conform and those who carry trauma caused by the society's focus on reproduction. To understand the function of the cannibalism, I will briefly discuss the story and explore how the idea of cannibalism as a displacement is connected to the spatial and temporal elements and how Natsuki's fantastical imagination, including resorting to cannibalism, works to produce survival and coping strategies for dealing with trauma—the process of recovering from trauma of sexual abuse and the heteronormative, reproductive-centered, capitalistic society.

*Earthlings* is a survival story for those who do not fit in to society. The story begins with Natsuki's visit to her grandfather's place in Akishino, Nagano, where she is away from home, surrounded by abundant nature, and where she may feel close to her imaginary Planet Popinpobopia. She bonds with her cousin Yuu because they both feel that they do not quite fit into the home or society. Natsuki's parents favor her older sister at home, whereas Yuu must grow up and take care of his divorced (and suicidal) mother.

Natsuki tells Yuu her secret that her plush toy named Piyyut comes from Planet Popinpobopia. She also believes that she is a magical girl, while Yuu sees himself as an alien. Every summer Natsuki looks forward to going to her grandfather's place to see Yuu. They commit to each other as a boyfriend and a girlfriend. At the age of ten, they make three marriage pledges to each other; the third pledge is "Survive, whatever it takes."[43] Their imaginations of being an alien and a magician help them cope with a hostile and stifling world. During sixth grade, Natsuki's teacher, Mr. Igasaki, at the "Juku" or "cram school," begins to molest Natsuki. [44] She tells her mother about her teacher's weird behaviors, but her mother does not believe her. At the summer festival, Natsuki is invited to the teacher's house and is forced to have oral sex. One day, she visits his house and uses her magical powers to escape from his abuse (murdering him without having any memory of the incident). In adulthood, she gets married to an asexual husband, Tomoya, as she does not want to engage in any sexual or reproductive activities. Both Natsuki and Tomoya get married to conform with the social expectations yet avoid the participation in the "Baby Factory." In the end, Natsuki, Tomoya, and Yuu start to live as aliens—Popinpobopians—in Natsuki's grandfather's place in Nagano.

In *Earthlings*, the element of cannibalism involves in the idea of displacement. As Aoyama notes, "[Cannibalism] is as a part of the Other, and for it to be represented, for us to experience it—and perhaps even participate in it—we have to undergo a displacement, a crossing of the frontier into the Other."[45] This description of the displacement is relevant to the nonconforming characters of Natsuki, Tomoya, and Yuu, who avoid living as Earthings, but choose to live as aliens. Cannibalism occurs only after they cross the border of the Earthling world (as a norm) to becoming nonconforming beings—aliens. The reader participates in experiencing how the three characters completely cross over to the alien perspective. Alien living is mainly concerned with providing the basic needs of food, sleep, and shelter without conforming to the productive/reproductive capitalistic society. The three of them live based on the basic time structure of daytime and nighttime, rather than the more complicated schedule dictated by living in society. Cannibalism happens not only out of the necessity for food consumption, but it is also connected to the need to defend themselves from Mr. Igasaki's parents, who intrude into their space seeking revenge for the death of their son. For Natsuki, anthropophagy is the process of recovery and healing from sexual abuse and the Earthling society, as she refuses to become a social tool. Cannibalism causes a mysterious pregnancy to occur in all three. In a sense, their mysterious pregnancy fits into Earthling society's expectations for being reproductive yet they are reproductive in a different way.

Aoyama argues that the displacement through cannibalism in the texts she discusses involves both space and time.[46] Considering the displacement, the movement within space as well as the change in the concept of time are intriguing features in terms of the process of changing and coping. For example, the movement between the geographic spaces of the urban area and the rural area, the space between the imaginary world (Popinpobopia aliens) and the real world (Earthlings), and the time between the Georgian calendar used by society and the Light/Dark Time used by the three characters are employed. Literary scholar Mina Qiao, in discussions of Ogawa Yōko's works, explains her idea of "liminal space" as follows, "A liminal space is a spatially peripheral and chronologically confused, self-contained world where conventions do not apply."[47] In the process of displacement in Murata's works, the transition between these spaces can be considered a liminal space. Cannibalism as displacement occurs in the rural area called Akishina in Nagano—Natsuki (and Yuu)'s grandfather's place—a place outside of childhood Natsuki's home and distanced from urban life and the human factory of the Earthlings. For Natsuki and Yuu, the place was a temporary sanctuary space in their childhood. Akishina is a geographical space as a peripheral but also a symbolic space where Natsuki and Yuu were able to share the imaginary world (Popinpobopia) and the real world (Earthlings). Later on, when Akishina becomes their alien world, the concept of the time changes. As mentioned earlier, they no longer need to follow the Georgian calendar for the reproductive and productive factory of the Earthlings. Instead, they focus on the Light/Dark Time for daily survival. Their imaginary and alien space does not apply standard conventions. Cannibalism occurs in this liminal space and is the ultimate method of survival for them. Murata employs this narrative device to create a liminal space for Natsuki's survival and coping strategies to flee danger and traumatic experiences.

Natsuki uses imaginary and supernatural methods such as magic, out-of-body experiences, and being an alien in the liminal space as coping mechanisms to deal with hostile and traumatic experiences. For example, trauma of sexual abuse and rape affects Natsuki in her childhood and adulthood. Out-of-body experiences help her temporarily escape from trauma. As noted above, during the summer festival, Mr. Igasaki invites her to come to his house and forces Natsuki to perform oral sex. In order to cope with the rape during the moment, she has an out-of-body experience:

> Suddenly my vision crumpled. Before I knew it, I had left my body and was looking down from the ceiling at Mr. Igasaki holding my head.
>
> Wow, I must have summoned a super strong magical power. I had no idea how, since I hadn't used my wand or mirror. But despite this spectacular magic, I felt no emotion whatsoever and simply watched my own body in silence from the ceiling.

Seeing Mr. Igasaki holding my skull and using my head as a tool, I vaguely understood. I'd thought I wasn't yet fully fledged member of the Factory, but actually I was already one of its tools after all.[48]

Mr. Igasaki forces Natsuki to perform oral sex even though she does not know what exactly he is doing to her. Natsuki's out-of-body experience allows her to escape from the trauma and to create a temporary distance, a liminal space, between her emotions and her body. This can be considered a temporary coping strategy, just like her and Yuu's pledge: "Survive whatever it takes." Natsuki also realizes that society considers her a sexual object whether she is aware of it or not, which makes her "one of [the Baby Factory's] tools." Afterward, Natsuki loses all sense of taste, and her ability to enjoy food does not return until she eats Mr. Igasaki's father's flesh.

Cannibalism happens at the climax of the story as the characters cross over from the Earthling world to the alien world. As mentioned above, cannibalism in this novel functions as a displacement of Earthling power to alien power—allowing Natsuki to regain her own power. After Natsuki, Yuu, and Tomoya adapt to their lives as aliens, Mr. Igasaki's parents come to their place in Nagano to avenge their son's death. The parents attack Natsuki, Yuu, and Tomoya, who kill them in self-defense. The shortage of food necessitates that the bodies be cut up and their flesh eaten for survival. While they manage to place the woman's flesh into the freezer, the man's flesh will not fit in the freezer, and so they decide to cook him as three different dishes: "Miso Soup with Man, Daikon Leaf and Man Stir-Fry, and Man Simmered in Sweetened Soy Source."[49] Similar to the "Ceremony of Life," the menu gives a sense of a mundane meal except for the fact that the dishes have been made with human flesh, but more importantly, Natsuki regains her sense of taste:

> It was the first time I'd felt such a fierce appetite since my mouth had been broken.

## "BON APPÉTIT!"

> I took a sip of the Miso Soup with Man and got quite a shock. "I can taste it!"

> "What do you mean? Of course you can! It's food, after all," Yuu said, amused, but I felt a surge of excitement at sensing taste on my tongue after such a long time.

I'd thought my mouth would never recover as long as I lived, but now it was my own again. The meaty soup filled my entire mouth with the strong flavor mixed in with the smell and slowly saturated each part of my body. Ecstatically, I munched on the Earthling. I felt as though I was eating for the first time in twenty-three years.[50]

Imagining eating the human flesh is visceral for many readers, yet this cannibalism scene is a significant turning point for Natsuki since her sense of taste is recovered. Consuming the flesh of the sexual abuser's father heals the trauma that she had endured for twenty-three years. Natsuki enjoys her sensation of not only taste, but also the smell and texture of the meat. This moment of displacement allows the power to shift and Natsuki to regain herself. As in Andrade's "Anthropophagite Manifesto," it is a shared moment of resistance with other alienated individuals in the society.

In the end, Natsuki, Yuu, and Tomoya all grow large bellies and conclude that they are pregnant. Using the same theme as "Ceremony of Life," cannibalism in this story causes mysterious pregnancy. Cannibalism is depicted as a method of survival and an alternative way of fitting into the societal expectations for nonconforming individuals. Yuu notes that any value, such as cannibalism or alienness, can be contagious and become a norm in the future: "'Don't worry,' Yuu said. 'This form of yourselves is also dormant with you, even if it isn't evident now. It can infect you at any time.' He smiled at them reassuringly. 'Tomorrow we will multiply. The day after we will multiply more.'"[51] His comment reminds us how cannibalism and fertility become normalized, as it is in the funeral rites in "Ceremony of Life." The taboo in the present can become the norm in the future, as any kind of value becoming a norm can "multiply."

## CANNIBALISM AS REPRODUCTIVE FOOD CONSUMPTION

Ono Miyuki (b.1985) began writing at an early age but turned to writing essays and fiction in recent years. She published a novella, "Pyua" [Pure], originally in *SF Magazine* in 2019, and her second fiction book, *Pure*, which is a collection of five stories including "Pyua," was published in 2020. *Pure* has also been nominated for the 2020 Sense of Gender Award. Similar to Murata's stories of cannibalism as a direct path to pregnancy, Ono's story tells of a compulsory reproductive system in which women must ingest men in order to become pregnant in a drastically depopulating world of the future. As Ono mentioned in a 2020 interview, she was inspired by the image of how the female praying mantis eats the male mantis after mating.[52] However, Ono's female cannibalistic trope is not a simple story of a power inversion between women and men or the women's utopia that is often depicted in alternative history or the future in speculative and science fiction. Certainly, it does not mark the cannibal female as "sexual attraction" or the racially other woman to be sexually liberated by the colonizers as is depicted in European and American literature.[53] Perhaps, it is similar to the image of the woman eating men in Japanese folk tales, such as the positive tales of *yamamba*, yet it is not a story of the female cannibals defeated by men nor is it a story of a woman who must be confined in the space of the mountain.[54] Ono's female cannibalism concerns a highly conforming reproductive-centered society reflecting the prevalence of the nation-state pronatal policies in contemporary Japan. In the world she creates in which cannibalistic reproduction is a norm, the protagonist who does not fit into society finds an alternative way to survive.

Similar to "Ceremony of Life," female cannibalism in Ono's story is institutionalized for pregnancy and childbearing. "Pure" begins with the scene of women hunting men for food and sexual consumption. The world of "Pure" is a sexually binaristic and strictly homosocial world between men and women. While men are used for labor and as a food resource, living in the special districts, women fight the society's enemies in wars and bear children. If women bear many children, they become an "honorary woman" who is exempt from universal conscription.[55] Women (with fangs, long nails, and scales on their bodies) have been genetically modified and evolved from human beings for the purposes of hunting and reproduction. In Planet Jung, young women (fifteen to eighteen years old) are trained to fight wars against their enemies and to hunt men for childbearing once a month. The protagonist, Yumi, does not quite fit into the cannibalistic reproductive-centered society. She hunts for men out of necessity and completes her institutionalized duties under surveillance, but she thinks that she might find another way of living. Cannibalism in this story is presented as a way to fit in to the world in which she resides. Yumi meets the man Eiji, but she does not eat him because he is raising abandoned "unevolved" (i.e., human-like) girls and because she likes him. In the end, Yumi chooses freely to have sex with and eat Eiji after one of her classmates attacks him. In the very end, for Yumi and two unevolved girls, cannibalism becomes solely a means of survival but not for a reproductive purpose. The slightly modified practice of cannibalism offers a small resistance to the coercive institutionalized reproductive practice. I will examine how Yumi rejects institutionalized cannibalism at three points in the story by means of minor resistance.

Yumi has discomfort with the (heterosexual) woman's roles that she must perform, including cannibalism, as she does not conform with the national duties. Ono herself commented in a 2020 interview on how women must play multiple roles in contemporary Japan: "I think what a contemporary woman is required to do is just like matching all six faces of Rubik's cube. First of all, she must work as the same as men; she must bear children; she must have an attractive appearance; she must be approved as a good wife, a wise mother. Even if all these requirements are satisfied, she is also told that she as a woman is not happy if her husband isn't making money."[56] Her comment reflects this fictional story in which women's roles are to fight to protect the nation and to bear children (to hunt men) for the nation. Instead, Yumi is more interested in looking at her friend Hitomi during the hunting and the cannibalistic moment. The story begins with Yumi admiring Hitomi's beautiful body, her ecstatic face caused by sexual pleasure, and her eating moment while Yumi is having sex with the man she had hunted. Yumi's image of Hitomi is erotic and descriptive:

> Hitomi shakes her body and raises herself up. Her glowing red body part is exposed when she spreads her legs wide open. Like a ripe pomegranate is fully open and its juice is dripping from it—Hitomi's center that swallows a penis in depth.
>
> It's beautiful, I think. Her genitalia, her smooth hip from there, her juicy breasts, her rich and wavy flaxen hair, her teary green eyes like a peridot gem, her strong muscular legs that place firmly on the ground and that her fingers dig into her skin.
>
> [...]
>
> Once I saw [the man's orgasmic face], my vagina that is supposed to be excited is getting cold and stiff like an iron pipe.
>
> [...]
>
> Soon after she checks that the man completely ejaculates, Hitomi rips the flesh from the man's throat with her two sharp fangs.[57]

The beginning sets up the tone of the story. Although Yumi does what is expected of her, she is not excited about sex with men for bearing a child. The detailed descriptions of Hitomi's body parts clearly show that Yumi likes to observe Hitomi's body and actions rather than having sex with the man. Yumi's sexuality does not fit into the imposed heterosexual reproductive system. Instead, Yumi experiences sexual and cannibalistic pleasure through watching Hitomi's body, as we do not see Yumi's eating and sex until the end of the story.

Yumi also does not eat or have sex with the man Eiji when she meets him. She instead communicates with him and gets to know him. Eiji's features remind Yumi of an image of Hitomi. Yumi eventually develops feelings for him and struggles with her desire to eat him. She begins to imagine the moment of enjoying Eiji's flesh,

> I want to embrace him and break his bones into pieces. Then I want to bite off the hard and chewy tendons fiercely and swallow all the body parts without leaving a piece. I want to bite his soft belly with my fangs, take all his organs out, chew them vigorously. I want to feel his warm blood coming through my throat, take in his hair, nails, and eyeballs as my nutrients, and absorb the entirety into my body.[58]

The description above illustrates how Yumi begins to desire him. She begins to fall in love. Particularly, she imagines how she wants to eat and chew each body part of his body. In contrast to how Miho tastes Yamamoto in Murata's "Ceremony of Life," Yumi's detailed and grotesque description seems less visceral because it is extreme. It highlights her affection and sexual feeling toward Eiji. Nonetheless, cannibal and sexual desire conflicts with her desire to see him and her respect for him and how he has raised the abandoned children.

Yumi can identify with Eiji since both Yumi and Eiji do not quite fit into society. Eiji has also escaped from the workplace and is raising the two abandoned female infants named alpha and beta who are unevolved, namely, similar to human beings in our society.[59] Yumi describes the two girls as "strange creatures," who have "no scales, no fangs, and no strong muscles" and who are called "'uncompleted' or 'ancestry misplaced' who possess a weaker body than men."[60] Unevolved females are killed after they are born because they "can't participate in wars, can't bear a child, and have no use."[61] This is reminiscent of the eugenics law in postwar Japan, as well as the politician's comment about there being "no use for menopausal women" if they are not reproductive. Nonreproductive people, like Yumi and Eiji, who do not conform are not valued in their reproductive society.

In the end, Yumi and Eiji's life with two girls does not last. Her classmate, Mami, is not happy with how Yumi can live naturally without conforming with society while Mami tries to follow the rules. Mami finds Eiji and has sex with him before Yumi gets there, leaving Eiji's neck bleeding severely. Yumi struggles with Mami and kills her. Yumi runs to Eiji. Before he dies, he asks Yumi to eat him and to take care of alpha and beta. She has sex with Eiji, and by her own choice, she eats him afterward.

In the very end, Yumi begins to live outside of the reproductive system and raise the two girls and a potential baby she might be carrying in her womb. Yumi hunts men at night and eats them with alpha and beta for survival. Yumi describes how she enjoys hunting and consuming men's flesh: "'Crunch,

crunch,' I feel crunchy noise in my head when a man's skull breaks. [. . .] I have no hesitation. Hunting is fun. The choking scent of blood. Sensation of how the heavy muscle fibers tear apart. Energy and mass that I take a living life. Nobody has taught me hunting is such fun in Planet Jung."[62] Yumi enjoys hunting and anthropophagy when it is her choice. Cannibalism becomes the practice of food consumption but no longer for a reproductive purpose. While alpha begins to grow fangs, beta begins to look like Yumi. Yumi's life with alpha, beta, and her baby is a method of resistance against and an alternative way of living outside of the institutionalized practice of cannibalism and reproduction.

## CONCLUSION

"My town is a factory for the production of human babies. People live in nests packed closely together. [. . .] The nests are lined up neatly in rows, and each contains a breeding pair of male and female humans and their babies. The breeding pairs raise their young inside their nests. I live in one of the nests too."[63] This is Natsuki's view of the normative world in Murata's *Earthlings*. All three works of Murata and Ono discussed here share worlds that are heteronormative, reproduction-driven, and reflect the state-imposed reproductive policies in contemporary Japan. Cannibalism in the texts is treated differently from the postcolonial speculative and science fiction that parodies and challenges models of colonization, as do the protozombie narratives in Brazilian literature. However, by using cannibalism, all the stories call into question the normalcy that creates hegemonic power in the reproductive-centered world. They parody, instead, the ways in which the Japanese government reinforces the values of women acting as childbearing machines and baby factories as a norm. In the end of Murata's "Ceremonies of Life," Miho conforms with anthropophagy and reproduction yet does so in a temporary and unique way by exerting volition and choice. Natsuki in Murata's *Earthlings* recovers her trauma of sexual abuse through anthropophagy. Three alienated characters are able to momentarily conform by becoming pregnant in a special, even magical way. In "Pure," while conforming at first to the practices of her society, Yumi lives and practices outside the normative cannibalistic reproductive society in the end. All of these characters have a momentary conforming moment, yet cannibalism still creates space for these unique individuals and a form of resistance, even though the resistance seems to be small. These forms of resistance depict a means of survival from and a coping strategy to deal with a highly conforming society.

## NOTES

1. Oswald de Andrade, "Anthropophagite Manifesto," (May 1928): para. 1, https://391.org/manifestos/1928-anthropophagite-manifesto-oswald-de-andrade/.
2. Lesilie Bary, "Oswald de Andrade's 'Cannibalist Manifesto,'" *Latin American Literary Review* 19, no. 38 (July-December 1991): 35, http://www.corner-college.com/udb/cproK3mKYQAndrade_Cannibalistic_Manifesto.pdf.
3. Tomoko Aoyama, *Reading Food in Modern Japanese Literature* (Honolulu: University of Hawai'i Press, 2008), 95.
4. "Ceremony of Life" was originally published in 2013 in *Shinchō* magazine and was published again as a collection of twelve stories in 2019.
5. Elizabeth M. Ginway, "Eating the Past: Proto-Zombies in Brazilian Fiction 1900–1955," *Alambique. Revista académica de ciencia ficción y fantasía/ Jornal acadêmico de ficção científica e fantasía* 6, Iss.1, Article 7 (2018): 1.
6. Ginway, "Eating the Past," 4.
7. Ibid., 10.
8. Aoyama, *Reading Food*, 96. Aoyama also refers to the idea of William Arens's *The Man Eating Myth* (1979).
9. Ibid., 96.
10. Ibid., 95.
11. Ibid.
12. Aoyama, *Reading Food*, 116.
13. Atsuko Sakaki, introduction to *The Woman with the Flying Head and Other Stories by Kurahashi Yumiko* (New York: Routledge, 2015), loc. 135 of 2590, Kindle. Sakaki cites Kurahashi's "Shōsetu no meiro to hiteisei" (trans. "The Labyrinth and Negativity in Fiction, "1966, translated by Dennis Keene) Kurahashi's idea of antinovel is described as "[a]t an uncertain time, in a place that is nowhere, somebody who is no one, for no reason, is about to do something—and in the end does nothing: this is my ideal of the novel."
14. Aoyama, *Reading Food*, 116–120. See Aoyama's discussion.
15. I had a wonderful opportunity to talk to the author Ono Miyuki on December 12, 2020, in the online book club meeting organized by East Asian subject librarian, Mitsutaka Nakamura, at Washington University in St. Louis. Ono mentioned that she was influenced by Hans Christian Andersen's "The Little Mermaid" (1837). See the interview with the Hayakawa publisher, "Gendai josei no ikizurasa."
16. Noriko Reider, "*Yamauba* and *Oni*-Women: Devouring and Helping *Yamauba* are Two Sides of the Same Coin," *Asian Ethnology* 78, no. 2 (2019): 405, 407, 422.
17. Reider, "*Yamauba* and *Oni*-Women," 417–422.
18. Ibid., 422.
19. Anna Specchio, "Eutopizing the Dystopia Gender Roles. Motherhood and Reproduction in Murata Sayaka's *Satsujin Shussan*," *Metacritic Journal for Comparative Studies and Theory* 4, iss. 1 (2018): 103.
20. While some translate *shōmetsu* as "Dwindling" in English versions of the title, I choose to use "Vanishing" because the word expresses a strong sense that sexual relations and family are completely disappearing. I also believe that "World

Vanishing" might be appropriate to capture the ambiguity of "vanishing," thanks to Laurel Taylor's suggestion.

21. Anna Specchio, "No Sex and the Paradise City: A Critical Reading of Murata Sayaka's *Shōmetsu sekai*, *International Journal of Afro-Asiatic Studies* 24, no. 2 (2020): 376, 391.

22. Murata Sayaka, "Seimei-shiki" [Ceremony of Life], in *Seimei-shiki* [Ceremony of Life], (Tokyo: Kawade shobō, 2019), 13.

23. Aoyama, *Reading Food*, 95.

24. Funerary anthropophagy was historically practiced in some cultures and groups in our societies but is no longer considered, by any means, common practice.

25. Murata, "Seimei-shiki," 16. I use my own translation of "Seimeishiki" throughout the chapter.

26. Ibid., 17.

27. Ibid., 18.

28. Water strider is "*amenbo*" in Japanese; the creature is usually not considered to be food, but the first two syllables of the word—*ame*—sound the same as a candy and thus seems sweet to a child.

29. Murata, "Seimei-shiki," 11–12.

30. Ibid., 14.

31. Ibid., 22.

32. Ibid.

33. Ibid.

34. Cabinet Office, Government of Japan, "Kodomo/ kosodate bijon" [Future Visions for Children/Childrearing] 2010, accessed February 21, 2021, https://www.cao.go.jp/shoushi/shoushika/family/vision/pdf/honbun.pdf. In terms of the "three" related acts, the Cabinet Office stresses three essential moral attitudes: 1. "Embrace human lives and growth"; 2. "Help those who are in need"; 3. "Support everyday lives."

35. Cabinet Office, "*Kodomo/kosodate bijon*."

36. There are many other pronatal policies: *konkatsu* or commercialization of marriage, *rankatsu* or egg freezing for women at early ages, *sankyū papa* project or paternal leave for childcare.

37. Murata, "Seimei-shiki," 33.

38. Ibid., 34.

39. Ibid., 38–39.

40. Ibid., 39.

41. Ibid., 48–49.

42. Murata Sayaka, "Live Online Q&A with Sayaka Murata," interview, Cheltenham Literature Festival, Oct. 4, 2020. The rhetoric of women's wombs as childbearing machines, which strongly resonates in contemporary Japan due to the current low birth rate, is reinforced by nationalistic sentiment. Several news items have reported on well-known politicians evaluating women's worth in terms of their reproductive capabilities. For example, the former Tokyo governor, Ishihara Shintarō, asserted in 2001 that menopausal women are of no use, and the former finance minister Yanagisawa Hakuo referred directly to women as childbearing machines in 2007. In

2014, when the female politician Shiomura Ayaka, who was unmarried and had no children, was presenting her concerns about the state's emphasis on pregnancy, childbirth, and fertility, a few assemblymen in the Tokyo Metropolitan Assembly yelled at her to get married soon and give birth. On a 2015 television show, the former prime minister, Suga Yasuhide, congratulated a famous male actor/singer and female actress on their marriage and encouraged the actress to bear many children to counter the low birth rate.

43. Murata Sayaka, *Earthlings* (2018), Translated by Ginney Tapley Takemori. (New York: Grove Press, 2020), 30. I use Ginny Tapley's (2020) translation of *Earthlings* throughout the chapter.

44. In Japan, many children attend after school, on weekends, or during the breaks "Juku," which is often translated as "cram school." It is a private tutoring or prep school that helps students prepare for entrance exams that are required by the Japanese school system.

45. Aoyama, *Reading Food*, 95.

46. Ibid., 95–96.

47. Mina Qiao, "Escaping the Physical: Liminal Body and Liminal Space in Ogawa Yōko's *Hotel Iris*," *U.S.-Japan Women's Journal* 55–56 (2019): 157.

48. Murata, *Earthlings*, 62–63.

49. Ibid., 237.

50. Ibid., 237–238.

51. Ibid., 246.

52. Ono Miyuki, "Gendai josei no ikizurasa o egaitara SF ni natta. 'Pyua' Ono Miyuki Intabyū" [When I imagine difficulties in life for contemporary women, the story has become science fiction. 'Pure,' Ono Miyuki's Interview]" interviewed by Mizoguchi Rikimaru, *Hayakawa Books & Magazines* (April 12, 2020), https://www.hayakawabooks.com/n/nc7a7e1c28017. I use my own translation of this work.

53. See cannibalism as "sexual attraction" in Arlette Bouloumié, "The Ogre in Literature," in *Companion to Literary Myths, Heroes and Archetypes*, ed. Pierre Brunel. trans. Wendy Allatson et al. (New York: Routledge, 1992), 921. The Jesuit missionary Jean de Lèry (*History of a Voyage to Land of Brazil, Otherwise Called America (etc.)*, 1578) links cannibalism and sexual liberation of native women. Cited in Peter Sands, "Cannibal Tropes in Gilman's Narrative of Discovery: The Food that Fuels the Nation" *Utopian Studies* 26, no.1, Special Issue: Utopia and Food (2015): 130.

54. Reider, "*Yamauba* and *Oni*-Women," 422.

55. Ono Miyuki, "Pyua" [Pure], in *Pyua* [Pure] (Tokyo: Hayakawa shobō, 2020), 13.

56. Ono, "Gendai josei no ikizurasa."

57. Ono, "Pyua," 7–9. I use my own translation of "Pyua" throughout.

58. Ibid., 36.

59. Ono's book includes a novella called "Eiji" that is a story about him prior to meeting Yumi.

60. Ono, "Pyua," 27.

61. Ibid.

62. Ono, "Pyua," 54.
63. Murata, *Earthlings*, 35–36.

## WORKS CITED

Andrade, Oswald de. "Anthropophagite Manifesto." May 1928. https://391.org/manifestos/1928-anthropophagite-manifesto-oswald-de-andrade/.

Aoyama, Tomoko. *Reading Food in Modern Japanese Literature*. Honolulu: University of Hawai'i Press, 2008.

Arens, William. *The Man-Eating Myth: Anthropology & Anthropophagy*. New York: Oxford University Press, 1979.

Bary, Leslie. "Oswald de Andrade's 'Cannibalist Manifesto.'" *Latin American Literary Review* 19, no. 38 (July-December 1991): 38–47. http://www.cornercollege.com/udb/cproK3mKYQAndrade_Cannibalistic_Manifesto.pdf.

Bouloutmié, Arlette. "The Ogre in Literature." In *Companion to Literary Myths, Heroes and Archetypes*, ed. Pierre Brunel. trans. Wendy Allatson, Jusith Hayward, and Trista Selous, 912–924. New York: Routledge, 1992.

Cabinet Office, Government of Japan. "Kodomo/ kosodate bijon" [Future Visions for Children/Childrearing]. 2010. Accessed February 21, 2021. https://www8.cao.go.jp/shoushi/shoushika/family/vision/pdf/honbun.pdf.

Ginway, Elizabeth M. "Eating the Past: Proto-Zombies in Brazilian Fiction 1900–1955." *Alambique. Revista académica de ciencia ficción y fantasía/ Jornal acadêmico de ficção científica e fantasía* 6, iss.1, Article 7 (2018): 1–14.

Murata Sayaka. *Earthlings*. Translated by Ginney Tapley Takemori. New York: Grove Press, 2020.

——. "Live Online Q&A with Sayaka Murata." Interview. Cheltenham Literature Festival. Oct. 4, 2020.

——. "Satsujin shussan" [Birth Murder]. Tokyo: Kōdansha, 2014.

——. "Seimei-shiki" [Ceremony of Life]. In *Seimei-shiki* [Ceremony of Life], 7–49. Tokyo: Kawade shobō, 2019.

——. *Shōmetsu sekai* [World Vanishing]. Tokyo: Kawadeshobō, 2015.

Ono Miyuki. "Gendai josei no ikizurasa o egaitara SF ni natta. 'Pyua' Ono Miyuki Intabyū" [When I imagine difficulties in life for contemporary women, the story has become science fiction. 'Pure,' Ono Miyuki's Interview]." By Mizoguchi Rikimaru. *Hayakawa Books & Magazines*. April 12, 2020. https://www.hayakawa-books.com/n/nc7a7e1c28017.

——. "Pyua" [Pure]. In *Pyua* [Pure], 5–56. Tokyo: Hayakawa shobō, 2020.

Qiao, Mina. "Escaping the Physical: Liminal Body and Liminal Space in Ogawa Yōko's *Hotel Iris*." *U.S.-Japan Women's Journal* 55–56 (2019): 153–173.

Reider, Noriko. "*Yamauba* and *Oni*-Women: Devouring and Helping *Yamauba* are Two Sides of the Same Coin." *Asian Ethnology* 78, no. 2 (2019): 403–427.

Sakaki, Atsuko, trans. Introduction to *The Woman with the Flying Head and Other Stories by Kurahashi Yumiko*. New York: Routledge, 2015. Kindle.

Sands, Peter. "Cannibal Tropes in Gilman's Narrative of Discovery: The Food that Fuels the Nation." *Utopian Studies* 26, no.1, Special Issue: Utopia and Food (2015): 125–142.

Specchio, Anna. "Eutopizing the Dystopia. Gender Roles, Motherhood and Reproduction in Murata Sayaka's *Satsujin Shussan*" *Metacritic Journal for Comparative Studies and Theory* 4, Iss. 1 (2018): 94–108.

——. "No Sex and the Paradise City: A Critical Reading of Murata Sayaka's *Shōmetsu sekai*." *International Journal of Afro-Asiatic Studies* 24, no. 2 (2020): 373–396.

*Chapter Five*

# Ports in a Storm
## *The Poetics of Space in Hino Keizō*

### Amanda C. Seaman

As he walks through the business district of Ōtemachi at night, on the way to a nearby hotel bar, the unnamed but clearly autobiographical narrator of Hino Keizō's 1996 story "Hashigo no tatsu machi" (City of the Ascending Ladder, translated into English as "Jacob's Tokyo Ladder") finds once-familiar streets uncanny and strange, a sensation reinforced by the sight of a mysterious figure clad in a long black raincoat.[1] Unable to resist the urge to follow this figure in black, he grows more and more unnerved, increasingly unable to recognize his surroundings. Suddenly, as he rounds the corner, a familiar sight looms up behind the trees of the Imperial Palace: "Before me, as I stood there stock-still and baffled, within my field of vision I saw a silver Tokyo Tower rising up straight and true, yet somehow like an illusion—the abrupt intrusion of a separate "reality."[2] Just as suddenly as he appeared, the dark figure vanishes. Initially, Hino's* own anxiety abates as well; he continues on his way to the Imperial Hotel, no longer frightened by the again-recognizable urban landscape around him. Nevertheless, the memory of the "bizarre state in which I had been so vulnerable, the strange character in the black raincoat—I never knew its sex—and its abrupt disappearance" nags at him, and exactly a week later a cancerous lump is detected in his kidney, sending Hino* into a state of shock. After receiving his diagnosis and returning to work, he again finds himself unable to recognize the streets and buildings that he had passed through so many times before, and cannot help wondering if his earlier encounter was a surreptitious warning. "Perhaps," he muses, "the mysterious figure that continued to walk several paces ahead of me was an accommodating harbinger of my impending fate."[3]

The dark sense of foreboding produced by our narrator's unexpected nighttime vision foreshadows how the experience of illness will transform his relationship to physical space as a whole. Death, here manifested as an uncanny figure clad in black, disrupts his sense of equilibrium and perception of the world around him, visibly altering previously familiar city spaces. Even after it disappears, he remembers its presence and cannot push it out of his mind, and upon being given his cancer diagnosis he recognizes the profound ways in which bodily affliction and the psychic imbalance that it provokes are manifested in equally profound transformations in his perception of the world, transformations that blur the boundaries between sense and imagination and challenge his very ability to distinguish "reality" from "illusion." After entering the hospital and beginning treatment, this blurring and confusion become even more profound, as Hino* finds that his mind can no longer make sense of his own body or of the world containing it, things and places that he thought he knew so well. Even after recovering from surgery, his relationship to space continues to be a fraught one as he continues to experience hallucinations, fantastical irruptions of his mind into the perceptions provided by his senses that he cannot fully comprehend nor describe. Ultimately, it is only by focusing on a singular place—the Tokyo Tower—and affirming both its this-worldly reality as well as its universal significance as a metaphorical bridge between heaven and earth that Hino* is able to reground himself and reintegrate his sense of being, both in time and in the world.

The importance of space and place in "Jacob's Tokyo Ladder" is typical of many of the works of Hino Keizō (1929–2002), who had a long career as an author, cultural critic, and journalist. Although he is known in English-language scholarship primarily as an "environmental writer" due to the focus upon nature and its degradation in his most famous work, the novel *Yume no shima* (Island of Dreams), such a characterization only scratches the surface of his far more wide-ranging literary oeuvre.[4] Hino's enduring concern for issues of space and place may have been rooted in his own peripatetic childhood and adolescence; born in Tokyo in what is now Setagaya Ward, he moved with his family to the Japanese colony of Korea, living first in provincial Gyeongsangnam-do and later in the colonial capital, Keijō (now Seoul). In the aftermath of World War II, his family was repatriated to Japan, where they settled in his father's hometown of Fukushima in Hiroshima Prefecture. After attending university in Tokyo and earning a literature degree, he became a foreign correspondent for the *Yomiuri Shinbun*, covering South Korea and the war in Vietnam. In the 1970s, he began a new career as an author, garnering a number of Japan's top literary awards (including the Akutagawa Prize in 1975, the Tanizaki Prize in 1986, and the Noma Prize in 1993) for his writing in the decades that followed. In 1990, Hino was diagnosed with kidney cancer. Following surgery to remove the tumor, he received a course of immunotherapy, a treatment regime that had become more common by that time. Although Hino went into remission, however, he never fully recovered his earlier vigor, eventually succumbing to aggressive colon cancer in 2002.

In the pages that follow, I will look more closely at the major work that emerged from Hino's initial struggles with this illness—the short story collection *Dangai no toshi* (A Year on the Brink), which won the Itō Sei Prize in 1992—and the complex ways in which urban space is deployed there as backdrop, stage, and metaphor for the author's physical and emotional journey with and through affliction. In each of the collection's stories, Hino explores spaces and places that simultaneously anchor him in the here-and-now and sustain him in his struggles, while also pointing him toward more transcendent meanings and realities. For Hino*, the nothingness represented by impending death takes on apparently tangible form, as in his vision of the mysterious man in black, disturbing and displacing the world of perceptible experience—his neighborhood, the city itself, and even his hospital room. Illness does more than simply constrain his movement through the world—it prevents him from finding or creating meaning from the spaces around him, which are displaced by phantasies that emphasize his bodily fragility even as they blur the boundaries between that body and its material surroundings. Ultimately, it is only through regrounding himself spatially and experientially that he is able to avoid falling prey to despair and death, a fate figured as loss of, separation from, and disaggregation of the things and places he has known.

## HINO AND CITY SPACE

Japanese critics know Hino Keizō as a writer for whom urban spaces—in particular, those of Tokyo—functioned not simply as backdrops or settings, but as metaphorically-charged characters in their own right. As Suga Atsuko notes in her review of *Dangai no toshi*, Hino's fictional city frequently contains surrealistic "urban blind spots" where incongruous features, feelings, or experiences are juxtaposed with otherwise normal city spaces.[5] In his writing, Hino often alludes to striking visual representations of cities and cityscapes to enhance his own verbal ones. For example, in "Jacob's Tokyo Ladder," nighttime Tokyo is described as being transformed into a place like those depicted by Giorgio di Chirico, whose work focuses on solitary towers and cityscapes, or "Monsù Desiderido," the *nom de plume* assumed by two early seventeenth-century painters (Didier Barra and François de Nomé) whose works include "strange architectural fantasies, with crumbling buildings under stormy skies" in which only one or two lonely, tiny figures appear.[6] Hino brings a similar sensibility to his exploration of the modern buildings of the city, describing them as something quite different than the square steel and concrete cubes to which they normally are compared. In his stories, he pays special attention to Tokyo's skyscrapers built during the bustling 1980s, specifying them by name and location in a way that makes it seem as if they stand alone, the sole inhabitants of a city that in fact is home to many millions of people. Looming above them all, however, both physically and metaphorically, is the thousand-foot-tall Tokyo Tower, a modern icon built in 1958 and seen by Hino as the most utterly extraneous—and for that reason, uniquely beautiful—feature of the cityscape.

Hino's descriptions of the new gleaming buildings of Tokyo stand in contrast to the gradual disintegration of his own body, implicitly likened to the darkness and decay of traditional edifices such as Meiji Shrine. In a metaphorical sense, cities are akin to individual living beings, with skyscrapers embodying their aspirations and metaphysical qualities; as he declares in the collection's final story, "[C]ities are microcosms of our consciousness, and the tower is the focus that pulls the microcosm upwards."[7] As his illness progresses, Hino's fictional avatar finds himself and his thoughts confined to smaller and smaller spaces—his house, his hospital room, the view from his window. Nevertheless, throughout *Dangai no toshi* the city continues to be not simply a place in which Hino exists, but a point of anchorage keeping him from being swept away by the turbulent and frightening waves of disease and delusion.

This connection of the body to contemporary city space—one that valorizes that space as a counterweight to Hino's fragile and tenuous physical existence—offers a more positive appraisal of the city than that found in earlier works such as *Island of Dreams*. There, as Matthew Strecher has observed, Hino emphasized "the vacuousness of Tokyo in the post-modern era, describing the metropolis as a beautiful shell, bereft of any human warmth."[8] Hino's approach to the city in *Dangai no toshi* also is at odds with recent scholarly work about Tokyo, which dwells less on the city's physical present than on traces and memories of its history, such as the ways in which place names like Asakusa, Ueno, or Ginza are used to evoke times past or to designate individual or collective sites of memory. The more recent cityscape, on the other hand, tends to be treated as nondescript and unremarkable, the product of ruthless rebuilding efforts after a series of natural and manmade disasters.[9]

In Hino's illness narratives, however, Tokyo is emphatically not a site of memory or nostalgia, paralleling Hino's disinterest in exploring his own past. Rather, it is a physical rather than imagined or remembered place, with real buildings and lived-in spaces. Perhaps most importantly, it is a site of industry, activity, and production, highlighted by Hino's frequent name-checking of buildings identified either with corporate enterprise (e.g., NEC and National) or with city and national government. With the onset and advance of disease, it is these dynamic and forward-moving aspects of urban life that become increasingly alien to Hino's* own daily experience of convalescence, isolation, and interiority. Focused on the current and future state of his body and mind, and his inability to find familiarity or meaning in his surrounding, he literally and symbolically struggles to assimilate his un-productive body to the bustling world outside.

## GIVING WAY: ILLNESS AND DIS-LOCATION

In the five stories that make up *Dangai no toshi* (Year on the Precipice)— "Tōkyō tawā ga suita" (Tokyo Tower Saved Me), "Bokushi-kan" (The Parsonage), "Dansō ni yuramekau shiroku te no hira no mine" (The Group of White Palm Prints on the Cliff), "Okujō no kage-tachi" (Ghosts on the Roof), and "Unkai no sakame" (A Rift in the Sea of Clouds)—he narrates in quasi-diaristic fashion his diagnosis, surgery, and recovery from kidney cancer.[10] Narrated (like the later story "Jacob's Tokyo Ladder") by a fictionalized version of Hino himself (referred to here and elsewhere as Hino*), nearly always in the first person, these stories trace a journey from the streets of Tokyo to the examination rooms and suites of Hino's* hospital, into his innermost thoughts, fears, and nightmares, to a river in rural Okutama, and then to Okinawa, returning in the end to the Tokyo skyline. The first story, "Tokyo Tower Saved Me," becomes a touchstone for Hino, adumbrating themes of place and illness that will be developed and explored in the rest of the collection. In it, Hino* has his first brush with mortality, and the accompanying distortions of meaning and place that define his illness. The anesthesia and pain medication administered to Hino* turn out to be a dry run for death and the terror that it provokes, leaving him both scared and scarred by the experience.

As the story opens, Hino* is planning a trip to Africa to explore the origins of early humans, and decides to have a physical exam before his departure. Due to his history of kidney stones, the doctor performs an ultrasound on Hino's* kidneys. Concerned by an unusual shadow on the film, the doctor orders a battery of other tests, culminating with a PET scan that confirms the presence of a mass in the kidney. Beset with anxiety, Hino* attempts to distract himself with work and everyday activities, putting off exploratory surgery out of fear that it will reveal that his mysterious lump is cancerous. Finally acceding to his doctors' wishes, he agrees to undergo the procedure; afterward, he recalls lying awake at night as his operation approached, haunted by the realization that "his body and the boundary between life and death were before his eyes."[11] In an attempt to reimpose some sense of order, Hino* insists on being able to choose where he will be treated. He does not want to go back to Yoyogi Hospital (the provider preferred by his employer), not only because he cannot have a private room there but also because he hates its location, adjacent to the heavily-wooded precincts of Meiji Shrine. As he observes, "The energy at that locale does not work for me. [. . .] Ever since I was a child, old-style Japanese shrines and shadows have always made me uneasy."[12] Instead, he manages to get admitted to the newer Keio University Hospital, where he is given a sixth-floor room with a view in the new wing. "Above all else," says Hino*, "I can look out the window. On the left side, there is the roof of the old building; on the right, there is the cityscape from Aoyama to Akasaka with Tokyo Tower in the center, and I can see part of the woods of Jingu Gaien."[13] As his surgery approaches, the unimpeded sight of wide urban vistas offers Hino a respite from the shadow of disease looming ahead of him. "Outside my window," he recalls, "the rich green forests . . . glowed in the sunset. White clouds drifted in the unusually blue sky . . . I pondered this surprising world, where a beautiful summer evening and cancerous cells can exist together."[14]

Things are quite different the next morning when he gets ready for his surgery, as smog now obscures his view of the Tokyo skyline. A similar blurring affects his mind and his perceptions, one made more acute by the drugs administered to him every three hours in the ICU following his procedure. Hino's* attitude to pain medication, we discover, is a complicated and ambivalent one. As a young man, he was forced to endure intense pain after appendicitis surgery, when his doctors told him to "deal with it" and refused to give him a shot. Yet while he is happy that medical practice has moved away from such "moral masochism," and indeed worries lest he be denied adequate pain management during his current hospitalization, he is troubled by the effects of the medications now being administered to him. While the sedatives used for a routine endoscopy had produced the "pleasure of slowly floating in a kind of metaphysical, cosmic hallucinatory world,"[15] the drugs given to Hino* in the ICU and during his recovery utterly tear through his consciousness, severing his awareness of and connection to space and time:

> Not just the pain from my wound, but the very presence of my body itself, disappeared. Yet far from losing consciousness, I began to feel an intense confusion, as if I suddenly was on a roller coaster. Hallucinations of every kind sprang from my consciousness and began to fly around . . . Various shapes pop out one after another from every side of the infinite darkness, and they seem to hit my face, flowing to the left and the right.[16]

After the first onslaught of these formless hallucinations, which Hino* concludes must be products of some deep, primordial part of his mind, he manages to ascertain that he still is alive, although he cannot remember the shape, sound, or physical appearance of what he has experienced. Upon returning to his room from the ICU, the hallucinations return in new and even more vivid form:

> At first, completely meaningless hallucinatory images attacked me at high speed. On the second and third days after my operation, they overlapped with actual things that I was seeing around me, mixing and melting together, and it became difficult to differentiate between hallucinations and actual objects, visions and reality. Hallucination and reality unapologetically existed side-by-side.[17]

In between these troubling hallucinatory episodes, Hino* seeks solace in the view from his hospital window, that had so impressed him when he first arrived. The first thing he sees is the Tokyo Tower, framed between two clusters of buildings, and a series of other familiar landmarks:

> the Aoyama Itchome Twin Buildings, the corporate headquarters of National, the ANA Hotel, and the headquarters of NEC in Tamachi, all with their television towers. [. . .] I was impressed and reaffirmed by those buildings, the sky and the lights that I have seen every night. I found them all again.[18]

By locating and naming the buildings that he recognizes, Hino* is able to reorient himself and remind himself that he is anchored in the reality of the modern city, reassuring him that he has not been fundamentally changed by his surgery. Just as he concludes that that all is as it should be, however, he shifts his gaze to the roof of the hospital annex building across the street. To his amazement, ten to twenty people are sitting on the railing that runs around the top of the building, all of them dressed in white garments like medieval monks' robes. Some of the faces seem vaguely familiar, while others are utterly unrecognizable. Shaken by the sight of these strange apparitions, Hino* wonders why some of them look vaguely familiar. Suddenly, he is filled with the sense that these are ghosts, spirits of people he once knew who now are dead—a reminder that all is not well, and that he is being treated for a terminal illness. Sitting at the cusp of death himself, the world of the dead now can more easily spill into his still-living existence. Soon, the ghostly figures are joined by what seem to be giant tigers and bears flying through the sky, ones whose appearance calls to mind science fiction classics like *Forbidden Planet* in which "an invisible alien monster is caught in a powerful electromagnetic trap, its face visible only as a reddish blob, its body a vague sparkling shape flashing in the sky."[19]

Notably, Hino* is not frightened by these fantastic visions. "There is no danger of being harmed," he comments, "and there is no sense that I am being cursed by dark grudges . . . these are not malicious Japanese-style ghosts"[20]— an attitude prompted in part by the apparitions' juxtaposition against familiar, concrete spaces and places like the hospital or the buildings of Tokyo itself.

What does scare him, however, is the appearance of strange Japanese characters within the red lights of those same buildings:

> The red lights don't look like red lights. They become red letters. Skyscrapers and TV antennae as far as the eye can see—all of them have red signs. They are Chinese or Japanese characters. This made me realize once again that we are not looking at images per se. The lights are not simply red dots; they have a meaning that is closely related to the meaning of the building or TV tower. The reverse is also true. There is no pure meaning. Meaning has an image. No, meaning is image, or image is meaning. As someone who works with words and characters, I always took it for granted that words and characters are things with a long and true history. Maybe you misread an unclear character, and the red light looks like a kanji . . . I couldn't say anything.[21]

As the narrator ponders this profoundly incoherent situation, one in which he cannot make any sense of the objects around him or even recognize the connection between those objects and the words meant to denote them, he realizes that, far from being imposed upon him from outside, it is being generated from within his own mind. Meaning, in other words, is in danger of disappearing completely, swept away by images that rush at him too quickly to be understood, much less controlled—a particularly terrifying fate for a writer and thinker.

The spatialized nature of Hino's* hallucinations, divided into interior, formless visions swirling about in his consciousness and apparitions that appear to exist outside of his body, flitting in and through the exterior world, recalls Aristotle's notion of *phantasia*, roughly equivalent to our modern concepts of "dream," "vision" as well as "hallucination." As we have seen, however, Hino's* struggle with the overwhelming discombobulation caused by these *phantasia* gives way to a caesura between word and image. This situation goes beyond ancient psychology's definition of *phantasia* as irruptions of images proper to the intellect (what we would call "imaginary" ones) into the cognitive space normally ruled by images produced through sense perception, representing instead a far more fundamental rupture in the very facilities essential for reasoning and meaning-making, one that continues to afflict Hino* as he struggles later on to recall and interpret his hallucinations. Were the ghosts he saw solid, or semitransparent, or actually invisible? Why did they all appear to be male? Could he find a deeper significance in the flying lions and bears, just like people used to find lions and bears hidden in the starry sky? Even months later, Hino* continues to labor against a nagging sense that the world is coming apart, complaining that "tall buildings overlap the forest, and the TV towers are cut off halfway . . . cars pass through the walls of the old hospital building under my eyes."[22]

As the title of Hino's story "Tōkyō tawā ga suita" makes clear, what saves Hino* from being overwhelmed by his hallucinations and the psychic breakdown they both herald and produce is the presence of the Tokyo Tower, which he described as the most significant part of being hospitalized, "A modest but jewel-like experience of consciousness,"[23] which also plays a starring role in "Jacob's Tokyo Ladder." Time after time, amidst the assaults of various imaginary terrors, "illusion(s) summoned from [his] fluctuating consciousness," he fixes his gaze on the solitary tower rising up in the middle of the cityscape outside his window, secure in his knowledge that it truly and utterly exists, its colors striking and true.[24]

> I was terribly impressed by the orange and silver colors of the illumination of Tokyo Tower. It was not flashy and overbearing, and it contains a little sadness. The platinum color is crisp and sharp; it is cultured—almost a holy symbol ... it is wrapped in dignity and elegance.[25]

The space around the tower strikes him as a magical precinct, housing a precious edifice likened to the "spires of Gothic cathedrals, clock towers in the middle of the road, obelisks, pagodas, ziggurats, sacred trees, pyramids ... a form of prayer inseparable from the holy things of people who tried to hold something certain."[26] As Hino later put it in "Jacob's Tokyo Tower,"

> Even when uncanny, chaotically shifting hallucinatory images dominated my conscious vision—eyes open or closed—Tokyo Tower continued to look the same as always and continued to talk to me: *Only a vertical shaft running from heavens to earth will remained unchanged, no matter how much everything else falls into mad chaos*, an image drawn explicitly from Jacob's vision of the heavenly ladder in the book of Genesis.[27]

Tokyo Tower, however, is at one and the same time a metaphor, a symbol of the connection between the heaven and the earth, as well as something implacably *real* in a way that nothing else has been for Hino* before. While the hallucinations are rushing at him at an uncontrolled rate, he cannot control them or make sense of them. The view of Tokyo Tower calms him because it possesses at one and the same time a this-world solidity as well as a unique meaning. Built in 1958 as a communications platform, it was the tallest structure in Japan during Hino's lifetime, a potent symbol of Japan's recovery from war and its industrial prowess.[28] At the same time, it was and is an edifice largely divorced from commercial or governmental interests or activities, helping to explain why Hino might have employed it as a secular analog to cultic and religious structures meant to bridge the space between this world and one above and beyond it. Ultimately, feeling like there is a heaven—a place beyond the spaces of the earth—is what gives Hino* the ability to control the images and to see that even though he is sick, there is a place of comfort and peace beyond himself, unaffected by the chaos afflicting his body and mind.

## SEARCHING FOR THE SUBLIME

In the collection's final story, "Unkai no sakame" (A Rift in the Sea of Clouds), Hino* has decided to fulfill a speaking obligation in Okinawa, one delayed for over a year because of his cancer. Although he does not want to travel because he is worried about the lingering effects of his illness and his reduced stamina, he nevertheless boards an airplane and travels to Naha. Okinawa's semitropical climate reminds him of Vietnam, where he had been assigned years before as a correspondent for the *Yomiuri Shinbun*, and the red hibiscus and white-walled houses around him fill him with nostalgia. Despite his fatigue and diminished concentration, Hino* manages to pull himself together and complete his presentation before returning to the airport and boarding his return flight. Before the airplane even takes off, he quickly falls into a deep sleep, awakening to the sight of the sun setting below him, shining up through the clouds.

While the plot of this story is simple enough—a man goes on a trip and returns—the emotional journey it details is a far more complex one, as Hino struggles to comprehend the concept and reality of nothingness, and how he might stave it off. Sitting in an outpatient clinic as the story begins, waiting to receive his cancer treatment injections, Hino* finds the clinic's clean, bright interior calling to mind Ernest Hemingway's "A Clean, Well-Lighted Place" (1933), a simple yet affecting story about an old man drinking alone in a café staffed by two waiters—a young man impatient for him to pay his tab and leave, and an older one who ends up joining the man for one more round. While Hemingway's story confronts issues—aging, loneliness, the fleeting nature of youth—with which our author himself was grappling, it is the old waiter's final, wry parody of the Lord's Prayer to which he is particularly drawn:

> He knew it was all *nada y pues nada y nada y pues nada*. Our *nada* who art in *nada*, *nada* be thy name thy kingdom *nada* thy will be *nada* in *nada* as it is in *nada*. Give us this *nada* our daily *nada* and *nada* us our *nada* as we *nada* our *nadas* and *nada* us not in *nada* but deliver us from *nada*; *pues nada*. Hail nothing full of nothing, nothing is with thee.[29]

In his translation of Hemingway's text, Hino renders both the Spanish *nada* and the English "nothing" with the same Japanese word, *mu* (無), a choice that not only emphasizes the passage's nihilistic message, but also transposes Hemingway's Christian frame of reference by evoking the Buddhist notion of "nothing-ness" or "void-ness" (*Sūnyatā*), the ultimate destination of all existence in which individuality and appearance are dissolved into complete truth and self-less reality.[30] These reflections on death and nothingness are given even greater poignancy when Hino* sees a woman in the clinic's radiology department, emaciated yet still beautiful, whose vacant stare draws him to her:

> While we often are quick to use words like "despair" or "despairingly," there was not even a spark of life in this woman's eyes. She was staring at something I could not see, something that I thought I could perceive but that I was afraid to put into words. I felt deeply and painfully that this thing exists in the world, even if it can't be pointed to on any map. . . . I was confused, but felt like I had touched something real that I couldn't fully comprehend. I quietly left the place.[31]

What the dying woman is looking at, he realizes, is death—a realization that makes Hino* aware of his own mortality. He knows that she is farther down the same path that he is travelling, a path that leads to something at once very real yet also place-less.

Sitting in the airplane to Okinawa, his thoughts turn obsessively inward, circling from the dead-eyed woman to how kidney cancer can metastasize into the lungs, to his failure to quit smoking, and back to the woman again. Trapped high in the air, in a space even more confined than his hospital room, he cannot write the speech that he has to give the next day. Even when he reaches the ground, Hino* remains unable to recenter or ground himself, or to find security and meaning in tall buildings as he once had done. Sitting in his Naha hotel room, observing the nondescript office blocks that now fill the skyline, he thinks back to the days when the city was home to only one or two tall buildings, "new towers that pierced the heavens.

> In the middle of so many ten-story buildings clinging to the ground, the fifty-story skyscrapers looked like verticality incarnate. If anything, the view of their tops cloaked in clouds . . . reminded me of the Big Wild Goose Pagoda and the Little Wild Goose Pagoda in the ancient Chinese city of Xi'an. . . . For me, those few skyscrapers were towers of the unconscious within a mythic imagination."[32]

In this passage, Hino's* comparison of Tokyo's first skyscrapers to two Tang-era Chinese pagodas, built to house sacred Buddhist relics brought from India on the Silk Road, emphasizes the profound, quasi-religious role they play within his psyche. What made these towers so special, however, quite apart from their cultic role, was their solitary size and splendor, provoking feelings of awe among city dwellers as well as travelers approaching them across the high plateaus. Now, the mythic scale of such buildings has been attenuated by their sheer numbers; Tokyo's rapidly growing skyline now makes him shudder, as do blithe comments that the city's skyscrapers are "more beautiful than Mt. Fuji."[33]

Despite his inability to find any solace or release from his obsessive ruminations on emptiness, meaninglessness, and death, Hino* nonetheless manages to deliver a successful talk to his hosts before returning to the airport and boarding the flight back to Tokyo. As soon as he is seated, he immediately falls into a sleep so profound that he does not hear the flight attendants' instructions or the roar of the plane's engines upon take-off— "an unexpectedly deep sleep, like when I had general anesthesia before my surgery." Unlike that experience, however, he has no dreams or hallucinations; as he recalls, "Despite the absolute absence of any kind of self-consciousness, I experienced a vague, deep peace, as if a greater consciousness were quietly witnessing a 'dreamless sleep.' Indeed, it seemed like the energy scattered outside of me was rapidly focused within."[34] Upon awakening, Hino* feels utterly transformed. Looking around him at the familiar airplane surroundings, Sensing the presence of a "stronger something or other" amidst the familiar surroundings of the aircraft, he looks out the window at a sea of darkening clouds below, resembling a newly-plowed field:

> In the distance, the ridges of the clouds seem to have elongated cuts, and from beneath them an intense light is shining upward. Perhaps the sun is setting under the sea of clouds, sinking into the horizon, and its last rays are emanating outward. You can't see the sunset under the sea of clouds; only the rays of light shine brightly towards the heavens.[35]

Mesmerized by seeing a sunset in this way, Hino* notes how much brighter and purer the colors appear from above: "A nearly vermillion red, yellow mixed with vermillion, an orange verging on gold . . . and then a blue that seems to pass through the sky. Primary colors, but so very different from the primary colors you can see on earth."[36]

This intense vision of "eerily pure primary colors . . . [whose] brilliance is too great, even destructive" initially fills him not with aesthetic appreciation, but with fearful awe.[37] Yet as Hino* continues to gaze upon the sunset, feeling like he is looking into the "depths of his consciousness," he suddenly recalls a passage from the Tibetan "Book of the Dead" (*Bardo Thodol*) describing how the transition between life and death is heralded by a profound vision of the deepest red. Now, he realizes that the light shining upon him is something even more intense: a deep orange, "a color of even higher energy than red or vermillion."[38] In an instant, the colors of the sunset disappear, replaced by nighttime darkness as his plane descends into the Tokyo. Observing the lights of the megalopolis spread out below him, a sight that once filled him with awe, Hino* now finds himself unmoved; "Tokyo," he remarks dryly, "didn't seem very bright anymore."[39] Despite his initial misgivings, then, Hino* ultimately is happy that he went to Okinawa. Suspended between Tokyo and Naha, between the heavens and the earth, he finally is able to escape from the nothingness, the *nada*, that had threatened to overwhelm him at the clinic before his trip. Returning from an empty, deathlike sleep to the familiar world of Tokyo through the mediation of an intense, liminal vision of brilliant sunlight, Hino* thus reverses the voyage of life, transition, and dissolution described in the "Book of the Dead," regaining his center and his sense of meaning in the process.

## PLACES OF MEANING AND THE MEANING OF PLACES

Throughout Hino's literary career, spaces and places have served as occasions and provocations for metaphorical reveries, with the city's buildings and above all towers particularly ripe for interpretation. As described in *Dango no toshi*, however, illness changed the author's relationship to these spaces, as he struggled both to recognize them and to control their meanings. When he was first recovering from cancer, Tokyo Tower comforted him, reminding him of the connection between heaven and earth and offering a point of anchorage against the turbulent onset of hallucinatory visions. As we might expect from a well-travelled and widely-read cultural critic, Hino draws on a wide variety of sources to give meaning to the structures around him, with metaphor playing a central role in his literary and psychological endeavor to understand his illness and his fear of death and what happens afterward. In the words of anthropologist Gregory Bateson, "Metaphor is not just pretty poetry, it is not either good or bad logic, but is in fact the logic upon which the biological world has been built, the main characteristic and organizing glue of this world of mental process."[40] These sentiments are ones fully shared by Hino, who read Bateson and who drew upon the latter's insights regarding the irruption of the symbolic into the rational realm in "Tokyo Tower Saved Me."

Religious traditions are among the primary sources that Hino draws on to make sense of mortality, death, and the spaces in which life and death unfold. His approach to heaven and its angelic messengers in "Tokyo Tower" draws deeply from Christian images and beliefs, influences also evident in allusions to the Holy Land (in "Ghosts on the Roof") or descriptions of an incongruous church in the hills of Okutama (in "The Parsonage"). Buddhism plays an even more central role in Hino's reflections on death and dying, most notably in discussions of the seeds of consciousness (*shuji*), nothing-ness (*mu*), and the passage from death to afterlife in the *Tibetan Book of the Dead*. At the same time, Hino's reflections on illness and dying are equally informed by a range of secular mythopoeses, ranging from film (*Blade Runner* and *2001: A Space Odyssey*) to poetry (Dante's *Inferno*) to fiction (the Brontës and Hemingway), and even to children's literature (the surreal world of Moomin and his friends).[41]

Taken as a whole, this rich body of religious, philosophical, and literary material is placed in service of one central project—namely, to impose form and meaning on the seemingly formless and random experience of sickness and the prospect of death. In *Illness and Metaphor*, Susan Sontag memorably notes that there are two kingdoms: the kingdom of the sick and the kingdom of the well. She says, "Illness is the night-side of the life, a more onerous citizenship. Everyone who is born holds dual citizenship, in the kingdom of the well and in the kingdom the sick. Although we all prefer to use only the good passport, sooner or later each of us is obliged, at for a spell, to identify ourselves of that other place."[42] Seen in these terms, Hino Keizō's stories can be read as dispatches from the kingdom of the sick, a place where changes to one's physical body are accompanied by transformations in perception and the very ability to find meaning in the world.

Being an inhabitant of the kingdom of the sick also changes Hino's* relationship to space. Expanding upon themes adumbrated in *Island of Dreams*, the stories in *Dangai no toshi* explore how being ill affects the body spatially, as illness limits one's movements and changes how the sick person sees, moves through, and understands the world around him or her. For Hino*, the hospital, his home, and even the view from his window take on radically different meanings as he spends more time in them. Rather than being a place to have a checkup and leave, the hospital is now a place to which he is confined, and in which death is a constant companion, a fact that alters his fundamental sense of space. Recalling his convalescence in "The Group of White Palm Prints on the Cliff," Hino highlights this transformation in how he understood his physical surroundings and their relationship to himself:

> I realized that a surprisingly complex space can be created inside and around my palm simply by slowly bending and stretching my five fingers . . . the small changes in the space created by my five fingers are very real and very large . . . I felt that the space of the entire hospital room had been transformed just as much as the view outside my window.[43]

In turn, the journey from sickness into health also is a journey through space, as Hino* travels through the city and its environs, and ultimately to Okinawa, in an attempt to make sense of his new reality.

While Hino Keizō's treatment of these themes is original in its execution and conceptual breadth, his attention to the physical and spatial contexts of illness and affliction is not a new phenomenon within Japanese letters. Indeed, there is a long history of writing about one's ailments and recuperation, beginning with diaristic accounts from the Tokugawa era and continuing through the Meiji period and into the present, where illness has featured in memoirs, autobiographies, and fiction.[44] Within this tradition, the confining qualities of illness play a particularly important role in works by the Meiji novelists Masaoka Shiki (1867–1902) and Natsume Sōseki (1867–1916), both of whom focus on the ways in which their surroundings shaped their sickness, convalescence, and recovery. Shiki, who suffered from tuberculosis that slowly ate away his spine, was shut in a small house with a garden for the last seven years of his life, enduring pain so severe that he barely could move. The frustration produced by these experiences emerge in his poetry as well as his self-writing; as he described in the 1902 essay "Notes from My Six-Foot Sickbed," a serialized diary published in the newspaper *Nihon*, his world was a very small one:

> A six foot sick bed—this is my world. And this sick bed six feet long is too big for me. Sometimes I have only to stretch my arm a bit to touch the tatami, but at other times I can't even relax by pushing my legs outside the covers. In extreme cases I am tormented by such terrible pain that I'm unable to move my body so much as an inch or even half an inch. Racked by pain, anguish, shrieks and morphine I search for a way out, helplessly craving a little peace on a road that leads to death.[45]

Shiki's suffering and illness here are given emphatically spatial dimensions, delineated by his room and the bed within it—circumstances that lead him to transform that room into a miniature world of its own, the site as well as the object of his literary efforts as well as his paintings, which take as their subjects the fruits and flowers found in the garden outside his window.

While Shiki's small world was one to which he retreated after falling ill, remaining there until his death, another famous literary sufferer, Natsume Sōseki, had his convalescence cut short. While recuperating from stomach ulcers at the hot springs of Shuzen-ji, on the Ito Peninsula, Sōseki's quiet days of writing and thought ended when complications from his condition led to severe bleeding and a coma. After regaining his strength, he was transferred to a Tokyo hospital by his doctors, an experience described by Sōseki in a series of thirty-two short essays published in the *Asahi Shinbun* in 1911 and later anthologized as *Omoidasu koto nado* (*Recollections*). In them, Sōseki explored the philosophical, literary, and cultural implications of his illness and the near-death experience that he underwent, augmenting his memories with a number of *kanshi,* Chinese poetry, and haiku in order to more fully and poetically express his feelings about sickness and death.[46] Notably, Sōseki's illness memoir is bookended by a journey—his departure from Shuzen-ji for Tokyo, which opens and closes the collection and which serves as the organizing occasion for his reflections on what he endured and what it meant. Moreover, while Sōseki makes occasional forays into the precincts of philosophy, represented by William James and Friedrich Nietzsche, and his primary frame of reference is a literary (and especially Dostoevskian) one, it is the quiet world of Shuzen-ji that provides him with his most profound insights into the value and fleeting nature of life:

> The sky was deep and clear. The sun's rays filled the whole blue canopy of heaven. I lay silent and alone, basking in the reflected warmth of that infinity. A cloud of dragonflies appeared. I wrote in my diary, "Rather than people; the sky. Rather words, silence.. . . Coming to my shoulders seeking friendship, the red dragon-flies."[47]

Almost eighty years later, Hino's work on illness and space continues to explore these themes, focusing however on the ways in which illness transforms one's place in the world, and thus one's consciousness and very self. While Sōseki's muses are Nietzsche and Dostoevsky, Hino's are Moomin and Tarkofsky. Nonetheless, both express a similar desire: to find meaning in illness, to define themselves and their suffering, and to anchor those experiences in and through the world around them.

## NOTES

1. Given that the narrator of this and the other stories discussed here is a thinly veiled version of Hino himself, he will be referred to here and *passim* as Hino*, to distinguish him from the author *per se*.
2. Hino Keizō, "Jacob's Tokyo Ladder," in *Tokyo Stories: A Literary Stroll,* trans. and ed. Lawrence Rogers (Berkeley: University of California Press, 2002), 53.
3. Hino, "Jacob's Tokyo Ladder" 53.
4. See e.g., Karen Thornber, *Ecoambiguity: Environmental Crises and East Asian Literatures* (Ann Arbor: University of Michigan Press, 2012), 485 and Mark Pendleton, "On Mobius Strips, Ruins and Memory: The Intertwining of Places and Times in Hino Keizō's Tokyo," in Barbara E. Thornbury and Evelyn Schulz, eds. *Tokyo: Memory, Imagination and the City* (Lanham, MD: Lexington Books, 2018), 45–67.

5. Suga Atsuko, "Kyokō to genjitsu o ōraisuru tōbyōki ga shinobsu sonzairon," *Bungakukai* 5 (1992): 280.
6. "Monsù Desiderio," in *The Oxford Dictionary of Art*, 3rd ed., ed. Ian Chilvers (New York: Oxford University Press, 2004), 478.
7. Hino Keizō, "Unkai no sakame," in *Dangai no toshi* (Tokyo: Chūō Kōronsha, 1992),165.
8. Matthew Strecher, "Purely Mass or Massively Pure? The Division Between 'Pure' and 'Mass' Literature," *Monumenta Nipponica* 51/3 (1996): 368.
9. See e.g., Rio Otomo, "Redrawing a Map of Motherhood," *Japan Forum* 29/2 (2017): 180–195, as well as the introduction to *Tokyo: Memory, Imagination and the City*, ed. Thornbury and Schultz.
10. Hino Keizō, *Dangai no toshi* (Tokyo: Chūō Kōronsha, 1992); all translations from this work *passim* are my own.
11. Hino, "Okujō no kage-tachi" (Ghosts on the Roof), in *Dangai no toshi*, 106.
12. Hino, "Tōkyō tawā ga suita" (Tokyo Tower Saved Me), in *Dangai no toshi*, 15.
13. Hino, "Tōkyō tawā ga suita," 24.
14. Ibid., 30.
15. Ibid., 35.
16. Ibid., 36.
17. Ibid., 45.
18. Ibid., 47–48.
19. Ibid., 53.
20. Ibid., 54–55.
21. Ibid., 56.
22. Hino, "Dansō ni yurameku shiroku te no hira no mine" (The Group of White Palm Prints on the Cliff), in *Dangai no toshi*, 145.
23. Hino, "Tōkyō tawā ga suita," 62.
24. Ibid., 62.
25. Ibid., 47.
26. Ibid., 64.
27. Hino, "Jacob's Tokyo Ladder," 54; cf. Genesis 28:12, "And he dreamed, and behold a ladder set up on the earth, and the top of it reached to heaven: and behold the angels of God ascending and descending on it."
28. Tamaki Mihic, "Tokyo Memory, Imagination and the City (Review)," *Japanese Studies* 39:1 (2019): 141.
29. Ernest Hemingway, "A Clean, Well-Lighted Place," in *Winner Take Nothing* (New York: Charles Scribner's Sons, 1933), 23–24.
30. On this see Paul Williams, "Buddhist Concept of Emptiness," *Routledge Encyclopedia of Philosophy*, 1998, accessed 17 May 2021; https://www.rep.routledge.com/articles/thematic/buddhist-concept-of-emptiness/v-1.
31. Hino, "Unkai no sakame" (A Rift in the Sea of Clouds), in *Dangai no toshi*, 161.
32. Ibid., 166.
33. Ibid.
34. Ibid., 170.
35. Ibid., 171.

36. Ibid., 172–173.
37. Ibid., 173.
38. Ibid., 175.
39. Ibid., 177.
40. Gregory Bateson and Mary Catherine Bateson, *Angels Fear: Towards an Epistemology of the Sacred* (New York: Macmillan, 1987), 30.
41. See in particular, "Dansō ni yurameku shiroku te no hira no mine" pages 139–140 where Hino's ruminations on ancient man's awareness of death lead him to reflect on the motif of grass in Tarkosky's films and from there to the black grass-like figures of the hattifattener creatures in Moominland.
42. Susan Sontag, *Illness and Metaphor* (New York: Picador Press, 1990), 3.
43. Hino, "Dansō ni yurameku," 133.
44. W. Evan Young, "Domesticating Medicine: The Production of Familial Knowledge in Nineteenth-Century Japan," *Historia Scientiarum* 27/2 (2018): 132.
45. Masaoka Shiki, "Byōshō rokushaku" (A Six-Foot Sickbed), quoted in Donald Keene, *A Winter Sun Shines In: A Life of Masaoka Shiki* (New York: Columbia University Press, 2003), 171–172.
46. See Maria Flutsch, "Time, Death and the Empire: Natsume Sōseki's *Omoidasu koto nado (Remembrances)*," *Japanese Studies* 23/3 (2003), esp. 245–249.
47. Natsume Sōseki, *Recollections* (*Omoidasu koto nado*) trans. Maria Flutsch (London: Sōseki Museum in London, 1997), 76.

## WORKS CITED

Bateson, Gregory and Mary Catherine Bateson. *Angels Fear: Towards an Epistemology of the Sacred.* New York: Macmillan, 1987.
Flutsch, Maria. "Time, Death and the Empire: Natsume Sōseki's *Omoidasu koto nado (Remembrances)*," *Japanese Studies* 23, no.3 (2003): 239–250.
Hemingway, Ernest. "A Clean, Well-Lighted Place." In *Winner Take Nothing.* 15–24. New York: Charles Scribner's Sons, 1933.
Hino Keizō. "Jacob's Tokyo Ladder." In *Tokyo Stories: A Literary Stroll.* Trans. and ed. Lawrence Rogers. 46–57. Berkeley: University of California Press, 2002.
———. "Dansō ni yurameku shiroku te no hira no mine." In *Dangai no toshi.* 123–150.Tokyo: Chuo koronsha, 1992.
———. "Okujō no kage-tachi." In *Dangai no toshi* 95–122.Tokyo: Chuo koronsha, 1992.
———. "Tōkyō tawā ga suita." In *Dangai no toshi.* 5–68. Tokyo: Chuo konosha, 1992.
———. "Unkai no sakame." In *Dangai no toshi.* 124–178. Tokyo: Chuo koronsha, 1992.
Keene, Donald. *A Winter Sun Shines In: A Life of Masaoka Shiki.* New York: Columbia University Press, 2003.
Mihic, Tamaki. "Tokyo Memory, Imagination and the City (Review)," *Japanese Studies* 39, no.1 (2019): 141–142.

Natsume, Sōseki, *Recollections* (*Omoidasu koto nado*). Trans. Maria Flutsch, London: Sōseki Museum in London, 1997.

Otomo, Rio. "Redrawing a Map of Motherhood," *Japan Forum* 29, no.2 (2017): 180–195.

*The Oxford Dictionary of Art*, 3rd ed., ed. Ian Chilvers. New York: Oxford University Press, 2004.

Pendleton, Mark. "On Mobius Strips, Ruins and Memory: The Intertwining of Places and Times in Hino Keizō's Tokyo." In Barbara E. Thornbury and Evelyn Schulz, eds. *Tokyo: Memory, Imagination and the City.* 45–67. Lanham, MD: Lexington Books, 2018.

Sontag, Susan. *Illness and Metaphor.* New York: Picador Press, 1990.

Suga Atsuko, "Kyokō to genjitsu o ōraisuru tōbyōki ga shinobsu sonzairon," *Bungakukai* 5 (1992): 278–281.

Thornber, Karen. *Ecoambiguity: Environmental Crises and East Asian Literatures.* Ann Arbor: University of Michigan Press, 2012.

Williams, Paul. "Buddhist Concept of Emptiness," *Routledge Encyclopedia of Philosophy*, 1998. Accessed 17 May 2021; https://www.rep.routledge.com/articles/thematic/buddhist-concept-of-emptiness/v-1.

Young, W. Evan. "Domesticating Medicine: The Production of Familial Knowledge in Nineteenth-Century Japan," *Historia Scientiarum* 27, no. 2 (2018): 127–149.

*Chapter Six*

# The Foreign Land outside Japan
## An Attempted Solution to Abjection in Murakami Ryū's Fiction

Francesca Bianco

### INTRODUCTION

A recurring theme in Murakami Ryū's (b.1952) literature, the foreign land is a place of fantasy for the characters and a means through which they attempt to rebuild their identities shattered by abjection, namely their rejection of Japanese moral values and identity. The Japanese cities in the narratives, which represent the physical body of Japanese society, are the focus of violence and destruction of the characters; and the foreign land, by comparison, is imagined as a desirable substitute for the boring and asphyxiating Japanese metropolis. The characters of Murakami's fictional worlds are outcasts that cannot conform to the normative system imposed by Japanese society, instead, they find in the foreign land that contrasts Japan a locus in which they can reconstruct their identities shattered by their repulsion of Japan. Murakami utilizes the characters' destructive acts against the city to manifest a critique of contemporary Japanese society.

Critics usually associate the images, videos, memories, and accounts coming from characters who have lived abroad or have been in contact with elements extraneous to Japan with the strong influence that Murakami received from Western culture in his youth, growing up near the American military base in Sasebo.[1] However, the foreign land functions due to the process of destruction and detachment from Japan and its values. The explicit or implicit presence of a foreign land, a place perceived as "not Japan," slowly becomes part of the identity of the characters. As Barbara Flauto points out, "Murakami shows his interest in 'other worlds,' which he envisions as alternatives to an oppressively 'normal' Japan."[2]

In Murakami's stories, the foreign land is created as a psychological entity rather than a physical setting in which the characters act and the events take place. In other words, the characters have not physically departed from Japan. Such a foreign land is usually evoked either as a distant memory or a pure conjecture about what it is felt this foreign place should be: a projection created in the minds of the characters who try to realize their fantasies in different ways. For this reason, and because of the impossibility of Murakami's characters to fully detach themselves from their Japanese identities, their departure for the foreign land and their reconstruction of identities is almost always a failed attempt.

Murakami Ryū's ability to portray Japanese society with lucid criticism of its more common and defining aspects is the most recognizable trait of his writings. His works are defined as "problematic" because they oppose the status quo that Japan has achieved after the end of the war and American occupation.[3] The 1960s–1970s student movements, the incidents triggered by the United Red Army, and Mishima Yukio's (1925–1970) attempted coup d'état historically marked the historical importance of this period and had a profound effect on young citizens like Murakami, making him question the modernization process of his country. Heavy use of drugs, promiscuity, and the violence experienced by his characters represent a generation of young people seeking to discard everything that Japan as a society embodies. For Sandra Buckley, "[Murakami's] rendering of Japanese post-war youth culture is grounded in the complexity of the day-to-day negotiations of difference and identification."[4] Many of the escapades represented in Murakami's novels are inspired by the author's personal experiences in his troubled years as a student. Ōoka Makoto defines Murakami's works as an example of a literary tradition that portrays the distorted reality in young people's eyes through psychedelia.[5] Psychoactive substance abuse dominates the main characters of Murakami's fiction. From his debut in the literary world, with *Kagiranaku tōmei ni chikai burū* (1976; *Almost Transparent Blue*, 1977), Murakami had his protagonists rebel against what Carl Cassegrd terms "the boredom of naturalized modernity."[6] The Japanese status quo embodies the evil "boredom" for those inhabiting Murakami's literary worlds. Therefore, this aversion for Japanese society drives the main protagonists to violence or destruction. In *Almost Transparent Blue*, the main character Ryū, like his friends, directs violence toward himself through excessive use of drugs, almost experiencing a lethal overdose. Stephen Snyder gives a perfect description of the unsettling conditions of the people appearing in Murakami's novels: "The mundane represents a kind of threat from which they must flee, anxiety for which they seek therapy in violent conditions and degraded situations."[7]

The need to escape from the threat posed by society generates violent acts from the characters with the specific aim of destroying what they see as its physical representation. Social outcasts excluded by their family, the characters of Murakami's literary world attempt to fight the Japan they inhabit in the only way they know how: by destroying themselves and Japan itself. For those born and raised in the very society they despise, rejecting Japanese society means repudiating part of their own identity, which is directly or indirectly constructed upon the distinctive values rooted in a nation's moral compass. Consequently, the process of destruction is split in two: an outward and an inward movement.

The outward movement of destruction envisions the whole of Japanese society as a physical place, namely the city; hence any disruptive act must be directed toward the city, especially, in almost every Murakami's work, Tokyo. Margaret Hillenbrand reveals a literary tradition in which "the image of the metropolis becomes the natural flashpoint for literary antagonism toward the state apparatus," defining it as a common theme in postwar Asian literature.[8] Tokyo, as the capital of political, economic, and cultural activities, symbolizes Japan as a nation in Murakami's narratives. It is also the epitome of Japanese modern cities, envisioned as a conglomerate of the most repulsive and lurid experiences. The maladies of modern urban living, such as superficiality and hypocrisy, generate a sensation of disdain in the protagonists, and their endeavor to refuse these social norms fuels the urgency to destroy the metropolis.

The inward movement, on the other hand, is directly addressed toward the identity of the characters and their attempts to remove what they recognize as Japanese in themselves. Murakami's characters seek in the decadent lifestyle a way to repudiate moral norms, to underpin their identification with Euro-American culture, and to explore spaces other than Japan that embody their way of detaching themselves from the preestablished order in Japanese society.

## ABJECTION AND THE FOREIGN LAND

The disavowal of Japan affects both the outer and inner space of Murakami's characters, resulting in their sense of dissociation from the cities in which they live and their own identity. Julia Kristeva sees abjection as "[e]ssentially different from 'uncanniness,' more violent, too, [. . .] elaborated through a failure to recognize its kin; nothing is familiar, not even the shadow of a memory."[9] For Kristeva, abjection happens within the self, which rejects what she calls "the foundations of its own being." She adds:

> The abjection of self would be the culminating form of that experience of the subject to which it is revealed that all its objects are based merely on the inaugural loss that laid the foundations of its own being. There is nothing like the abjection of self to show that all abjection is in fact recognition of the want on which any being, meaning, language, or desire is founded.[10]

Desperate and anguished, the self refuses to identify with what constitutes its own identity. Besides this, Kristeva indicates "the place" as a focal point for the self that feels abjection. She claims that the self will question its place: "'Where am I?' instead of 'Who am I?.'" Because "space that engrosses the dejected, the excluded, is never one, nor homogeneous, nor totalizable, but essentially divisible, foldable, and catastrophic."[11]

The place constitutes the physical body with which the self that is feeling the abjection can interact. For Murakami's characters, the place of their Japanese identity, the modern city, is the physical body toward which they can manifest their abjection. Within the textual frame, the city represents anguish vis-à-vis the asphyxiating society that must be repudiated. Abjection explains the outward and inward movement of destruction in Murakami's characters: the destruction of place is an outlet for the rejection of identity. The city represents the moral values generated by society that shape the individual's ethical system.

Kawamoto Saburō points out that the city, in its literary depictions, is the locus of the modern identity crisis portrayed in Murakami's novels, stating that "there is no space for the representation of the self but the realistic representation of the city, and the self is lost in its background."[12] The city is represented as fractured, and Tokyo is a showcase of ugly social reality. The characters who inhabit Murakami's fictional world experience Tokyo at its worst: filthy streets in Shinjuku, cage-like hotel rooms that evoke claustrophobia, parks infested with drug addicts and homeless people. Since the cityscape in its various aspects becomes the fractured place that embodies society as a whole, dissociation with the city is tantamount to a rejection of society and the self. Through sexual transgression and violence, the protagonists express their sense of abjection in relation to Tokyo and, by extension, Japan.

The existence of a physical body symbolizing abjection constitutes the leitmotiv of Murakami's characters. Repulsion following the identity crisis caused by abjection leads the characters to destroy the tangible form of Japanese society which they despise, that is the city.[13] *Koinrokkā Beibīzu (1980; Coin Locker Babies, 2013)*, one of Murakami's most iconic novels, is the perfect example of this disdain toward Japanese society. In the novel, two orphaned protagonists, Kiku and Hashi, raised together as brothers, confront their abjection concerning the society that has discarded them as their mothers have. For Kiku and Hashi, abandoned in a coin locker a few hours after their birth, the metal landscape framed by the box of the coin locker represents both the physical trap in which they find themselves and their vision of Tokyo. In a scene of gameplay in the orphanage, Hashi re-creates a model of a house and has the coin locker as the central element in his composition. "The taillight [where the coin locker was] was perfect: a bright orange plastic reflector covered the tiny light bulb, the chrome casing was spotless, and the red and blue wires had been carefully wrapped in a neat ball. The coin lockers shone at the heart of Hashi's kingdom."[14] The coin locker is the symbol of what constitutes Kiku's and Hashi's identities, the foundations of their being, but also a memento of their abjection, which they wish to destroy along with the city of Tokyo that contains it.

In the story, Tokyo is described as a living creature, stressing how the place, in its role of representing Japanese society, is envisioned as a physical body to be maimed:

> The physiological systems and organs mapped out on the dummy were just like those of the city: the raw materials flowing into the city were food coming down the throat; power plants were the city's lungs, and the government offices and businesses were the digestive system, absorbing all available resources; the wires strung everywhere were the nervous system, streets were veins and arteries, and the people, cells; the harbor was a gaping mouth, and the runway out at the airport, a tongue.[15]

Kiku, physically repulsed by the mere existence of Tokyo, feels an impelling force that drives him to annihilate the city to regain control over his identity, while Hashi is subdued by madness, unable to forgive his mother who abandoned him in a coin locker. Their hatred for the world revolves around their wish to destroy Tokyo, and the novel ends with the depiction of the city as a wasteland after the whole area has been poisoned with the toxin DATURA. Stephen Snyder describes the final scene of the novel as the manifestation of "ultimate abjection," revealing how the theme of the novel centers on the identity crisis due to abjection.[16]

The annihilation of Tokyo and Japan results from abjection and the subsequent identity crisis. But we also see an attempt to reframe a new identity in Murakami's stories through the presence of the foreign land. A foreign land, an alternative space to Tokyo-Japan, stands as a possible solution to the abjection of the desperate characters that populate Murakami's literary world. Their fractured identity, following the destruction of the physical body of Tokyo-Japan, seeks a way of rebuilding itself and creating new foundations within something that is not Japan. A foreign land becomes the perfect solution for the shattered identity of Murakami's characters. Imagined as an ideal, different from the refused and maimed physical body of the city, this new place is where they try to find their peace.

In *Coin Locker Babies*, the character Anemone fantasizes about a foreign land in which to rebel against reality. Like her boyfriend Kiku, Anemone too feels disdain and disgust toward the city of Tokyo, which drives her to help Kiku poison the city. For her, "the whole city stinks of age and stagnation and boredom," and she hopes to turn Tokyo into a boiling swamp.[17] She therefore redesigns her apartment to resemble a tropical paradise for her pet, a crocodile, while listening to British pop music such as that of David Bowie. Inspired by what a perfect habitat for a crocodile might be, Anemone tries to create a foreign place within her home, decorating it with exotic plants and setting a swamp-like temperature, hoping to make her pet, and herself, believe that they are not in Japan. The tragic death of the crocodile leads Anemone to abandon her apartment, declaring her attempt to create a foreign land in her imagination as a way of fighting the evil boredom of Tokyo as a failure.

In *Almost Transparent Blue* and *In za miso sūpu* (1997; *In the Miso Soup*, 2006), America is the foreign land the characters dreamed of, showing the fascination the characters have developed for American popular culture. They have an image of America that stems from their partial encounter with its culture, through movies, fashion brands, or music. They idolize the foreign land as superior to Japan and fantasize about living there. These characters, as Christian Perwein states, "have a picture of America in their heads that is exclusively their own. None of them ever sets foot there and experiences the real America for themselves. [. . .] [T]hey keep living with an imagined America in their heads that they construct themselves."[18] Their fantasies of America remain flimsy, just like Anemone's tropical fantasy.

In "Penraito" ("Penlight"), a story published in *Topazu* (1988; *Tokyo Decadence: 15 Stories*, 2016), the unnamed narrator is a young prostitute who converses with a voice in her head named Kiyomi, who personifies the protagonist's unfulfilled desires. Kiyomi claims that, when she was alive, she was a famous and beautiful pianist and singer with many suitors. But most importantly, she tells the protagonist stories about her life abroad: Hong Kong, Canada, and Spain, all places where Kiyomi has spent wonderful days but unattainable to the young prostitute. Although Kiyomi is only a projection of the disaffected mind of the narrator, this alter-ego possesses significant experience and knowledge of the world. In the following scene, the narrator distracts herself from the pain and humiliation of her daily work by fantasizing about Kiyomi's romantic adventure in Hong Kong.

Kiyomi, I say to the other person inside me. It happened again. He says I'm a pig.

*What do you expect? You are a pig. What a view from up here, though! It's like the hotel I stayed at in Hong Kong.*

You've been to Hong Kong?

*I've been everywhere. In Hong Kong, a man from Sumitomo Bank named Kawamura took me to a private club. [. . .]*

Where did you meet this man Kawamura?

*At the hotel, the Mandarin Palace in Kowloon, in the tea lounge. He came up and introduced himself. A real gentleman. Tall too, and single.*[19]

For the narrator, Kiyomi is glamorous and sophisticated and has traveled the world. In creating Kiyomi, the narrator also creates her vision of the foreign, imagining it and shaping it to be a better place than the only one she knows: the miserable and dirty city of Tokyo. Through Kiyomi's memories, the protagonist envisions an imaginary place outside Japan, underlying by comparison, the gruesome setting and encounters she experiences in her everyday life in Tokyo.

In the short story "Cauntā de nondeiru toki, itsumo omō no daga, bātendā to iu no wa nanto sūkō na shokugyō na no darō" ("Whenever I sit at the bar drinking like this") from the same collection, the protagonist reminisces about dirty and poor foreign places he visited and compares the life of some young children in Calcutta with those in Japan:

> "The children all go out to beg every morning, and the father works at some construction site twice a week or so, makes about two dollars a day, just enough to eat. But the thing is, they're happy. Cheerful."
>
> "They're cheerful?"
>
> "The children's faces just glow. Infinitely happier than the Japanese kids you see trudging back and forth to 'cramming schools' every night."[20]

Through the stereotypical image of poverty in Calcutta, Murakami highlights the flaws of an unhappy country. Considering the extreme comparison between the privileged conditions of Japanese kids and the impoverished life of young children in Calcutta, the protagonist, in praising the latter, produces an ironic literary outcome. The comparison returns later in the text when the protagonist, nagged by his mistress, recalls the sight of a beggar in Calcutta and immediately envies him: "All [the beggar] needs to do is survive."[21] The memories of these places and encounters, embodying the most stereotypical set of fixed images of those foreign lands, are only used to criticize Japan since the character is reluctant to challenge his Japanese identity. All the observations and comparisons end at a superficial level.

For the characters in Murakami's writings, the purpose of the foreign land is to reframe their identities based on this imaginary space built through a mixture of common knowledge and stereotype. Limiting his analysis to the relationship between Japan and America, Tatsumi Takayuki observes a socio-psychological phenomenon in the Japanese that he calls Occidentalism: "The Japanese tried to import a huge number of Anglo-American cultural products and unwittingly misread their Occidentalism as genuine internationalism."[22] We see this in Murakami's characters, not only concerning American culture but with regard to Western and non-Western foreign places as well. The characters' visions of foreign land submerge a conglomerate of beliefs about the exotic, as opposed to what Japan embodies. The image of the foreign land is not authentic, but functions to serve as an antithesis to Japan. This creation of a foreign land runs parallel to what Edward Said describes as the creation of the "Orient" as a set of romanticized images and fixed beliefs used by the West.[23] Without the implications of the power relationship between Occident and Orient, the foreign land is only a romanticized fantasy created by those who have never actually experienced the foreign: it counterbalances Japan's boring and suffocating urban modernity. All the foreign places mentioned by Murakami's characters are bearers of stereotypical features, representing "a significant discursive Other for Japan's identity construction."[24] Scholars have analyzed how using the Other in different media is important to reinforce the idea of "Japanese uniqueness."[25] On the contrary, the purpose of Orientalism and Occidentalism in Murakami's fiction is related to a form of criticism: Japanese identity emerges as differing from the Other, but in this comparison, the Other always results as holder of distinctive features preferred by the characters. The foreign land created through this system of stereotypes is the product of a vision of the world purely structured on the Japanese system of values and identity, rendering the characters incapable of addressing their abjection regarding Japan. How the Other is envisioned by Murakami's characters is still strongly related to them being Japanese, and they imagine those exotic places following the common pattern designed by their own culture. In *In the Miso Soup*, one of the hostesses Kenji meets with his customer Frank expresses her desire to go to America to visit "Niketown." Kenji, seeing Frank puzzled regarding what this "Niketown" is, explains that it is just a big shopping mall displayed in several commercials aired in Japan, and that "[o]nly the Japanese make a big deal about Niketown."[26] For the hostess, the shopping mall is emblematic of the whole of the United

States and is real only for Japanese people but is unknown to Americans. In short, the abjection toward Japan cannot be confronted if the characters' visions of a foreign land are based on Japanese culture they nonetheless want to distance themselves from. The characters, still firmly anchored to the Japanese norms, while talking about a place that stems from the stereotypical images produced by their culture, are not really confronting their repulsion for Japan. The abjection is thus left unsolved.

## THE OUTSIDE LAND INSIDE JAPAN

Besides places outside Japan and places that exist in the real world, in some texts, Murakami develops a foreign land that is a place existing inside Japan, but it constitutes something recognized as differing from it on the societal level. This foreign place is indeed an outside land within the Japanese borders, and, in the textual framework, it functions for the characters as a possible solution to abjection, while for Murakami it represents a means of launching a fierce critique of Japan.

*Coin Locker Babies*, as one of Murakami's most representative books, forms a perfect container of examples within this discourse. In the novel, Toxitown is an enclosed area of the city that normal citizens would not wish to approach. Still formally part of the Tokyo municipality, this land had been poisoned and contaminated and is now home to prostitutes, the homeless, and criminals. The police patrol its borders, marked off by barbed wire, but once inside, anarchy reigns. A place forgotten by society, Toxitown is an environment for the rejected, or more probably for those who have rejected the outside world, and it embodies an "*akusho*," an evil place.[27] The characters move and live in this rundown setting, in any case preferable to the moderate yet abhorrent modern city. With its own rules and hierarchy whose hallmark is violence, Toxitown coexists with Tokyo, sharing the same land but constituting, in practice, another different place:

> The warning, however, didn't have much effect on traffic in and out of Toxitown, since the people it was meant to scare off were interested in the new territory precisely because it was one place in Tokyo where police jurisdiction didn't extend. And once the area had been colonized by gangsters and hoods, other types began to collect there too; drifters and vagrants, the deinstitutionalized mentally ill, lower-class whores, male prostitutes, wanted criminals, degenerates, cripples, and runaways all took up residence in Toxitown, and an odd sort of society began to form.[28]

Hashi hides in Toxitown, living there and working as a rent boy, waiting for his break as a singer, and when Kiku finds him, he sees a different person: Toxitown has changed Hashi, or, more probably, he can reveal his true self only in this place, finally refusing society and its morality. For Kuroko Kazuo, "by setting the 'ruins' of 'Toxitown' in the middle of Tokyo, Murakami uses this credible and possible 'other world' to affirm the importance of attacking reality."[29] Kuroko points out the relevance that stems from the internal positions of these "other places" that can be found in Murakami's literature: the "*akusho*," in reality, is just "an out of ordinary world," and its privileged position inside Japan is perfect to fulfill the characters' desire for destruction and the writer's desire to criticize society.[30] Hillenbrand too points out how Toxitown represents "a barely camouflaged critique of the state and its destructive infringements into the lives of the nation's subjects."[31] Nevertheless, Hashi abandons Toxitown once he becomes a singer and immediately wishes the places of his past had never existed:

> Hashi almost wished this world within barbed wire had somehow vanished in the interim. And not just this place; he would be better off without any of the old scenery—the island down south, Kuwayama's crummy house, the slope where the cannas bloomed in summer, Milk's doghouse, the beach, the orphanage, the rows of cherry trees, the sandbox, the chapel, everything. But why? It was simple: because he, Hashi, had become a singer.[32]

This passage shows that the abjection is not solved with the mere existence of Toxitown: Hashi still desperately tries to find his place in Tokyo and cannot completely dissociate from what he despises.

The development of the foreign land as a literary means of critiquing Japan continues in other novels, and the concept of the foreign land inside Japan assumes political overtones. In *Hantō o deyo (2005; From Fatherland with Love*, 2013), we see a fractured Japan in which Fukuoka and Kyushu claim independence from the central power of the Capitol under the control of the North Korean Koryo Expeditionary Force. The presence of a group of foreign characters, the North Korean soldiers, creates an interesting split whereby the military group sees Japan as a foreign place, comparing it with their home villages. The citizens of Fukuoka, on the other hand, witness the creation of a foreign land they can compare with Japan as their original homeland. For the North Korean characters, the first approach with Japanese society is shocking. Having shaped a specific set of mental images of Japan gleaned from occupation during World War II, the contrast between what they believed about Japan and what it is now produces a sense of disdain that fuels their desire to destroy its society. Having felt a "mixture of animosity and grudging respect" for a country that "had once fought so fiercely against the West," they now have to face reality, understanding that "Japan had degenerated into a country that was little more than America's servile, tail-wagging lapdog."³³ Like Murakami's other characters who live with their abjection, feeling disgust for Japanese society, the North Korean soldiers look upon the decadence of Japanese morals and the country's evil system, judging the people as weak and corrupt. In the same paradigm seen above, the modern city represents the degeneration of an immoral society, and the characters are ready to maim its physical body as a way of purging it.

The plan to occupy Fukuoka proceeds, and defining borders are set up. Every movement is controlled by the Koryo and the Japanese Self-Defense Forces dispatched along the confines of Kyushu. After an attempt to kill several North Korean soldiers, resulting in the murder of several Fukuoka citizens by the SDF, the Fukuokans start to view the central government with disdain, and their attitude toward the invaders starts to become less hostile. There seems to be a real possibility that the international community may recognize Kyushu as an independent region, and prospects of prosperity arise. But the attempt to set up a foreign land inside Japan is undermined by a group of outcasts and young misfits who attack the hotel where the Koryo has made its headquarters. This group, led by the poet Ishihara, is made up of eighteen boys who "socially isolated themselves through a systematic invisibilization."³⁴ The youths were discarded after being labeled as "defective" for not conforming to social norms, and they feel a sense of repulsion for society:

> They'd been under constraint and pressure from the moment they first became aware of their surroundings, threatened with punishment if they didn't follow orders. And they'd had it engraved on their minds, with the edged tools of fear and pain, that they were powerless. Everyone in this world was a hostage to some form of violence; it was just that most people never realized it.³⁵

For Oh Sejong, the youths' status as outsiders is marked by their names being written in katakana, used "to stress the peculiarity of their isolated and invisible existence."³⁶ Tateno, Shinohara, and the other young boys under Ishihara's roof had, in one way or another, committed heinous crimes for which they are too young to be held fully accountable. They have run away from the institutes or homes where they have been held in search of freedom in the abandoned building managed by Ishihara and Takei. The area surrounding the building is a sort of no man's land, and their existence is silently accepted by the local government, happy that the responsibility for these defective youths no longer lies with them. Once the Koryo show interest in the abandoned area to build new apartments for the soldiers, Ishihara's boys start to plot the destruction of the hotel. Just like Toxitown, the area in which the young boys live represents a sort of foreign land within Japan's borders, where those who despise society can live on their terms. The creation of a politically and socially recognizable foreign land, the Koryo-ruled Kyushu region, results in a menace for the peaceful equilibrium gained by the group of outcasts, and for this reason alone the attempt to create a politically and societally foreign place inside Japan cannot be accomplished textually. Interestingly, those who despise society as Murakami's other characters do are the ones who oppose the actual creation of a new State within the confines of the Japanese borders. Before the appearance of the Koryo Expeditionary Force, the group itself, driven by its hatred toward Japanese society, is planning to attack the established order: "Takei was an admirable financial manager for the group. But his real purpose in financing Ishihara was to start a revolution in Japan, and he seriously intended to employ the youths as soldiers in his struggle."[37] Indeed, the desire to destroy Japan is actively cultivated, and some even say that Ishihara and his friend Nobue "had once committed murders and even blown-up a section of Tokyo with a bomb of mind-boggling proportions, just for fun."[38] Nevertheless, the need to demolish the country is set aside when the ownership of their own land is threatened by an external force. The community created by Ishihara represents a microcosm interrupted only momentarily by Fukuoka's authority, and the young boys interact with other citizens only when they leave their building and its surrounding area. Somehow, and albeit imperfectly, they had already created a foreign land, a protected environment under their rule inside Fukuoka's borders. It is no coincidence that Takei's guerrilla plan is only directed against North Korean soldiers, and appeared merely as a daydream that would never come about.

The failure to create a concrete alternative to Japan is marked by the destruction of the Sea Hawk Hotel by Ishihara's boys. The aim was to protect their own place, partially distant from the societal order, but still officially under its control, and the young boys destroy the Koryo headquarters. The hotel, built to resemble an artificial foreign land, a fake representation of South Pacific island paradises and African jungles, crumbles like the dream to create a foreign land in place of corrupt modern Japanese society. The conclusion embodies the impossibility for Ishihara's boys to completely reject Japan and to solve their abjection: after the death of their companions and the destruction of the hotel, Ishihara's few surviving members continue to live in their abandoned building as though nothing had happened, and the project to preserve their heroic deeds through Ishihara's poems would never take shape.

The story that most closely creates a foreign land acting as a valid alternative to Japan is *Kibō no kuni no ekusodasu* (2000; *Exodus to the Land of Hope*). In the novel, a group of high school students decide to move away from Japanese society and establish a new city near Napporo, Hokkaido. They create a new currency and strengthen their financial autonomy through their web-based company called ASUNARO. The element in the literary discourse that probably marks their achievement of dissociating themselves from Japan is that they manage to create a newly established order inside Japan without resorting to violence. Shimizu Yoshinori points out how the absence of a destructive element is important in the effective realization of the exodus: "Peculiarly [for Murakami's writings], and almost fundamentally, it is an independent movement able to achieve its purpose without the need to oppose or fight the Japanese government."[39]

The story starts with the discovery by a group of international reporters of a couple of young Japanese boys in Pakistan fighting for the Pashtun guerrilla. The brief recorded interview with one of the Japanese boys in a shabby clinic sparks a shocking reaction in Japanese public opinion, with everyone wondering how boys as young as this could leave Japan and join a bloody war in which they have no interest. The interviewed boy, ultimately identified by the name "Namamugi" in the novel, clearly states his abjection, and how he now identifies as a member of the Pashtun tribe: to questions of the CNN reporter regarding his nationality, he replies "I was Japanese once. [. . .] Now I am a Pashtun."[40]

Dissociating from his Japanese identity, Namamugi decided to leave Japan behind, not seeing in the destruction of the physical land a possible solution to his abjection. The only way open to him was to reinvent himself by reaching a real foreign country, speaking a different language, and joining what he believes is a just cause: the Pashtun guerrilla movement. Namamugi, like Murakami's other characters, despises Japan, and while answering the reporter's questions, he explains the reason behind his choices in a powerful speech.

"Don't you miss Japan?"

"I already forgot that place."

"Forgot? Why?"

"There's nothing in that country; it is already dead. I don't think about Japan anymore."

"What does this place have?"

"It's got everything, all the joy of living, the love of family, friendship, respect, pride, all these things. It is true that we have enemies, but there is no bullying or being bullied here."[41]

For Namamugi, Japan is a place without love, joy, or hope. In a society in which everyone bullies or is bullied, surviving cold everyday life is impossible, and it leads the self to internal death. The foreign land wins in this comparison, no matter how difficult the hardship to bear in order to live outside the easy comfort of Japan is.

Namamugi is the one who inspires the younger generation in his former homeland to leave Japan too, and soon all the flights for Pakistan are crowded with high school students trying to mimic his actions. But they are rapidly blocked by the police, who stop flights and send them back home. The only possible solution is to abandon the idea of leaving Japan, and, at that precise moment, ASUNARO and the project to create a new societal community take form. "Their real exodus begins the moment they give up fleeing Japan."[42]

The younger generation fiercely criticizes Japanese society, and this is expressed by their desire to abandon it: mature enough to be aware of the unhappy and unjust aspects of Japan and the asphyxiating air of its cityscapes, these youths begin an exodus toward a new possibility, seen as "the land of hope." The concept of hope, said to be lacking in Japan by one of the main characters, is identified by Kuroko as "the freedom of the soul": "The primordial condition, fundamental for humanity to live in this world, is 'the freedom of the soul,' and if restrained, everyone would harbor bitter feelings of hopelessness and dissatisfaction toward their society."[43] The protagonists cannot be considered totally outcasts such as Kiku or Hashi in *Coin Locker Babies*, Ishihara's boys in *Fatherland with Love*, or the other protagonists in Murakami's works, but they too represent an invisible category of Japanese society, living under the established order. Hideo Nakamura, one of the boys who try to catch a flight to reach Pakistan, tells the narrator of the novel a story: one day he goes to school, and he meets his friends that, as though he is not there, start to ignore him without a valid reason. The existence of bullying in the form of intentional banishment is what leads Nakamura to stop attending school, underlying a real problem that Japanese society still cannot solve. The face of this unhappy country is that of bullying, and the feelings that brought Namamugi to leave Japan to join the Pashtun war are shared among the dropout students that refuse to continue studying to avoid the pressure of this hostile society. Excluded by their peers and adults, the students in this novel, like an ostracized population, must dream of an exodus to a better and happier place different from Japan.

The students in *Exodus to the Land of Hope* still see themselves as members of their society, which is why they shun violence as a means of destroying Japan. Their revolution appears moderate compared with the destruction of Tokyo or Fukuoka in the novels discussed above, but, in the end, it is more successful because they do not try to take revenge by maiming the body of their society, nor do they try to change it. Being too young to actively modify the established order directly, the students do not even try to protest against what they think is corrupt; they just take what they can and depart once a greater community has been created on the ASUNARO network. Cassegrd analyzes the absence of violence or rebellion against mainstream society as a way of humiliating the adult generation, culminating in the decision to abandon their societal order.[44] They simply leave Japan behind, and from what they build inside its borders, they make Japanese society evolve into a better and happier version.

The absence of any attempt by the students to improve the society they live in could be due to Murakami Ryū's disappointment in the educational system and the ineffectiveness of the angry student movements during his youth. In an interview, Murakami reveals his disillusionment with Japanese society, unable to change because student activism has failed to achieve its purpose:

> I was beginning to suspect that leftist radicalism, democracy, and other common ideologies in our country were not authentic. Those ideas were taking root here and rapidly losing their original spirit. To be honest, I do think there was something genuine in the leftist movement immediately after the war, but everything soon degenerated, resulting in stability but without real change. What a disappointment: nothing was real, the students' struggle in the late sixties ended in nothing.[45]

Having been an activist for what was felt to be a just cause in his student years, and having seen no sign of any effect on modern society, Murakami shows the ineffectiveness of destroying Japan as means of changing it. In this novel then, he develops the concept of the foreign land not as a mere object of comparison with Japanese society, but as its evolution. In *Exodus to the Land of Hope*, there is no longer any need to make comparisons: Japan is the land of hopelessness, its younger generation decides to leave it behind, depriving it of a future, to build a real land of hope. For the characters, that this land of hope is geographically still inside the Japanese borders symbolizes the final acceptance of their Japanese identity and the possibility of transforming it into something better, not simply replacing it or attempting to change it through destruction. This new foreign land, marked by silent acceptance, the absence of violence, and the characters' positive hope to create something better is the solution to abjection in Murakami's writings.

## CONCLUSION

Starting from Murakami's criticism of Japanese society, the foreign land in the literary context represents the outcast characters in an attempt to find a solution to their abjection. The outward and inward movements of destruction result from their abjection: the physical body of the city is the outlet for the desire to destroy the society they inhabit and the identity crisis takes place; the imaginary foreign land is the place where the process of reconstruction of the self can happen.

"The apocalyptic rejection of the world" of the protagonists in Murakami Ryū's literature represents their attempt to free themselves of the sense of abjection toward the place that should represent the primary source of contact between reality and their own identity.[46] The construction of the foreign land, which takes place through stereotypes or common knowledge, fixed images, or a confused memory of the outside, is the equivalent to the reconstruction of their identity.

Nevertheless, this attempt often seems to fail because the characters cannot completely shut out their Japanese identities: in *Coin Locker Babies*, Toxitown is an outlawed foreign land, and even if for a moment Hashi seems to reinvent himself through this space, he still runs away from it as soon as he becomes a singer, trying to find his place in Tokyo among the "normal" people. The use of violence to destroy Tokyo gives a moment of relief to Kiku and Hashi, but they accept madness as a flawed solution to their abjection and it does not help the two rebuild themselves and be free of Japan.

*Almost Transparent Blue*, *In the Miso Soup*, and the stories in *Tokyo Decadence* contain a kaleidoscope of decadent situations, and the characters find a pathetic form of consolation in imagining a foreign land in a far better situation than their own. Tokyo is a city to be disdained; it can only offer profligate and immoral experiences. But abjection is still not solved because the foreign land is only mental, merely a fantasy place built upon Orientalism and Occidentalism, used to find a moment of solace, and the characters cannot truly rest and reinvent themselves there.

Recourse to violence is useless in shaping the foreign land, as exemplified by *From Fatherland with Love*. Occupation by the Koryo Expeditionary Force prepares Fukuoka to be the place where the foreign land can be founded, but the boys in Ishihara's group prevent it from coming into being. Still not ready to discard their identity and their place, the boys kill several North Korean soldiers, putting an end to the foundation of the foreign land. The emblematic ending of the novel clearly suggests a refusal to find a full solution to their abjection regarding Japan and to start the process of reframing: for Kuroko, the nihilistic attitude of the characters will always prevent them actually attempting to change the status quo, and the fact that neither Ishihara nor anyone else will write or talk about what they have done is the culmination of their refusal to face their abjection.[47]

None of the stories mentioned above manage to depict the replacement of Japan with a foreign land in which the characters can find a real solution to their sense of abjection. Kawanishi Masaaki reveals the futility of the characters' actions and their inability to actually destroy and completely erase the society they despise: the novels end in the same condition in which they started, and society appears unchanged.[48] The only promising attempt to solve this abjection is the land of hope created in *Exodus to the Land of Hope*, where the absence of violence and the sense of indolence is underscored by the silent and pragmatic migration of the younger generation. The foreign land in *Exodus* solves the feeling of abjection: the students take with them what is useful in their Japanese identity, and rather than destroy it, rebuilding it from zero, they use it as the basis for constructing something new, thus bringing about a positive evolution.

## NOTES

1. Many literary critics identify American culture as one of the main factors influencing writers like Murakami Ryū and Murakami Haruki. Glynne Walley, for example, traces the same pattern in both writers stemming from their close contact with American culture. See Glynne Walley, "Two Murakamis and Their American Influence," *Japan Quarterly* 44, no. 1 (1997): 41–50.

2. Barbara Flauto, "Perdita d'identità e critica sociale: il mondo estremo di Murakami Ryū," *Il Giappone* 47 (2007): 155.

3. Kuroko Kazuo, *Murakami Ryū: 'kiki' ni kō suru sōzōryoku*, (Tokyo: Bensei Shuppan, 2009), ii. Kuroko uses the word "Mondaisaku" to describe how Murakami's works are considered in relation to the societal discourse they depict.

4. Sandra Buckley, ed., *Encyclopedia of Contemporary Japanese Culture*, (London: Routledge, 2002), 335. In her analysis, Sandra Buckley stresses the opposition reserved to Murakami Ryū by the literary establishment that accuses his writings of lacking intellectual and literary resonance.

5. Ōoka Makoto, "Bungaku ni arawareta mayakuteki kankaku o megutte," in *Gunzō Nihon no Sakka 29: Murakami Ryū*, ed. Akira Nogami, (Tokyo: Shōgakukan, 1998), 35. Ōoka gives a wonderful portrayal of how Murakami's first novel embodies the frailty of modern Japanese moral values, recognizing a tradition of writers and poets that contested the normative system in the same manner of Murakami.

6. Carl Cassegrd, *Shock and Naturalization in Contemporary Japanese Literature*, (Leiden: Brill, 2007), 189. Cassegrd identifies "modernity" as the problematic aspect of contemporary Japan: the ordinary is what Murakami's characters try to fight, living in a constant repetition of experiences that would be considered shocking by the standard members of the society.

7. Stephen Snyder, "Extreme Imagination: The Fiction of Murakami Ryū," in *Ōe and beyond: fiction in contemporary Japan*, ed. Stephen Snyder and Phillip Gabriel, (Honolulu: University of Hawai'i Press, 1999), 201.

8. Margaret Hillenbrand, *Literature, Modernity, and the Practice of Resistance: Japanese and Taiwanese Fiction, 1960–1990*, (Leiden: Brill, 2007), 175. Margaret identifies the aversion for the cityscape and extreme sexual practices as literary products of a social condition caused by the postwar modernity in which the

family has disintegrated in this setting. She recognizes the same literary pattern not only in Japanese writers like Murakami Ryū and Yoshimoto Banana, but also in Taiwanese writers.

9. Julia Kristeva, *Power of Horrors: An Essay on Abjection*, trans. Leon S. Roudiez, (New York: Columbia University Press, 1982), 5.

10. Ibid., 5.

11. Ibid., 8.

12. Kawamoto Saburō, "Toshi no naka no sakkatachi: Murakami Haruki to Murakami Ryū o megutte," in *Gunzō Nihon no Sakka 29: Murakami Ryū*, ed. Akira Nogami, (Tokyo: Shōgakukan, 1998), 41.

13. Kuroko, *Murakami Ryū*, 63. Kuroko talks about the "desire of destruction" ("hakai nebō"), as a main feature in Murakami's literature. For him, this desire stems from the resentment the characters feel toward society, while Murakami criticizes the capitalistic aspect of Japan.

14. Murakami Ryū, *Koinrokkā Beibīzu*, (Tokyo: Kōdansha, 1980). Murakami Ryū, *Coin Locker Babies*, trans. Stephen Snyder, (London: Pushkin Press, 2013), 11, Kindle ed.

15. Ibid., 89.

16. Snyder, "Extreme Imagination," 211.

17. *Coin Locker Babies*, 129.

18. Christian Perwein, Transnational Japanese-American Ambiguities in Select Works of Murakami Ryu, *Nanzan Review of American Studies* 40 (2018): 8–9.

19. Murakami Ryū, *Topazu*, (Tokyo: Kadokawa Shoten, 1988). Murakami Ryū, *Tokyo Decadence: 15 Stories*, trans. Ralph McCarthy, (Kumamoto: Kurodahan Press, 2016), ch. 7, Kindle ed.

20. Murakami Ryū, *Hashire! Takahashi*, (Tokyo: Kōdansha, 1986). *Tokyo Decadence: 15 Stories*, ch. 1.

21. Ibid., ch. 1.

22. Tatsumi Takayuki, "The Japanoid Manifesto: Toward a New Poetics of Invisible Culture," *Review of Contemporary Fiction* 22, no. 2 (2002): 13.

23. Edward W. Said, *Orientalism*, (New York: Vintage Books, 1979 [1978]).

24. Kawai Yuko, "Using Diaspora: Orientalism, Japanese Nationalism, and the Japanese Brazilian Diaspora," in *Intercultural Masquerade: New Orientalism, New Occidentalism, Old Exoticism*, ed. Regis Machart, Fred Dervin and Minghui Gao, (London: Higher Education Press, 2016), 99. Kawai describes how representation of the Other, in his analysis of the Japanese-Brazilian community, serves to strengthen national identity. Murakami reverses this process, using Orientalism and Occidentalism to criticize Japanese identity.

25. Kawai's analysis focuses on Japanese TV shows and their representation of the Japanese-Brazilian community as the "Other," while Millie Creighton inquiries into the use of the Western foreigner in advertisement. See Millie R. Creighton, "Imaging the Other in Japanese Advertising Campaigns," in *Occidentalism: Images of the West*, ed. James G. Carrier, (Oxford: Calendor Press, 2003), 135–160. In both examples, the Other is a means through which Japan and Japanese values appear superior, and the foreign serves only for this process.

26. Murakami Ryū, *In za miso sūpu*, (Tokyo: Gentōsha, 1997). Murakami Ryū, *In the Miso Soup*, trans. Ralph McCarthy, (London: Bloomsbury), 24.
27. Snyder, "Extreme Imagination," 210.
28. *Coin Locker Babies*, 53.
29. Kuroko, *Murakami Ryū*, 65.
30. Ibid., 66.
31. Hillenbrand, *Literature, Modernity, and the Practice of Resistance*, 212–213.
32. *Coin Locker Babies*, 156–157.
33. Murakami Ryū, *Hantō o deyo*, (Tokyo: Gentōsha, 2005). Murakami Ryū, *From Fatherland with Love*, trans. Ralph McCarthy, Ginny Taply Takemori, Charles De Wolf, (London: Pushkin Press, 2013), ch. 3, Kindle ed.
34. Oh Sejong. 2019. "Teikoku o hikitsugu bungaku keishiki: 1992 nen ikō no nihon gendai bungaku ni okeru kitachōsen hyōshō, Murakami Ryū 'Hantō o deyo' o chūshin ni," *Kōbe-shi gaikokugo daigaku gaikokugaku kenkyū* 93 (2019): 170.
35. *From Fatherland with Love*, ch. 5.
36. Oh, "Teikoku o hikitsugu bungaku keishiki," 170.
37. *From Fatherland with Love*, intro. 2.
38. Ibid., intro. 2.
39. Shimizu Yoshinori, "Quattordicenni alla frontiera: L'esodo nel paese della speranza di Murakami Ryū e Kafka sulla spiaggia di Murakami Haruki," trans. Gianluca Coci, in *Japan Pop: Parole, immagini, suoni dal Giappone contemporaneo*, (Rome: Aracne Editrice, 2013), 72.
40. Murakami Ryū, *Kibō no kuni no ekusodasu*, in *Hajimete no bungaku*, (Tokyo: Bungeishunjū, 2006), 161–162.
41. Ibid., 164.
42. Shimizu, "Quattordicenni alla frontiera," 73.
43. Kuroko, *Murakami Ryū*, 45–46.
44. Cassegrd, *Shock and Naturalization*, 205.
45. Murakami Ryū, "La forza rigeneratrice della musica, del cinema e delle relazioni interpersonali," interview by Shimizu Yoshinori and Gianluca Coci, in *Japan Pop: parole, immagini, suoni dal Giappone contemporaneo*, (Rome: Aracne Editrice, 2013), 88–89.
46. Cassegrd, *Shock and Naturalization*, 206.
47. Kuroko, *Murakami Ryū*, 232.
48. Kawanishi Masaaki, "Hon o yomu: Koinrokkā Beibīzu," in *Gunzō Nihon no Sakka 29*, 132.

# WORKS CITED

Buckley, Sandra, ed. *Encyclopedia of Contemporary Japanese Culture*. London: Routledge, 2002.
Carrier, James G., ed. *Occidentalism: Images of the West*. Oxford: Calendor Press, 2003.

Cassegrd, Carl. *Shock and Naturalization in Contemporary Japanese Literature.* Leiden: Brill, 2007.

Creighton, Millie R. "Imaging the Other in Japanese Advertising Campaign," in *Occidentalism: Images of the West*, edited by James G. Carrier, 135–160. Oxford: Calendor Press, 2003.

Flauto, Barbara. "Perdita d'identità e critica sociale: il mondo estremo di Murakami Ryū." *Il Giappone* 47 (2007): 149–169.

Hillenbrand, Margaret. *Literature, Modernity, and the Practice of Resistance: Japanese and Taiwanese Fiction, 1960–1990.* Leiden: Brill, 2007.

Kawai, Yuko. "Using Diaspora: Orientalism, Japanese Nationalism, and the Japanese Brazilian Diaspora." In *Intercultural Masquerade: New Orientalism, New Occidentalism, Old Exoticism.* Edited by Regis Machart, Fred Dervin and Minghui Gao, 97–117. London: Higher Education Press, 2016.

Kawamoto, Saburō. "Toshi no naka no sakkatachi: Murakami Haruki to Murakami Ryū o megutte." In *Gunzō Nihon no Sakka 29: Murakami Ryū.* Edited by Akira Nogami, 40–55. Tokyo: Shōgakukan, 1998.

Kawanishi, Masaaki. "Hon o yomu: Koinrokkā Beibīzu," in *Gunzō Nihon no Sakka 29: Murakami Ryū.* Edited by Akira Nogami, 130–136. Tokyo: Shōgakukan, 1998.

Kristeva, Julia. *Power of Horrors: An Essay on Abjection.* Translated by Leon S. Roudiez. New York: Columbia University Press, 1982.

Kuroko, Kazuo. *Murakami Ryū: 'kiki' ni kō suru sōzōryoku.* Tokyo: Bensei Shuppan, 2009.

Murakami, Ryū. *Kagiranaku tōmei ni chikai burū.* Tokyo: Kōdansha, 1976.

———. *Koinrokkā Beibīzu.* Tokyo: Kōdansha, 1980.

———. *Hashire! Takahashi.* Tokyo: Kōdansha, 1986.

———. *Topazu.* Tokyo: Kadokawa Shoten, 1988.

———. *In za miso sūpu.* Tokyo: Gentōsha, 1997.

———. *In the Miso Soup.* Translated by Ralph McCarthy. London: Bloomsbury, 2003.

———. *Hantō o deyo.* Tokyo: Gentōsha, 2005.

———. *Kibō no kuni no ekusodasu*, in *Hajimete Bungaku.* Tokyo: Bungeishunjū, 2006 [2000].

———. *Coin Locker Babies.* Translated by Stephen Snyder. London: Kindle ed., Pushkin Press, 2013.

———. *From Fatherland with Love.* Translated by Ralph McCarthy, Ginny Taply Takemori, Charles De Wolf. London: Kindle ed., Pushkin Press, 2013.

———. "La forza rigeneratrice della musica, del cinema e delle relazioni interpersonali." Interview by Shimizu Yoshinori and Gianluca Coci, in *Japan Pop: parole, immagini, suoni dal Giappone contemporaneo*, 87–97. Rome: Aracne Editrice, 2013.

———. *Tokyo Decadence: 15 Stories.* Translated by Ralph McCarthy. Kumamoto: Kindle ed., Kurodahan Press 2016.

Oh, Sejong. "Teikoku o hikitsugu bungakukeishiki: 1992 nen ikō no nihon gendai bungaku ni okeru kitachōsen hyōshō, Murakami Ryū 'Hantō o deyo' o chūshin ni." *Kōbe-shi gaikokugo daigaku gaikokugaku kenkyū* 93 (2019): 167–180.

Ōoka, Makoto. "Bungaku ni arawareta mayakuteki kankaku o megutte." In *Gunzō Nihon no Sakka 29: Murakami Ryū*. Edited by Akira Nogami, 35–38. Tokyo: Shōgakukan, 1998.
Perwein, Christian. "Transnational Japanese-American Ambiguities in Select Works of Murakami Ryū." *Nanzan Review of American Studies* 40 (2018): 3–21.
Said, Edward W. *Orientalism*. New York: Vintage Books, 1979 [1978].
Shimizu, Yoshinori. "Quattordicenni alla frontiera: L'esodo nel paese della speranza di Mirakami Ryū e Kafka sulla spiaggia di Murakami Haruki." In *Japan Pop: Parole, immagini, suoni dal Giappone contemporaneo*. Edited and translated by Gianluca Coci, 61–85. Rome: Aracne Editrice, 2014.
Snyder, Stephen. "Extreme Imagination: The Fiction of Murakami Ryū." In *Ōe and beyond: fiction in contemporary Japan*. Edited by Stephen Snyder and Phillip Gabriel, 199–218. Honolulu: University of Hawai'i Press, 1999.
Tatsumi, Takayuki. "The Japanoid Manifesto: Toward a New Poetics of Invisible Culture." *Review of Contemporary Fiction* 22, no. 2 (2002): 12–18.
Walley, Glynne. "Two Murakamis and Their American Influence." *Japan Quarterly* 44, no. 1 (1997): 41–50.

*Chapter Seven*

# The Fantastical Space of Exile in Tawada Yōko's *Memoirs of a Polar Bear*

Barbara Hartley

## CREATING A PHANTASMAGORICAL EXILIC SPACE

Reveling in representations of the fantastical space is one of many pleasures experienced by readers of the Tawada Yōko (b. 1960) text. Even her narrative arcs that conform to "real life" are characterized by liminal elements that undermine sociolinguistic certitude or predictability and thereby draw readers inexorably into a fantasy realm.

With three generations of animal protagonists, *Memoirs of a Polar Bear* (Portobello, 2017; translated from the German, *Etüden im Schnee*, 2014; written initially in Japanese as *Yuki no renshūsei* [lit. the snow apprentice], 2010–2011) is an overtly fantastical literary production. In addition to an unnamed performing bear, now turned writer, whose building superintendent reads the *Sarashina nikki* in Russian translation, the work features this bear's daughter, Tosca (sometimes Toska), as she authors the life-narrative of her trainer when the latter loses her job. We also meet Tosca's son, Knut, who, rejected by his mother after his birth, becomes a global celebrity feted by the press. This plot synopsis suggests a teleological clarity and neatness of form. Nevertheless, Tomoko Takeuchi Slutsky points out that, with its tendency to "subvert and obfuscate [any] definite dualism," the novel is "exciting to read" because of the very way in which relationships between "original and copy, reality and fiction, are vexed, inverted, muddled and complicated."[1] This, of course, is Tawada's signature style.

The fantastical space of *Memoirs of a Polar Bear* permits the humorous yet poignant narration of the travails of the life of the exile. While Suzuko Mousel Knott explains that "polar bear movement within habitats is in practice a form of nomadism" and that "[i]ndividual bears never truly settle in one place," each bear in Tawada's tale has nonetheless been removed or born outside the polar habitat and forced into foreign terrains.[2] In narrating their tales, the text dismantles contemporary myths of inclusivity, while also contesting the value of putatively beneficial modern structures that, in fact, harshly constrain those marked as "other" or "outsider." Notions of exile are embedded not merely in tropes overtly associated with exclusion and mobility, but also in less obvious concepts, including the hegemonic parameters of maternity that Tawada contests in her narratives. Furthermore, the phantasmagorical is often profiled in *Memoirs of a Polar Bear* through the use of the dream as a narrative strategy evoking exile and unfamiliar space.

Some scholars argue that attributing human traits to animals replicates prejudice and stereotypes. In addition to discussing the relationship between exile and the fantastical in Tawada's text, I will consider problems that arise when depicting human-like polar bears. It is my contention that, far from entrenching hegemony, Tawada's account accords with theories of critical anthropomorphism that permit the creation of an alternate literary space. While her presentation of interspecies relations might be the most fantastical element of the novel, there is a sense that these exchanges between animal and human offer possibilities for real-life futures. In this sense, *Memoirs of a Polar Bear* seeks to profile and to ameliorate the circumstances of animal and human exiles alike. Before providing a brief summary of the text and background on Tawada herself, I will elaborate upon the three language versions of the text and the use of Susan Bernofsky's English translation for this discussion.

## POLAR BEAR REPRESENTATIONS IN A THREE-WAY LANGUAGE SPACE

In addition to presenting readers with a variety of peripatetic protagonists, Tawada has long written about language shift, often as an interrogation of hegemonic readings of nation and state. As Jordan A.Y. Smith reminds readers with reference to Susan Bernofsky's "fluent, lucid translation" from German into English, it is "easy to forget" that "there are two 'originals'" behind the English version of Tawada's novel.[3] Douglas Slaymaker points out that, in the case of *Memoirs of a Polar Bear*, which he refers to as *The Snow*

*Apprentice* in a direct rendering of the Japanese title, neither language version authored by Tawada is "a translation of the other."[4] Rather, the relationship between the two recalls the observation made by the writing bear, when her original Russian is translated into German by a "Slavist named Eisberg who lived in Berlin,"[5] that "the original and its translation began to play a fugue [canon], though as far as I could see, it was more like a game of Cat and Mouse than a sublime musical form."[6] Slaymaker suggests that, like this "Cat and Mouse," Tawada's texts "form two versions of the same narrative line, fighting in two languages, pushing and pulling."[7] The oppressive imperative generated is evident from the bear's comment: "As the mouse being pursued, I had to run faster and faster so the cat wouldn't catch me."[8] This race to evade capture suggests the sense of exile that I argue underpins this novel and also Tawada's cultural production in general.

No translation can capture every element of its source text. Nevertheless, as Gayatri Chakravorty Spivak famously points out, while "impossible," translation is "in every possible sense [. . .] necessary."[9] The "impossibility" of translation is particularly evident when considering the work of Tawada who deploys sophisticated levels of "ambiguity and slipperiness of meaning."[10] The "impossibility" of comfortably reading across the three versions of Tawada's narrative is apparent from Douglas Slaymaker's insightful discussion of various slippages between the Japanese original and English translation of the novel. Noting that this text is redolent with Tawada's "especially clever facility" to move between languages, Slaymaker is adamant that this is "a profound technical feat," rather than any literary "trick."[11] Confirming that he is in no way critical of Bernofsky's "masterful" translation and acknowledging that he does not read the German from which the English version was authored,[12] Slaymaker elucidates various aspects of the Japanese text that might defy even the most gifted translator. In addition to the inability of English to fully capture the "rich mimetic vocabulary" of Japanese,[13] he is interested in the way in which "the natural-sounding use of passive voice" can "defer the question of naming the species and gender of the narrator."[14] Discussing this point at some length, Slaymaker also considers what is lost in translation by the fact that the English words "hand" and "paw" are covered by the same expression, "*te*," in Japanese.[15] The need to distinguish between these in English removes the suspension of distinction of species that the Japanese permits. Particularly significant is the fact that the Japanese reader will reasonably assume that the narrator is a person while, through the use of the expression "paw-hand," the English language reader is alerted at the outset to the existence of the narrating bear. This alert is supported by the English title of the novel—*Memoirs of a Polar Bear*—which draws on neither the Japanese title, which Slaymaker notes translates as *The*

*Snow Apprentice*, or the German, which translates into English as "etudes in snow." Meaning "technical exercise," the term "etudes," in music at least, often appears as "studies."

Smith raises a further translation issue by speculating that the name of a key animal trainer character referred to as Ursula (from the word bear) in the Japanese (Uruzura) and German versions was "translated" in English to "Barbara."[16] This change, Smith suggests, while referencing a conversation between himself and author Tawada, was made to evoke the Davey Crocket song lyrics that tell of the frontier hero killing "himself a bar [rather than bear] when he was only three." He concludes that the translation might be thought of as "American" as much as English.[17]

In spite of these issues, there is no doubt, to borrow from Slaymaker, that Bernofsky's translation is "masterful." I will therefore use her words for the citations given below while triangulating these against similar passages that appear in the original Japanese text.[18]

## ACROSS THREE GENERATIONS OF POLAR BEARS

The story line of Tawada's text involves three generations of polar bears. The first is unnamed, the second is her daughter, Tosca, while the third is Tosca's son, Knut. Various commentaries explain how in 2006 a polar bear cub named Knut was born at the Berlin Zoo.[19] Like his Tawada tale counterpart, Knut was rejected by his mother. This real-life Knut was raised by caretaker, Thomas Dörflein. Noting how "[t]he entire nation was moved by images of the little polar bear," Sabine Peschel observes that: "the resulting 'Knutmania' led to a 2007 *Vanity Fair* cover with actor Leonardo DiCaprio shot by famed photographer Annie Leibovitz, a film and plush likenesses."[20] A resident of Berlin at the time, Tawada was surely bemused by the ruckus surrounding this bear whom, in a discussion declaring Tawada's novel to be a queering of zoopoetics, Eve Hoffman argues may well be "the most famous animal ever to inhabit a German zoo."[21] While Knott explains how Tawada gave a reading of her novel in German at the National History Museum in Berlin beside the preserved body of polar bear Knut who died in 2010,[22] the author structures her narrative to first introduce the bear who gave birth to Knut's mother.

The novel commences with this unnamed bear recalling, reconstructing through memory, her childhood, which she begins to commit to paper when unable to recall her mother. Reference was previously made to the bear's building superintendent reading a Russian translation of *Sarashina nikki* (Sarashina Diary), one of Japan's classic Heian era (794–1185) texts. Douglas

Slaymaker argues that there is "a genre question hidden in this exchange," a message that might be missed by a non-Japanese reader.[23] Slaymaker explains that while it is one thing to invoke a "diary," a "n*ikki*" is "a much more personal kind of memoir." In other words, there is an intimacy to the bear's recollections that might be absent in a more pedestrian account of one's past. Although the bear was raised by a man named Ivan (Yvan) to ride a bicycle and perform with the Moscow Circus, she is now a retired circus performer working in circus administration. Knott links this fact to the novel's intertextual reference to the Red Peter ape—discussed further below—who undertakes clerical work in a short story by Franz Kafka (1883–1924).[24] Eventually, the bear takes the autobiography to an editor named Sea Lion, a fan from her circus days who had "claimed to be hopelessly in love with me."[25] Notwithstanding his former crush, Sea Lion's ethical stance is highly suspect in terms of respecting the intentions of the writerly bear. Although the pair had once "wound up kissing," she is now a "miserable former circus star" standing "defenceless before the bloodthirsty publisher, clutching my virginal work."[26] Sea Lion unilaterally gives the first instalment of her material a title that he believes will increase sales. When the bear intersperses political observations throughout her work, Sea Lion objects.

Eventually, in danger of internment because of this political commentary, the bear is assisted to relocate to West Germany. During the lifetime of her daughter, Tosca, the bear's writing had been long out of print to become "one of the many cultural objects left out of the official archive through the process of selection."[27] Throughout her own lifetime, however, this writing brings fame although limited fortune. When attacked by West German neo-Nazis who hear her say the word "Moscow,"[28] the bear emigrates to Canada where Tosca, a surviving twin, is born. In her discerning reading of Tawada's novel, Elizabeth McNeill uses the term "grandmother" to refer to this bear.[29] Tawada, at one point at least, also deploys the term when depicting the vision of a "beautiful aged queen"[30] who explains to Knut that he has "an infinitely long line of ancestors."[31] Since, in the Western hegemon particularly, the grandmother is often depicted as sessile and passive, the use of this term appears to be inappropriate in terms of the mobile bear's active persona.

The second section of the novel concerns Tosca who trained as a classical ballerina. Initially, her youthful-looking, circus-veteran trainer, Barbara (Ursula, as noted above, in the German and Uruzura in the Japanese language novels respectively), relates her tale. By the section's close, with Barbara unwell and "reluctant to leave her narrow bed" after "almost fifty years [. . .] in the circus world,"[32] narrator roles are reversed and Tosca becomes the storyteller. Punctuating her fantasy tale with historical elements, Tawada borrows from the narrative of the real-life Knut's real-life mother, Tosca, who performed with the Staatszirkus, State Circus, of the German Democratic Republic (GDR).

A feature of the circus performance of Tosca and Barbara was the exchange of a sugar cube from the mouth of one to the other. This was billed as "The Kiss of Death." While Magras suggests a sexual frisson,[33] I argue that the intimacy displayed in this and other activities in which the bear and her trainer engage is much more than physical. In fact, the relationship depicts a complete collapse of the border between animal and human life. Importantly, this intimacy infers exile. After Knut's birth, Tosca rejects stereotypical maternity to instead "narrat[e] the [magnificent] tale of my friend Barbara."[34] With Barbara's death in March 2010, Tosca longs for her companion. This longing is not, however, for their shared circus life. Rather she wishes to "go on conversing with [Barbara] at the North Pole of our dreams."[35] Thus, the pair come together in dreams, perhaps the exemplar fantasy realm and also the realm that sustains the exile. Accordingly, when providing her "bear's-eye-view" of "The Kiss of Death," Tosca does not recall the canvas walls of the circus tent and certainly not the space in which the two rehearsed. Rather, she remembers how the color of "the sugar gleaming in the cave of [Barbara's] mouth" reminded her of "snow" and filled her with "longing for the far-off North Pole."[36] McNeill explains that Tosca and Barbara have three shared dreams in which the two communicate with perfect ease.[37] Since McNeill further points out that Tawada never designates the "common" language shared by the pair,[38] we can conclude that linguistic forms are ultimately irrelevant.

The third section of the narrative focuses on Knut who, abandoned by Tosca at birth, is raised by an environmental campaigner named Matthias. As a fictional representation of the real-life Thomas Dörflein, Matthias devotes himself to the newborn bear. Since, with the exception of event attendance at a plush city venue, the fictional Knut—like his real-life counterpart—was born and spent the entirety of his life at the Berlin Zoo, his narrative might appear to have limited connection to exile. Knut, however, is involved in a project related to climate-change, one of the greatest contemporary causes of refugee movement. Although Tawada critiques the bear's appropriation for this purpose, exile and movement through space thus comprise the very underpinnings of Knut's tale. Magras, furthermore, points out that, with the Zoo giftshop exploiting "every Knut-related merchandising opportunity," the section is a "trenchant" critique of capitalism.[39] Knott, moreover, notes that even the first writing bear's flight to freedom was contingent upon her capacity to achieve literary marketplace success.[40] Capital, too, has played an aggressive role in the spread of globalization, evoking the exiled worker upon whom corporations generate their billions. Capital's obsessive extraction of fossil fuel has also contributed majorly to climate change. It is no surprise therefore that, when balancing atop an ice floe, the bear of the first section feels the "ice melt away from second to second beneath my feet."[41]

Toward the close of the novel, Knut becomes friendly with a spectral-like presence named Michael who, following Matthias's sudden death (real-life carer, Dörflein, died unexpectedly in 2008), appears in mysterious fashion. While Knott correctly points out that hallucinations of this nature are symptomatic of the anti-NMDA receptor encephalitis that caused the real-life Knut's death,[42] the appearance of Michael, and also of "nightly visits from [the bear's] writing grandmother,"[43] add a further magical realist dimension to the tale. With a voice that "only a bee can achieve with her honey,"[44] and believing as a child that "it was normal not to get any dinner if I didn't do well in my song and dance training,"[45] this figure is clearly a representation of singer Michael Jackson (1958–2009). In Tawada's novel, Michael visits Knut both before and after the former's death, a report of which Knut reads in a newspaper. Michael never returns once Knut informs him that the papers are saying "horrible things about you too."[46] The novel concludes as Knut drifts away from life and wonders if Michael will visit again. The bear also longs for the North Pole, "as sweet and nourishing as [mother's] milk,"[47] while watching "little white leaves" of snow fly past.[48] This snow is a "spaceship" that "lifted me up and flew off as fast as it could in the direction of the skull—the cranium of the earth," perhaps also a metaphor for the longed-for North Pole. Noting that the lunar references of the novel's opening "connect the narrator to [the story] of Callisto in Ovid's Metamorphoses, a nymph-turned-bear in mythology as well as Jupiter's second-largest moon," McNeill points out that the reference to the snow as a "spaceship" links the novel's first paragraph to its last.[49] In an extraordinary real-life example of the collapse of species distinction, the encephalitis that took Knut's life was "an autoimmune disease thought to exist only in humans."[50] After a Berlin neurologist read Knut's autopsy report and found "striking symptomatic parallels" with human patients, tests on tissue samples from Knut's brain revealed the precise cause of the bear's death.[51]

McNeill argues that each generation of bears "reflect[s] on how bodies are written and read in their respective societies."[52] This occurs as "their own bodies circulate through historically contingent processes of exile and migration." While there are powerful dream and fantasy elements, the qualifier "historically contingent" confirms that Tawada's novel also provides real-life social commentary. It is from this perspective that there is strong condemnation of the gendered nature of social relations for both bear and human women.

## NOVELIST BECOMING ANIMAL

Tawada Yōko was born in Japan. As Yonaha Keiko explains,[53] after graduating in Russian literature from Waseda University, Tawada began living in Germany. The writer is therefore equally skilled at producing texts in German and Japanese and has been the recipient of prestigious literary/cultural awards in each place. While there could therefore be no more fitting novelist to produce a text that probes notions of exile and the mobility associated with that process, animals and their lives are also key to several Tawada texts.

One of Tawada's earliest prose works in Japanese, titled "The Bridegroom Was a Dog" (1993, Inumukoiri), featured a teacher whose questionable pedagogy included encouraging students to reuse tissues and to enjoy the feel of snot, "so soft, warm and wet."[54] In the grand tradition of *iruikon-intan* tales that depict marriage between a human and another form, this teacher also told of a princess promised in marriage to a dog. There is even a hint that a man who moves into her home may have become part-dog after being attacked by strays. It seems only logical that this interest in relations between species eventually became the ability to provide a totally convincing representation of a literate polar bear who is indistinguishable from the writer's human protagonists. Smith notes that, in addition to being a novelist, Tawada is also a "perhaps less known but equally important [. . .] cutting-edge poet."[55] While there is indeed a strong strand of lyricism throughout the novel, this is counter-balanced by a directness that both compels and confounds.

The trajectories of the lives of the three generations of polar bears featured in *Memoirs of a Polar Bear* can sometimes appear to overlap with the life of Tawada herself. For example, the bear of the novel's first section is a writer. Hoffman notes that this creature "shares the experiences of forced assimilation with many of Tawada's human protagonists."[56] Yet some of these are surely shared also with the author. Although pressured by her editor to write in her "own" (whatever that might mean) Russian language rather than German, with a view to a translation being produced for local markets, the bear refuses to have her identity fixed "as the 'foreigner' and reclaims her right for self-representation on her own terms."[57] The pressure to which this bear is subject is one "with which Yoko Tawada as a Japanese writer who writes and publishes her work in German is only too familiar, as she has often discussed in interviews and essays."[58] Yet there is no proprietary claim to sole ownership of her work in Tawada's resistance to the standardization of the publishing industry. McNeill, in fact, argues that Tawada regards even the "genre of autobiography" as one "in which one life writes another's life and one's story is never solely one's own."[59] Slutsky argues that this effect is particularly apparent in the second section of the Japanese version of the book where there is an interchangeability of "pronouns [. . .], identities and species."[60] Concluding that Tawada's novel "refuse[s] to enter 'the autobiographical pact,'" she speculates how, "by way of fragmentation and incongruity," the novel suggests "an alternate model" that disrupts understandings of autobiography as "a genre marked by a linear continuity of a person's life and static identity through time."[61] Given the "function and nature of memory," it furthermore follows that neither can autobiography "escape becoming a fiction."[62]

Further discussing the shared nature of textual production, McNeill interprets the polar bear's "reading aloud and writing down a literary text" as a way to "incorporat[e] another's story into one's own."[63] She proposes that reading does not merely transform the reader but also transforms the text. Ultimately, "life is transformed when life is written."[64] This, McNeill concludes,[65] is the "poetics of metamorphosis" practiced by both the writing bear of the novel's first section and by Tawada as author. Such metamorphosis arguably results from ongoing literary exchange often in a fantasy space with other real-life and fictional exilic wanderers.

Hegemonic interpretations seek to define language as an exclusive collection of words associated with a specific place. One of the principal elements of the *Nihonjinron*, theories of Japanese-ness, discourse that swept Japan in the postwar era, for example, was the claim that Japanese was a language that was "spoken natively only by [the Japanese] themselves."[66] In other words, this language was only truly accessible to those located from birth in Japan. Even returnees—Japanese who live temporarily outside the country—could be treated as suspect. Far from a marker of stasis, however, Tawada regards language as designating movement from place to place. Hoffman, too, explains how *Memoirs of a Polar Bear* abandons the usual assumptions attached to language to envision this entity "as a practice of embodiment that allows for mobility of the subject."[67] This decoupling of language from the sessility imposed by vested interests does not come without cost. As a novice writer, the bear declares that her desire to continue writing her autobiography is "three times the size of my fear of having my existence destroyed."[68] She later observes that not only was writing "a more dangerous acrobatic stunt than dancing atop a rolling ball," but that this activity "required as much strength as hunting."[69]

While costly, investment in linguistic mobility yields entry into otherwise inaccessible worlds. The bear explains that, with each sentence written, she was "transported to a place I hadn't known existed."[70] The prominence of fantasy and dream in Tawada's novel suggests that this unknown place might be metaphoric. Yet the specific locations referenced—Soviet Russia, East Germany, West Germany, Canada—equally suggest that it is literal. In fact, the association of writing to the spin of the ball on which the bear balances,[71] is linked in the English translation to the earth and the sun.[72] This suggestion that writing is the key to "knowing" the universe in all its magnificent wonder furthermore links to the cosmic elements of the novel's opening and closing passages discussed above.

## THE EXILIC STATE OF ANIMALS AND HUMANS INTERTWINED

With exile being a recurring theme in *Memoirs of a Polar Bear*, McNeill distinguishes between literary and political exile.[73] I would argue, however, that in this work the two become one. In Hoffman's words, furthermore, the protagonists of Tawada's tale "illegally" cross borders that are both "geographical and ideological."[74] The reference to illegality confirms how, whether or not violating the law of a particular land, there is an imperative to movement into a state of exile that cannot be suppressed. Exile, moreover, may be repeated. Seized with the desire to relocate to Canada when castigated in West Berlin for eating "an entire armful of [Canadian] salmon,"[75] the unnamed first protagonist dreams of "a frozen city in which the walls of all the buildings were made with transparent ice."[76] She thereupon reflects that with one "successful experience with exile under my belt, surely it would be possible for me to go into exile a second time."[77]

Tawada, furthermore, provides insights into the exiled subject herself and into the processes that she must undergo. Lamenting her inability, later overcome, to write, Tosca observes that her mother "was highly intelligent and infinitely inquisitive." That was why, Tosca continues, "she went into exile and wrote an autobiography."[78] This suggests that exile is truth-seeking. Furthermore, once "infinitely inquisitive" individuals, individuals who become bored with the way things are in the Japanese version, unearth information concealed by those in authority, the former become outcastes. If exile is often forced—Tosca, for example, was captured in Canada and removed to the GDR—it can also be voluntary, with an individual or group consciously deciding to detach. Although voluntary detachment can occur without foresight of the outcome, it can also be chosen in full knowledge of consequent suffering. Sometimes, exile results from third-party intervention. Arriving from the Soviet Union at Berlin-Schönefeld, the GDR airport, the bear is "deposited" in a "dainty little train headed for West Berlin." Suddenly aware that: "I am going into exile," she realizes that someone has saved her from dangers "I hadn't known existed."[79]

One element of Tawada's genius is her ability to associate exile with notions not generally linked with travel through space to unfamiliar territory. In *Memoirs of a Polar Bear,* even the issue of motherhood can be read through this lens. The observation by Magras that "'family' is not necessarily the clan you're born into but the people who love you" hints at the contestation of motherhood in Tawada's text.[80] Hoffman, citing Donna J. Haraway, argues that Tawada replaces the "hegemonic logic of heterosexual procreation" with notions of "making kin."[81] The relationship between Tosca and Barbara can particularly be seen in this light. For example, "Unlike some mothers of Homo Sapiens" who "treat their sons like capital,"[82] Tosca rejected Knut in favor of telling Barbara's story. Tosca's choice contests images of maternity that, like a Virgin Mother statue, are fixed in one place. Such images obscure that fact that, in addition to having the right to choose separation, many real-world mothers and children can only survive when apart.

Exile or even mere mobility in the novel can come with an ever-present threat. As Smith points out, when the circus travels to the United States, authorities ban the "Kiss of Death" performed by Tosca and Barbara.[83] Although "[o]stensibly due to health concerns," the bear later learns that the ban resulted from pressure applied by "conservative Christians" fearful of sexual fantasies involving bears.[84] Dismissing this "ridiculous exaggeration," Tosca concludes that, "for Homo Sapiens, pornography had its seat in the heads of adults."[85] While brilliantly displaying Tawada's incisively targeted, often laugh-out-loud, dead-pan humor, these words in no way detract from the chilling depiction by officialdom of the exile as depraved or perverted. Such a classification justifies inhumane treatment and contempt. In fact, those administering this inhumanity paradoxically feel all the more virtuously human for their cruelly punishing ways.

Hoffman suggests that, like other Tawada works, *Memoirs of a Polar Bear* deploys "the perspective of 'the outsider' to break the spell of habit."[86] She notes, however, that this is no "purely metaphorical reading" of "just another cultural outsider or stranger."[87] Rather, "the intimate and erotic entanglement between bear and human" creates the "provenance for new narratives that open different ways of communication and deep forms of understanding between species."[88] Slaymaker, too, notes that "particularly in the wake of the triple disasters of Northern Japan," Tawada has explored borders relating to "interspecies," in addition to those that involve "youth and age, male and female and [. . .] trauma, disaster, and health."[89] While interspecies exchange is critical to Tawada's narrative, she surely also advocates for new forms of exchange between humans.

There is an imperative to these new exchange forms given that, for many today, exile and movement are the default rather than minority positions and that those who remain in one place indefinitely are the exception and no longer—if they ever indeed were—the rule. As a "mobile, liminal space [. . .], a 'floating island'[90] from which the inhabitants never depart,"[91] the circus, too, evokes exile. For Smith, circus "nomadism" is "a metaphor for political flexibility" by means of which members can escape the "intense ideological scrutiny" of certain forms of government.[92] In the few years since the novel's publication, this issue has become even more pressing for the growing numbers of refugee/exiles across the world. Circus performers arguably provide a model for those who are dispossessed. Discriminated against from without and even within their own community, they possess a core strength that confronts head-on those who would erase them. And although Barbara eventually withdraws exhausted, she responds to the exploitation she experiences in the circus with her own "economic theory" based upon the principle that "all losses immediately turn into gains when you touch a horse."[93]

Since exiles are often bullied and harassed, we might expect the scene in the opening section of the novel in which, with her different appearance, the first polar bear protagonist is called names such as "snout-face" and "snow baby" at school.[94] Similarly, we perhaps understand how systematic exclusion saw Tosca unable to "land a role in a single production," even though she had "graduated from ballet school with top honours."[95] More disconcerting, however, is the fact that exiles themselves demean other exiles. The treatment of Knut by several Berlin Zoo animals suggests that this is particularly the case among those incarcerated and deprived of their freedom. When Knut tells of the pleasure of swimming, the arrogant sun bear disdainfully responds: "Swimming is a senseless activity. I have no time for silly little games."[96] The Canadian wolves, who had "frightened me right from the start,"[97] badger Knut for not looking like his human carer, Matthias. "Just look at my family," the head wolf declares. "All its members resemble each other like peas in a pod."[98] The brutal obsession with standardization on the part of those in power is clearly expressed through the wolf. For Magras, this section provides the "book's most devastating commentary."[99]

## BRINGING TOGETHER THE SPECIES IN EXILE

Although exile is a state to which both animals and humans are subject, we might ask whether, by depicting polar bears with human traits in *Memoirs of a Polar Bear*, Tawada is anthropomorphizing her subjects. Such an approach has been fiercely critiqued by theorists who include Sarah Guyer. To Guyer, anthropomorphism is a "rejection of pluralism, and the failure to appreciate nonhuman difference." She further argues that giving animals human characteristics is the "sticky residue of an exclusionary humanism" that is "often violent in its foreclosures, [. . .] papering over gaps in knowledge and knowability with unconscious assumptions and quaint attributions"[100]

Such attribution has been practiced from ancient times with the behavior of the alternately sage, mischievous, and deceptive animals found in Aesop's fables, for example, offering both salutary and exhortatory narratives for humans. By the time Aristotle established the groundwork for Western thinking three hundred years later, however, "the distinguishing trait" of the human, to borrow McNeill's words, was "rationality" or "logos—the faculty of discursive, as opposed to intuitive, language as well as reason."[101] It was this trait that unleashed the anthropomorphizing tendencies that deluded humans into believing that they possessed the "power to employ animals and plants as they wish."[102] Rene Descartes, for example, specifically found the animal "capacity for sensation" inferior to that of the human, thus depriving the former of either "critical or linguistic capability."[103] McNeill discusses how "only relatively recently" has critical attention been directed to this approach, with "contemporary theorists like Giorgio Agamben, Gilles Deleuze, and Donna J. Haraway" challenging any "clear distinction between 'human' and 'animal.'"[104]

Tawada dispenses with the discourses of these thinkers, discourses that can often be accessible only to specialists. Rather, she mounts a blazing critique of how those in power force those without power to submit to becoming a spectacle. Barbara, the circus trainer, declares for example:

> I love all mammals [animals], but I hated the popular circus numbers that put various beasts of prey onstage together. More specifically, I abhor the human stupidity and vanity that takes pride in forcing tigers, lions and leopards to sit nicely side by side. It reminds me of the government choreography that displays brightly garbed minorities in a parade, minorities granted a crumb of political autonomy in exchange for providing an optical simulation of cultural diversity in their country of residence.[105]

Recalling comments by Hoffman that the violence committed toward animals in Tawada's text "exceeds the treatment of actual animals and includes marginalized groups traditionally associated with animals (such as women and indigenous groups),"[106] the passage above evokes attempts to deny indigenous resilience and to replace this with an artifice that benefits central power structures. While focusing on circumpolar people,[107] and tying the practices of these groups—including Ainu people with their bear totem—to the "Kiss of Death" performance and also to shamanistic elements in the text,[108] Knott nonetheless notes how "Tawada provocatively positions the polar bears as ethnic minorities operating in a predominately human western world."[109] Barbara's words cited above thus recall the specularization of indigenous women such as Sarah (Saartje) Baartman (1775–1815) whereby essentialist aspects of women of color were constructed through scopophilic viewing by universalizing whites. Although Baartman may have participated in the process of public display that accompanied her entry into European society, the tragedy of her relocation to Paris dissipated any liberty she enjoyed. In Paris, fascination with her nonwhite physique saw her body retained for scientific purposes after her death. It is surely the same "human stupidity and vanity" abhorred by the narrator, and that coerced "tigers, lions and leopards" into "sitting nicely side by side," that sealed Baartman's fate.

    The closest animal/human relationship depicted is undoubtedly that of Tosca and Barbara. To Hoffman, the pair are linked by the trauma of "physical and emotional violence integral to the heteropatriarchal society."[110] Tosca was "mutilated" through "training," while Barbara apparently experienced sexual violence "during and after World War II."[111] Magras interestingly assesses the Tosca/Barbara chapter as the book's "weakest," a problem he attributes to the section being "bogged down with stories from Barbara's past."[112] These include one of an "aerial acrobat who taught her the tango."[113] Yet, such details often link the narrating human woman and the woman bear being narrated. It is, furthermore, while touching Tosca's belly that Barbara recalls her first tango lesson. The subsequent intertwining of the two women unfolds as follows:

> Tosca looked at me, faintly puzzled, but when I tugged at her arms, she took a step forward without hesitating. When I pushed against her, she took a step back. "Come to the cross, side step, forward step." It was an aerial acrobat who had taught me the tango. Her mother was from Cuba. As we danced, I fell down and our lips met.[114]

This tango reference is thus in no way superfluous. In addition to narrating the intimacy that develops between Tosca and Barbara, the passage also features a Cuban background tango teacher, possibly herself an exile in Europe. Oscar Conde observes that, although its reach extended beyond the marginalized, the tango was "a genuine creation of the popular classes, a product of hybridization and of the waves of immigrants who arrived in the port of Buenos Aries" between the late nineteenth and early twentieth centuries.[115] "Tango, Politics and the Musical of Exile," the title of Antonio Gomez's analysis of the tango's journey from the Rio de la Plata to Paris,[116] confirms that the dance belonged to those who left their homelands behind.

    Ultimately, Tawada's text rejects an Aristotelian-informed enlightenment interpretation of animal/human relationships that anthropomorphizes animal bodies while, recalling Guyer, "papering over gaps in knowledge and knowability with unconscious assumptions and quaint attribution." In fact, far from being what Steve Baker refers to, in a discussion of the limitations to the Deleuze-Guattari becoming-animal paradigm, as a mere "device of writing," Tawada's polar bears are "living beings" whose conditions of life are "of direct concern" to her as a writer.[117] As Smith notes: "In this mode, [Tawada's] animals are always already on par with humans, treated narratively as having characteristics such as a complex, humanlike consciousness."[118] This is evident in Tosca's wry observation that, not only were the "founders of the Roman Empire [. . .] suckled by a she-wolf," but "[a]ll heroes capable of earth-shattering deeds were adopted and nursed by animals."[119]

One particularly radical act occurs early in the book when the first polar bear protagonist declaratively utters the words, "I think." This statement defies animal and human distinctions by challenging the maxim often considered the very foundation of modern thought—"I think therefore I am" (Cogito ergo sum). Although Hoffman interprets the bear's statement as "alluding to the long history in literature and philosophy that excludes nonhuman animals from the production of language and meaning,"[120] these words, in fact, smash that history to bring down the entire enlightenment edifice. MacNeill perceptively notes that, by assuming a "shared capacity for thinking" and "shared knowledge of Western philosophy," there is an expectation that human readers will "finish [the bear's] statement."[121] Such an expectation "calls the reader into the polar bear's diegetic world and the polar bear into the reader's world."[122] This is but one example of how, rather than merely collapsing boundaries, Tawada removes these completely to introduce previously unimagined tropes and strategic literary creations. Commenting on eroticism in the images of cats by Carolee Schneemann (1939–2019), Baker points out that these animals "have their own perspective" and "their own vision of the world."[123] We can similarly read *Memoirs of a Polar Bear* as offering a fictional polar bear "perspective" and "vision of the world."

Ultimately, the collapse of species division evokes exile. In an encounter with Tosca's consciousness during a dream, Barbara finds herself in a place where "the grammars of many languages lost their colour." Instead, "they melted and combined, then froze solid again, they drifted in the ocean and joined the drifting floes of ice." It is at this point that Barbara "sat on the same iceberg as Tosca and understood every word she said to me."[124] This is no tidy drawing-room scene. Instead, the pair have detached from everything familiar to return to a state of nature in which they are terrifyingly set adrift while also liberated from the assumptions that constrain them. For exile offers opportunities that can never be accessed when enlightenment boundaries remain intact. Importantly, the relationship between Barbara and Tosca is no mere one-off. As the pair drift along together, a second iceberg floats by "with an Inuk and a snow hare sitting on it, immersed in conversation."[125] The possibilities suggested by Tosca's and Barbara's coming together are available to others too.

## WRITING ONESELF INTO EXILE

Like exile, writing is marked with danger. Lacking choice, however, the subject must often choose both. While textual production is usually associated with fixed points, writing brings the bear protagonist of the first section a consciousness of movement which, by evoking distant locations, also evokes exilic discourse. Having fallen asleep, the bear feels upon awakening that the "second half of life is beginning." Her goal at the "midpoint" of the "long-distance race" of her life is its "starting line," for "the place where the pain began is where it will end."[126]

In addition to problematizing space, Tawada's text disrupts hegemonic understandings of time. Time here is fluid—the opening passages begin with the writerly bear's earliest memories recalled while domiciled in a hotel room attending a conference in Kiev. These childhood recollections are no hagiography of early experiences. Rather, our bear counters claims that "spring makes [some] young again" by observing that a return to childhood is "not without indignities."[127] In fact, the childish past is "bitter honey" that stings the tongue.[128] The opening paragraph, for example, tells how not long after birth the bear was tortured and forced to stand on her hindlegs when an object was attached to her paws, a process that Slutsky interestingly reads through Judith Butler's theory of performativity. Hoffman notes that, in addition to disrupting "the reader's understanding of autobiographic writing as following a linear logic," the bear "writes her way backward, toward both the beginning and the ending of suffering."[129]

Certain tropes interrogate time and space simultaneously. It is writing that calls from the past the presence of Ivan, the first bear's original keeper. "Dead within me for so many years," Ivan returns to life "because I was writing about him."[130] Slaymaker, too, reminds us that "the past returns" when this bear "engage[s] in the act of writing."[131] Early memories recall Ivan's singing becoming "an abyss of endless lament." This singing evokes space and "perhaps my first longing for far-off lands." Our bear feels as if "distant places I'd never seen were drawing me to them, and I found myself torn between there and here."[132]

If chronological linearity is amorphous, so is generational distinction between Tawada's polar bears. We can therefore argue that being "torn between there and here"—a fitting exile mantra—is experienced by Tosca and Knut as much as the bear who precedes them. Notwithstanding the third bear's tragic encephalitic decline, the "beautiful, aged queen" who visits Knut in dreams declares, "I'm not only your grandmother, I'm also your great-grandmother and your great-great-grandmother. I am the superimposition of numerous ancestors."[133] Thus, a statement made with respect to one bear can often be applied to all. At the very least, individual bears have "doubles," with Slutsky pointing out that there was "another Tosca previous to the one ghost-writing for Ursula [Barbara]."[134]

## INTERTEXTUALITY, EXILE, AND SPACE

It is impossible to discuss *Memoirs of a Polar Bear* without reference to intertextuality. As Hoffman notes:

> [T]he novel alludes not only to a plethora of texts, legends, and shamanistic tales, from Franz Kafka's "A Report to an Academy" to the prevalence of bears in the mythology of many indigenous ethnic groups and religions, but also draws on the popular history in the German Democratic Republic and post-reunification Germany.[135]

Hoffman goes on to observe that, in addition to human and nonhuman animals in Tawada's text coming together to "share and shape historical spaces [and] times," they also share "narratives in conjunction with each other." The critic discusses how, when frequenting a bookshop, the first bear protagonist reads and scathingly critiques the ideas of the ape known as Red Peter featured in the 1917 Franz Kafka tale referred to above. In "a re-imaging and extension" that is "often characteristic of Tawada's writing,"[136] Red Peter's account of acquiring human characteristics in Kafka's narrative makes the bear narrator feel "sick to my stomach." Recalling being forced to stand upright as a child, she rejects any notion that walking on two legs is "progress."[137] Although McNeill argues that the bear misreads the report by Red Peter who merely "emulates humans in order to survive," she concludes that the focus on Kafka's text profiles the fact that the ape is effectively "a sterile interzone between human and animal."[138] This is in contrast to Tawada's polar bears "who fluidly cross and therefore question the traditional human-animal divide."[139]

Significant in terms of the relationship between exile and intertextuality is the discussion of *Atta Troll*, the Heinrich Heine (1797–1856) epic poem. Proclaimed by the German literature website to be "one of Heine's most challenging texts,"[140] *Atta Troll* narrates the travails of an escaped dancing bear pursued through the Spanish Pyrenees. A "Forest King" who once "ruled on mountain heights," the eponymous bear must now dance "in every marketplace/ For the people's pence."[141] As Atta Troll flees his oppressors, he is hunted in a manner that anticipates the fate of contemporary refugees forced into constant mobility.

In a humorous reference to the ideological appropriation of art, sometime narrator, Barbara, explains that "an East German playwright had crowbarred Heinrich Heine's epic poem [. . .] into a children's play."[142] In other words, Tawada suggests that, rather than endowing a text with the richness of previous reading experience, some intertextuality is forcibly controlled by powerful interests. Furthermore, although second-generation bear, Tosca, was offered the part of "Atta Troll's wife, the black bear Mumma," she declined on several grounds. Firstly, she did not agree that it "was less noble-minded" of the woman bear to remain captive while her partner fled. Perhaps more troubling, however, was the demand by the text that Mumma "bit[e] off and eat one of her youngest son's ears out of love." This, Tosca concluded, "was something that could never happen in nature." Furthermore, the narrator uses a "mocking tone" (*hihan saseru*) when speaking of the "success Mumma enjoyed in the capitalist city Paris and the white bear she took as a lover."[143]

The intertextual *Atta Troll* reference creates multiple narrative opportunities that include both profiling how the citation of a preexisting text can be compromised and permitting insights into Tosca's principled approach to the representation of her group. In Tawada's tale, the bear refuses to play a part that debases other bears. The perversely violent depiction of a mother who eats part of her child recalls the willingness with which white readers loved to be shocked by sensationalized claims of ritualized forms of violence among nonwhite communities. For all her concerns regarding hegemonic maternity, Tawada cannot allow these claims to pass unchallenged. Tosca also defends a woman's right to be cast as other than her male partner's shadow. While Atta Troll fled to freedom, Tosca refuses to condemn Mumma for not doing likewise.

There is, furthermore, a political dimension to the denunciation of the bear wife. One put-down relates to Black Mumma's "success" in the "capitalist city" Paris and the fact that she took a lover there of a different color. It is difficult to read this passage and not think, for example, of African Americans who found some respite in Paris from treatment meted out in their land of birth. Josephine Baker (1906–1975), for example, left the United States to become a dancing and singing sensation before her involvement with French men such as Joseph Bouillon (1908–1984). James Baldwin (1924–1987), too, departed his homeland to seek solace in Paris and later Provence and in his relationship with Swiss-born Lucien Happersberger (1932–2010).

## BEYOND EXILE

For polar bears, national identity has always been a foreign concept. It's common for them to get pregnant in Greenland, give birth in Canada, then raise the children in the Soviet Union. They possess no nationality, no passport. They never go into exile and cross national borders without a visa.[144]

The passage above, cited also by Knott when commenting on the "incongruity" of "polar bear nationality," is one of the most momentous in the fantastical space of *Memoirs of a Polar Bear*.[145] These words, in fact, provide oblique insights into the restraints that operate on the exile. As the reference to paraphernalia such as passports and visas demonstrates, authority expresses itself, often with justifications of the "security" of the citizenry, in a host of gate-keeping strategies designed to repel those regarded as "other" or "outside." These strategies come together to form an apparatus of repression that can appear impregnable. This is particularly the case for those whom Knott, citing feminist citizenship scholar, Ruth Lister, notes "carry their passport on their faces."[146] Notwithstanding that the protagonist bears appear more constrained with each generational iteration, *Memoirs of a Polar Bear* does offer hope. In addition to underground organizations seeking to remove the vulnerable from harm, potential is offered for relationships to exist beyond the reach of the hegemon. A bear and a woman who works in a circus or an Inuk and a snow hare sharing an ice floe and conversing together are testimony to this possibility. Declaring that each "belongs where he or she chooses, not in a Mondrian grid of pre-defined compartments," Magras acknowledges that heterodoxy is not without "its perils." More important, however, are "its benefits."[147] It is these benefits that Tawada advocates in her work. The real Knut passed away in 2011. Nevertheless, given that the fictional Knut was the last in a "long line of ancestors," he was undoubtedly as "highly intelligent" and "infinitely inquisitive" as the writing woman who bore his mother. The bear's spirit was therefore surely energized upon reaching "the cranium of our earth" with a determination to contest the Mondrian grids that constrain us all in conjunction with identity markers such as species, race, gender, and class. We can further hope that this inspiration was passed on even after his death to those of his own species and, indeed, to all sentient beings.

## NOTES

1. Tomoko Takeuchi Slutsky, "Staging of Self, Performance of Life." In *Tawada Yōko: On Writing and Rewriting*, ed. Douglas Slaymaker (Lanham and London: Lexington Books Kindle edition, 2020), 308–323, 308.

2. Suzuko Mousel Knott, "Transmigration and Cultural Memory in Yoko Tawada's *Etüden im Schnee*." In *Tawada Yōko: On Writing and Rewriting*, ed. Douglas Slaymaker (Lanham and London: Lexington Books Kindle edition, 2020), 284–306, 288).

3. Jordan A.Y. Smith, "Narration Between Species: Yōko Tawada's *Memoirs of a Polar Bear*, Translated by Susan Bernofsky." *Reading in Translation*, 21 February, 2017. https://readingintranslation.com/2017/02/21/narration-between-species-yoko-tawadas-memoirs-of-a-polar-bear-translated-by-susan-bernofsky/ (Accessed July 1, 2021).

4. Douglas Slaymaker, "The Hands of Bears, the Hands of Men." In *Tawada Yōko: On Writing and Rewriting*, ed. Douglas Slaymaker (Lanham and London: Lexington Books Kindle edition, 2020), 323–331, 325.

5. Tawada Yōko, *Memoirs of a Polar Bear*, trans. from German by Susan Bernofsky (London: Portobello Books, 2017), 32. Tawada Yōko, *Yuki no renshūsei* (Tokyo: Shinchōsha, 2011), 36. Cited in Slaymaker, "The Hands of Bears, the Hands of Men," 325.

6. Tawada, *Memoirs of a Polar Bear*, 32–33. Tawada, *Yuki no renshūsei*, 36.

7. Slaymaker, "The Hands of Bears, the Hands of Men," 325.

8. Tawada, *Memoirs of a Polar Bear*, 33; *Yuki no renshūsei*, 36.

9. Gayatri Chakavorty Spivak, "Translation as Culture," *Parallax* 6, no. 1, 13–24, 13,

10. Slaymaker, "The Hands of Bears, the Hands of Men," 328.

11. Ibid., 328.

12. Ibid., 326.

13. Ibid., 327.

14. Ibid., 326.

15. Ibid., 325–326.

16. Smith, "Narration Between Species."

17. Ibid.

18. As noted, the text was originally written in German, re-written (rather than translated) into Japanese and then translated from German into English. There is, therefore, a degree of slippage between the English and Japanese versions, both of which are, where possible, cited here. For example, "chiisa na densha" becomes "dainty train," although there is little in the Japanese to give the specific impression conveyed by the English word "dainty" (Tawada 2017, 38; 2011, 41). Similarly, on the same pages, the sentence: "Watashi wa nanika no kiken kara nogarerareta no kamo shirenai" becomes the partial English sentence: "to save me from a danger I hadn't known existed." A more literal translation might have been: "I had perhaps been diverted from some sort of danger." Any difference, however, is generally minor and therefore not noted. Appreciable differences are marked by square brackets within a quote.

19. Sabine Peschel, "100 German Must-Reads: Yoko Tawada: 'Memoirs of a Polar Bear.'" *Deutsche Welle* (dw.com), October, 2018. https://www.dw.com/en/yoko-tawada-memoirs-of-a-polar-bear/a-45620835 (Accessed July 1, 2021); Smith, "Narration Between Species."

20. Peschel, "100 German Must-Reads."

21. Eve Hoffman, "Queering the Interspecies Encounter: Yoko Tawada's *Memoirs of a Polar Bear*." In *What is Zoopoetics?: Texts, Bodies and Entanglement*, eds. Kári Driscoll and Eva Hoffman (E-book: Cham: Palgrave Macmillan, 2018), 149–165, 150.

22. Knott, "Transmigration and Cultural Memory," 284.
23. Slaymaker, "The Hands of Bears, the Hands of Men," 330.
24. Knott, "Transmigration and Cultural Memory," 292.
25. Tawada, *Memoirs of a Polar Bear*, 17; *Yuki no renshūsei*, 21.
26. Tawada, *Memoirs of a Polar Bear*, 18; *Yuki no renshūsei*, 22–23.
27. Knott, "Transmigration and Cultural Memory," 295.
28. Tawada, *Memoirs of a Polar Bear*, 64; *Yuki no renshūsei*, 67.
29. Elizabeth McNeill, "Writing and Reading (with) Polar Bears in Yoko Tawada's *Etüden im Schnee* (2014)," *The German Quarterly* 92, no. 1 (Winter), 51–67, 52.
30. Tawada, *Memoirs of a Polar Bear*, 213; *Yuki no renshūsei*, 215.
31. Tawada, *Memoirs of a Polar Bear*, 214; *Yuki no renshūsei*, 215.
32. Tawada, *Memoirs of a Polar Bear*, 163; *Yuki no renshūsei*, 163.
33. Michael Magras, "*Memoirs of a Polar Bear* by Yoko Tawada," *Kenyon Review*, June, 2017. https://kenyonreview.org/reviews/memoirs-of-a-polar-bear-by-yoko-tawada-738439/ (Accessed July 1, 2021).
34. Tawada, *Memoirs of a Polar Bear*, 164; *Yuki no renshūsei*, 163.
35. Tawada, *Memoirs of a Polar Bear*, 165; *Yuki no renshūsei*, 164.
36. Tawada, *Memoirs of a Polar Bear*, 165; *Yuki no renshūsei*, 164.
37. McNeill, "Writing and Reading (with) Polar Bears," 57–58.
38. Ibid., 58.
39. Magras, "*Memoirs of a Polar Bear*."
40. Knott, "Transmigration and Cultural Memory," 294.
41. Tawada, *Memoirs of a Polar Bear*, 73; *Yuki no renshūsei*, 75.
42. Knott, "Transmigration and Cultural Memory," 300.
43. Ibid.
44. Tawada, *Memoirs of a Polar Bear*, 239; *Yuki no renshūsei*, 241.
45. Tawada, *Memoirs of a Polar Bear*, 243; *Yuki no renshūsei*, 245.
46. Tawada, *Memoirs of a Polar Bear*, 250; *Yuki no renshūsei*, 252.
47. Tawada, *Memoirs of a Polar Bear*, 251; *Yuki no renshūsei*, 253.
48. Tawada, *Memoirs of a Polar Bear*, 252; *Yuki no renshūsei*, 253.
49. McNeill, "Writing and Reading (with) Polar Bears," 61–62.
50. Hanae Armitage, "Death of Beloved Polar Bear, Knut, Solved," *Science*, 27 August, 2015. https://www.sciencemag.org/news/2015/08/death-beloved-polar-bear-knut-solved (Accessed July 1, 2021).
51. Armitage, "Death of Beloved Polar Bear."
52. McNeill, "Writing and Reading (with) Polar Bears," 52.
53. Keiko Yonaha, "Kaisetsu" (Interpretation). In *Inumukoiri* (The Bridegroom Was a Dog) by Tawada Yōko (Tokyo: Kōdansha bunko, 1998), 138–147, 138.
54. Tawada Yōko, "The Bridegroom Was a Dog." In *The Bridegroom Was a Dog*, trans. Margaret Misutani (Tokyo, New York and London: Kodansha International, 2003), 7–62, 11.
55. Smith, "Narration Between Species."
56. Hoffman, "Queering the Interspecies Encounter," 156.
57. Ibid.
58. Ibid., 157.

59. McNeill, "Writing and Reading (with) Polar Bears," 62.
60. Slutsky, "Staging of Self, Performance of Life," 314.
61. Ibid.
62. Ibid., 319.
63. McNeill, "Writing and Reading (with) Polar Bears," 64.
64. Ibid.
65. Ibid.
66. Harumi Befu, *Hegemony of Homogeneity: An Anthropological Analysis of "Nihonjinron,"* (Rosanna, Vic.: Trans Pacific Press, 2001), 61.
67. Hoffman, "Queering the Interspecies Encounter," 158.
68. Tawada, *Memoirs of a Polar Bear*, 16; *Yuki no renshūsei*, 20.
69. Tawada, *Memoirs of a Polar Bear*, 30; *Yuki no renshūsei*, 34.
70. Tawada, *Memoirs of a Polar Bear*, 30; *Yuki no renshūsei*, 34.
71. Tawada, *Memoirs of a Polar Bear*, 30; *Yuki no renshūsei*, 34.
72. Tawada, *Memoirs of a Polar Bear*, 30.
73. McNeill, "Writing and Reading (with) Polar Bears," 52.
74. Hoffman, "Queering the Interspecies Encounter," 149.
75. Tawada, *Memoirs of a Polar Bear*, 44; *Yuki no renshūsei*, 47.
76. Tawada, *Memoirs of a Polar Bear*, 45; *Yuki no renshūsei*, 48.
77. Tawada, *Memoirs of a Polar Bear*, 45; *Yuki no renshūsei*, 48.
78. Tawada, *Memoirs of a Polar Bear*, 125; *Yuki no renshūsei*, 125.
79. Tawada, *Memoirs of a Polar Bear*, 38; *Yuki no renshūsei*, 41.
80. Magras, "*Memoirs of a Polar Bear*."
81. Hoffman, "Queering the Interspecies Encounter," 151.
82. Tawada, *Memoirs of a Polar Bear*, 164; *Yuki no renshūsei*, 163.
83. Smith, "Narration Between Species."
84. Tawada, *Memoirs of a Polar Bear*, 160; *Yuki no renshūsei*, 159.
85. Tawada, *Memoirs of a Polar Bear*, 160; *Yuki no renshūsei*, 159.
86. Hoffman, "Queering the Interspecies Encounter," 149–150.
87. Ibid., 150.
88. Ibid.
89. Slaymaker, "The Hands of Bears, the Hands of Men," 325.
90. Tawada, *Memoirs of a Polar Bear*, 161; *Yuki no renshūsei*, 160.
91. Smith, "Narration Between Species."
92. Ibid.
93. Tawada, *Memoirs of a Polar Bear*, 131; *Yuki no renshūsei*, 131.
94. Tawada, *Memoirs of a Polar Bear*, 7–8; *Yuki no renshūsei*, 12.
95. Tawada, *Memoirs of a Polar Bear*, 84; *Yuki no renshūsei*, 86.
96. Tawada, *Memoirs of a Polar Bear*, 221; *Yuki no renshūsei*, 222.
97. Tawada, *Memoirs of a Polar Bear*, 222; *Yuki no renshūsei*, 224.
98. Tawada, *Memoirs of a Polar Bear*, 222; *Yuki no renshūsei*, 224.
99. Magras, "*Memoirs of a Polar Bear*."
100. Sarah Guyer, "Critical Anthropomorphism After #MeToo: Reading *The Friend*," *Diacritics* 48.1 (2020), 30–50, 31.
101. McNeill, "Writing and Reading (with) Polar Bears," 53.

102. Ibid.
103. Ibid.
104. Ibid.
105. Tawada, *Memoirs of a Polar Bear*, 79; *Yuki no renshūsei*, 81.
106. Hoffman, "Queering the Interspecies Encounter," 155.
107. Knott, "Transmigration and Cultural Memory," 288.
108. Ibid., 296–297.
109. Ibid., 292.
110. Hoffman, "Queering the Interspecies Encounter," 161.
111. See, for example, Tawada, *Memoirs of a Polar Bear*, 140–2; *Yuki no renshūsei*, 141–142.
112. Magras, *Memoirs of a Polar Bear*.
113. Ibid.
114. Tawada, *Memoirs of a Polar Bear*, 106; *Yuki no renshūsei*, 108.
115. Oscar Conde, "*Lunfardo* in Tango: A Way of Speaking that Defines a Way of Being." In *Tango Lessons: Movement, Sound, Image and Text in Contemporary Practice*, ed. Marilyn G. Millar (Durham: Duke University Press, 2014), 33–59, 34.
116. Antonia Gomez, "Tango, Politics and the Musical of Exile." In *Tango Lessons: Movement, Sound, Image and Text in Contemporary Practice*, ed. Marilyn G. Millar (Durham: Duke University Press, 2014), 118–139, 118.
117. Steve Baker, "What Does Becoming Animal Look Like?" In *Representing Animals*, ed. Nigel Rothfels (Bloomington: Indiana University Press, 2002), 67–98, 95.
118. Smith, "Narration Between Species."
119. Tawada, *Memoirs of a Polar Bear*, 94; *Yuki no renshūsei*, 96.
120. Hoffman, "Queering the Interspecies Encounter," 155.
121. McNeill, "Writing and Reading (with) Polar Bears," 54.
122. Ibid.
123. Baker, "What Does Becoming Animal Look Like?", 73.
124. Tawada, *Memoirs of a Polar Bear*, 98; *Yuki no renshūsei*, 100.
125. Tawada, *Memoirs of a Polar Bear*, 98; *Yuki no renshūsei*, 100.
126. Tawada, *Memoirs of a Polar Bear*, 10; *Yuki no renshūsei*, 15.
127. Tawada, *Memoirs of a Polar Bear*, 9; *Yuki no renshūsei*, 13.
128. Tawada, *Memoirs of a Polar Bear*, 9; *Yuki no renshūsei*, 13–14.
129. Hoffman, "Queering the Interspecies Encounter," 161.
130. Tawada, *Memoirs of a Polar Bear*, 12; *Yuki no renshūsei*, 17.
131. Slaymaker, "The Hands of Bears, the Hands of Men," 329.
132. Tawada, *Memoirs of a Polar Bear*, 10; *Yuki no renshūsei*, 15.
133. Tawada, *Memoirs of a Polar Bear*, 213; *Yuki no renshūsei*, 215.
134. Slutsky, "Staging of Self, Performance of Life," 314.
135. Hoffman, "Queering the Interspecies Encounter," 150.
136. Knott, "Transmigration and Cultural Memory," 292.
137. Tawada, *Memoirs of a Polar Bear*, 51; *Yuki no renshūsei*, 53.
138. McNeill, "Writing and Reading (with) Polar Bears," 63.
139. Ibid., 62.

140. Anonymous, "Atta Troll," German Literature Website, comp. Ernest Schonfield, undated. https://sites.google.com/site/germanliterature/19th-century/heine/atta-troll (Accessed July 1, 2021).
141. Heinrich Heine, *Atta Troll*, trans. Herman Scheffauer (E-book: Project Guttenberg, 2010). https://www.gutenberg.org/files/31305/31305-h/31305-h.htm. (Accessed July 1, 2021).
142. Tawada, *Memoirs of a Polar Bear*, 87; *Yuki no renshūsei*, 89.
143. Tawada, *Memoirs of a Polar Bear*, 87–88; *Yuki no renshūsei*, 89–90.
144. Tawada, *Memoirs of a Polar Bear*, 86; *Yuki no renshūsei*, 88–89.
145. Knott, "Transmigration and Cultural Memory," 287.
146. Ibid., 286.
147. Magras, *"Memoirs of a Polar Bear."*

## WORKS CITED

Anonymous. Undated. "Atta Troll." *German Literature Website*, compiled by Ernest Schonfield. https://sites.google.com/site/germanliterature/19th-century/heine/atta-troll (Accessed July 1, 2021).

Armitage, Hanae. 2015. "Death of Beloved Polar Bear, Knut, Solved." *Science*, 27 August. https://www.sciencemag.org/news/2015/08/death-beloved-polar-bear-knut-solved (Accessed July 1, 2021).

Baker, Steve. 2002. "What Does Becoming-Animal Look Like?" In *Representing Animals*, edited by Nigel Rothfels, 67–98. Bloomington: Indiana University Press.

Befu, Harumi. 2001. *Hegemony of Homogeneity: An Anthropological Analysis of "Nihonjinron."* Rosanna, Vic.: Trans Pacific Press.

Gomez, Antonia. 2013. "Tango, Politics and the Musical of Exile." In *Tango Lessons: Movement, Sound, Image and Text in Contemporary Practice*, edited by Millar, Marilyn G., 118–39. Durham: Duke University Press.

Guyer, Sara. 2020. "Critical Anthropomorphism After #MeToo: Reading *The Friend*." *Diacritics* 48, Iss. 1: 30–50.

Heine, Heinrich. 2010. *Atta Troll*, translated by Herman Scheffauer. E-book: Project Guttenberg. https://www.gutenberg.org/files/31305/31305-h/31305-h.htm. (Accessed July 1, 2021).

Hoffman, Eva. 2018. "Queering the Interspecies Encounter: Yoko Tawada's *Memoirs of a Polar Bear*." In *What is Zoopoetics?: Texts, Bodies and Entanglement*, edited by Kári Driscoll and Eva Hoffman, 149–65. E-book: Cham: Palgrave Macmillan.

Knott, Suzuko Mousel. 2020. "Transmigration and Cultural Memory in Yoko Tawada's *Etüden im Schnee*." In *Tawada Yoko: On Writing and Rewriting*, edited by Douglas Slaymaker, 284-306. Lanham and London: Lexington Books Kindle edition.

Magras, Michael. 2017. *"Memoirs of a Polar Bear* by Yoko Tawada." *Kenyon Review*, June. https://kenyonreview.org/reviews/memoirs-of-a-polar-bear-by-yoko-tawada-738439/ (Accessed July 1, 2021).

McNeill, Elizabeth. 2019. "Writing and Reading (with) Polar Bears in Yoko Tawada's *Etüden im Schnee* (2014)." *The German Quarterly* 92, no. 1 (Winter): 51–67.

Peschel, Sabine. 2018. "100 German Must-Reads: Yoko Tawada: 'Memoirs of a Polar Bear.'" *Deutsche Welle* (dw.com), October. https://www.dw.com/en/yoko-tawada-memoirs-of-a-polar-bear/a-45620835 (Accessed July 1, 2021).

Slaymaker, Douglas. 2020. "The Hands of Bears, the Hands of Men." In *Tawada Yoko: On Writing and Rewriting*, edited by Douglas Slaymaker, 323–31. Lanham and London: Lexington Books Kindle edition.

Slutsky, Tomoko Takeuchi. 2020. "Staging of Self, Performance of Life." In *Tawada Yoko: On Writing and Rewriting*, edited by Douglas Slaymaker, 308–23. Lanham and London: Lexington Books Kindle edition.

Smith, Jordan A. Y. 2017. "Narration Between Species: Yoko Tawada's *Memoirs of a Polar Bear*, Translated by Susan Bernofsky." *Reading in Translation*, 21 February. https://readingintranslation.com/2017/02/21/narration-between-species-yoko-tawadas-memoirs-of-a-polar-bear-translated-by-susan-bernofsky/ (Accessed July 1, 2021).

Spivak, Gayatri Chakravorty. 2006. "Translation as Culture." *Parallax* 6, no.1: 13–24.

Tawada Yōko. 2003. "The Bridegroom Was a Dog." In *The Bridegroom Was a Dog*, translated by Margaret Misutani, 7–62. Tokyo, New York and London: Kodansha International.

———. 2011. *Yuki no renshūsei*, Tokyo: Shinchōsha.

———. 2017. *Memoirs of a Polar Bear*. Translated from German by Susan Bernofsky. London: Portobello Books.

Yonaha Keiko. 1998. "Kaisetsu" (Interpretation). In *Inumukoiri* (The Bridegroom Was a Dog) by Tawada Yōko, 138–47. Tokyo: Kōdansha bunko, 1998.

*Chapter Eight*

# Minding the Gap in Kawakami Hiromi

## Mina Qiao and Matthew C. Strecher

Kawakami Hiromi (b. 1958), who by her own account preferred "telling false tales" (*usobanashi*) to playing outside as a child, has always maintained a delicate balance between reality and the imaginary.[1] "The world of 'falsehood' is right beside the 'real' world, and in places the two overlap," writes Kawakami. "The doorway to the world of 'falsehood' is small, but its interior is unexpectedly spacious."[2] We sense that Kawakami herself is more comfortable in that realm of "falsehood" than in that of the everyday, intimately familiar with its landmarks, its puzzling inhabitants, its curiouser and curiouser flow of time and space. She is not out of her mind, but inside it.

Yet Kawakami lives and works in the real world. No doubt this is why she is able to juxtapose meaningfully the realities of modern life in Japan—housing developments (*danchi*), a tightly controlled society (*kanri shakai*), the widely touted groupism of modern Japan—with the tropes of Japan's ancient and recent past: animistic spirit belief, anthropomorphic legend, feudalist social structure, magic. Like Tawada Yōko, she draws on Japanese folklore, on myths of changelings (*henshin tan*), and of marriages between humans and animals (*irui kon'in tan*), yet she does so through the lens of modern experience. Like Murakami Haruki and Ogawa Yōko, she constructs mysterious spaces and the elements of absence. But Kawakami's approach is somewhat different from all these writers; the fantastical in her writing becomes a sense of strangeness that permeates the narratives, yet is fully internalized by the characters, to the extent that they no longer recognize the fantastical, whether in anthropomorphized animals or the invisible presence of humans. While Murakami's characters ponder and puzzle over the magical moments in their day, and Ogawa's agonize over the missing memories, language, or even body parts that form the absence at the center of her narratives, Kawakami's characters overlook the absences around them. The Kawakami narrative space is permeated with voids of every type, yet her protagonists are simply too detached to take notice of them.

This chapter will explore the void presented in Kawakami's writings by asking a simple question: What is missing, beyond the sudden vanishing of beings in the dreamscape? We will find, to anticipate our conclusions, that Kawakami simultaneously presents and ignores the disruption of reason and stability, highlights and downplays the magical. In so doing, she acknowledges a fundamental truth that underpins the work of other magical realist authors in this volume: that modernity, with its attendant repression of belief in the uncanny, leads contemporary Japanese to disregard traditional spirituality and its grounding in the natural world. Kawakami's apparently "light" stories conceal a much darker truth: that humanity is losing its capacity not only to form relationships amongst itself, but also to connect with its deeper roots in the natural world. It may be, in fact, that the evident imperturbability of Kawakami's various protagonists hints at a widespread tendency among those living in modern society to ignore what is being lost. We are inexorably being divorced from the historical, mythical, and spiritual roots that help us to recognize who and what we are, why we exist, and why we should care about it. The great irony of modern civilization is that we have the most advanced communications technology ever devised by humanity, and we have absolutely nothing to say, and no one to whom to say it.

Yet Kawakami appears unperturbed as her characters are unperturbed; amidst the most ordinary of circumstances—a day in a typical suburban housing unit, an afternoon picnic—the uncanny will come out. It is, rather, the reader who is challenged by Kawakami's "falsehoods"—talking bears, disappearing family members, girls who transform into foliage—and the reader who must decide whether all this is real. The author makes no comment, nor do her characters. This is classic magical realist tradecraft; as we sometimes tell students, the best way to distinguish fantasy from magical realist fiction is to consider whether we are tempted to imagine the characters in the story mad? In fantasy we never need to ask this question, for the rules of the fantasy world are established from the start: students at Hogwarts have magic wands, and their broomsticks can fly. In magical realism, however, the rules of the everyday world *should* apply, yet they are violated. Bears prepare salted fish for their honored guests. People can shrink to the size of a bean. The Night can be poured out of a coffee pot. As readers, we *have* to ask whether the characters who experience these things are mad, dreaming, or simply occupy a magical space we ourselves have yet to find. But never does the story lose its sense of the "falsehood." We can almost hear Kawakami, with a mischievous grin on her face, asking us: How far would you like me to push you today? What is your limit? And if our limit proves to be limitless, we might find our way into that "world of falsehood" that, Kawakami says, is just over our shoulder, waiting for us to rediscover it. Cécile Sakai notes that Kawakami's characters continue their daily lives while in constant dialogue with the other world, and the contrasts between two worlds grow less and less striking; in the end the everyday life ends up being fantastic, and reciprocally the fantastic becomes ordinary.[3] There is nothing and everything wrong with these spaces, and in time the astute reader comes to understand that, as dreamscapes, there is nothing untoward about them after all.

## TO SLEEP, NEIGH, PERCHANCE TO DREAM

We may prefer to imagine that the Kawakami protagonist is dreaming—that is our "out"—and in some cases this is precisely what is happening. In one of her earliest stories, "Atarayoki" (1996; "Record of a Night Too Brief"), she presents readers with a dreamscape that is almost poetic, a sequence of vignettes that, as Ninomiya Tomoyuki points out, alternate between stories of animals and stories of a quasi-scientific nature: "The odd-numbered sections . . . as their titles indicate, are tales of animals. The titles of the even-numbered sections . . . are made up of terminology from physics and biology and present the narrative of 'myself' and 'the girl.'"[4] While in this bizarre dreamscape, the narrator (who avoids the use even of the pronoun "I") transforms initially into a horse, and leaps across the darkening sky, neighing for all she is worth. She is given her name at the end of the first section:

> As I leapt I shouted, and it came out as neigh. It became a horse's neigh. I leapt onto a roof, neighing for all I was worth. Those who were observing from below applauded. Not to be outdone by their applause, I neighed again and again. My body became that of a horse, and was covered with black hair. "The night begins! The Night Horse has come!"[5]

But what exactly is "the Night Horse" here? Might it refer to the ancient Norse legend of the goddess Nótt, who rides her black-haired horse Hrímfaxi ("mane of frost") across the darkness every night, governing it as her son Dagr governs the brightness of day? Indeed, anything seems possible in this chaotically orderly prose poem of images and sensations, and while we do not seriously imagine that Kawakami is rewriting Norse myth into her dreamscape, we might, with some justification, suggest that she constructs a realm that reflects the mythic origins of humanity, and which lives always within the imagination alongside our dreams. We have asked, what is the Night Horse? Perhaps it would be better to ask, what is the Night? Is it a temporal period, between sunset and sunrise, during which all the little "critters" make their way out of subterranean hiding places to play? Or is it a metaphorical representation of the subconscious (sleep; as death might be seen as a metaphorical representation of the unconscious), from which our memories, fears and desires come out to play?

It is, of course, both.

We might surmise, in fact, that the transformation into a horse is merely a signal that no form is permanent, and that all things meld into one another in this realm. Indeed, the narrator later will be turned back into herself, and later she will be made a mud loach, burned into cinders, and transformed into new foliage. In fact, this story is really one of creation, and occupies a space between the mythic and the psychic; the narrator moves through her narrative like a creation goddess, both making and witnessing the making of the world. She participates in a ritual feast, then commits the taboo of leaving that feast. She inadvertently insults a Japanese macaque, and is pursued furiously by it when she is unable to speak and atone for her sin. She lies to a child and is made into a mud loach. She contemplates a herd of elephants forming themselves into mandalas, yet finds the process dull.

And all the while she pursues this mysterious *shōjo*, who increasingly resembles herself, and in time the narrator has some inkling that the *shōjo* is herself, a dreamscape version of herself. Alternately she loves and despises the *shōjo*, and is loved and despised by the *shōjo* in her turn. Finding the girl imprisoned in an impregnable box, she smashes the box, but destroys the girl within as well. Horrified, she begins a process of leapfrog reconstruction in which she remakes the girl, who then destroys and remakes her, and so forth. The two continue to trade places and to trade dominance, the one leading and the other following, neither achieving total control, but neither able to continue without the other. In Jungian terms, they become something like *persona* and shadow.

The tale culminates in their death and final transformation into the flora of the world itself. Dancing with the *shōjo*, the narrator is disgusted to find masses of red-capped mushroom-like things growing among her thinning hair. The emergence of this fungal growth signals the beginning of the end for the two, and a couple of chapters later, as the *shōjo* lies on the floor of the forest that has grown up from and around her, the narrator weeps for her transformation and the girl tells her, "'This is what finally happens to everything that is born . . . you're the same, you know.'"[6] With that, the two expire in a final kiss.

The tale—or the dream—ends with the dawn of civilization, as humans emerge to construct homes, farms, villages, and the narrator reawakens, this time in the form of a newt (*imori*). She emerges from her pond with her fellow newts, scavenging for food, and even biting the village's inhabitants as they sleep, then returns to the pond to lay eggs, and to sleep and dream. Perhaps she will dream she is a horse, and the whole thing will begin again.

What is of particular interest about this tale, as the above synopsis should suggest, is how the world inhabited by the narrator is both dreamscape—a fragment of the subconscious—and a realm of cosmic creation, a sacred ground in which ritual, creation, destruction, and reconstruction occur. It is a realm in which literally anything seems possible, in which the limitations of the physical world simply do not apply. It also appears to be a place in which desires are given free reign; the narrator is obviously attracted to the *shōjo* she encounters, and expresses both her love and her sexual desire for her. Yet she also freely acts upon feelings of jealousy, of anger, and even of violence. In this sacred space of creation, the narrator encounters herself, destroys herself, and remakes herself. The entire tale/dream may thus be read as an act of birth, death, and rebirth, or as a story of identity formation.

And whether we approach this literary space as a dreamscape or a mythic structure (or, more likely, as both), we may note the archetypal elements of birth, growth, transformation, decay, and death, though not necessarily in that order. It is a space that underlies all dreams, one that contains, in somewhat simplistic terms, those things that we all desire and fear. At the same time, Kawakami is careful to deny us any true basis for symbolic interpretation of this dream; convention might suggest the straightforward conclusion that the dreamer fears death and desires love; but in the absence of any background on the dreamer—and even of any concrete assurance that this is a dream—it is just as possible that he or she fears love and desires death. Or, perhaps we could say in classic Freudian terms that love and death are fundamentally linked, their roots bound together beneath the forest floor of our minds.

As the above will suggest, "Atarayoki" presents one of the more extreme magical landscapes in the Kawakami literary universe, yet, as in her other tales, it is presented with the same matter-of-fact calm as more realistic works such as *Sensei no kaban* (2001; *Strange Weather in Tokyo*) or *Kodōgu: Nakano shōten* (2005; *The Nakano Thrift Shop*). This may be the most striking aspect of Kawakami's use of literary space: whether she writes in the realistic, the magical realist, or as above, the full-on *surrealist* mode, her poker face never wavers. "When I'm writing one of my 'false tales,' my facial expression also takes on an air of falsehood,"[7] Kawakami writes mischievously in her afterword to this collection, but few readers would know that from her prose.

## THE HOLLOW IN COMMUNITY

Within the same collection as "Atarayoki" is a somewhat more coherent tale, one in which the realistic is effectively layered with the "falsehoods" for which Kawakami is so well-known. The entire narrative of "Kieru" (1996; trans. 2017 as "Missing" but perhaps better expressed as "vanishing") takes place in a *danchi*, the modern urban and suburban housing projects that seem to emblemize postwar urban Japan. It is worth noting that in many ways the *danchi* is a modern form of the old communal villages that once formed the hub of local life for Japanese, and each *danchi* will typically have its own playground, its own meeting hall, and a small council of representatives, not unlike a condominium unit might in the United States. Neighbors know one another, look out for one another, and also watch one another. The buildings themselves may range from a collection of duplexes and triplexes to high-rise *manshon*—derived from the English word "mansion" and a thoroughly euphemistic term for what are, in effect, two- and three-bedroom condos of about 1,000 to 1,200 square feet. Such housing is the dream for many urban and suburban Japanese, offering a compromise between private home ownership (or simply low-rent urban housing) and a sense (or perhaps an illusion) of close-knit community.[8] At the same time, *danchi* represent one of the defining cultural symbols of the Shōwa era isolation of the nuclear family, the collapse of community, and merely a new fantasy for Japanese urbanization. According to Oda Mistuo, the suburban *danchi*, as well as my-home-ism, is just one more commodity in the capitalist system of mass production and mass consumption.[9] "Behind this business mode, there is no space for living, but only a place of commodity."[10] For this reason, Wakabayashi Mikio argues, such housing developments have been violently severed from history and tradition.[11]

Kawakami's tale layers the modern atmosphere of the *danchi*, with its shared communal spaces, upon older practices of communities involving religious rites and observances, village festivals, and of course, intervillage relations. "Kieru" concerns an extended family—parents and their grown children, and a nonsense-speaking family deity called "Goshiki"—and its efforts to conclude an arranged marriage with the daughter—Hiroko—of a family from the neighboring Hikari *danchi*. And while arranged marriage was by no means as anachronistic as it might sound at the time of this story's writing, accounting for some 25–30 percent of all Japanese marriages at the start of the 1990s,[12] we see in the negotiations between the two families a sort of modern-day alliance being concluded between the two *danchi*, whose peculiar customs (or *kimari*, as Kawakami has it) contrast with one another.

What makes this story strange are precisely those *kimari*. Some of these are merely bizarre; it is customary, for instance, in the narrator's *danchi* to protect the entire community during its annual summer festival from a voracious species of stinging insect by selecting sacrificial members of the community to attract the insects' attention. Other *kimari* are more severe. There is, for instance, a rule governing all the *danchi* that exactly five persons must occupy each dwelling, neither more nor less. No explanation is given for this, no origin for the rule, but it means that when a new member marries into a family, another must be cast out. The matter is made more complicated by the fact that families are strictly forbidden from simply exchanging members to maintain their numbers. "So when Hiroko comes to our house, my next older brother can't just go over to her place and marry her younger sister."[13]

All of this is presented to the reader in a most matter-of-fact tone, as though it were nothing at all that such rules are in place, unexplained and unquestioned. The closest thing to an explanation we have is a mysterious character called "Ten-san," an old woman who not only acts as the go-between for the two families' marriage negotiations, but provides rulings on what is and is not permitted. Her age is uncertain, but it is believed that she has been performing this role—something between a spiritual leader and a central authority—since the days even before the birth of the narrator's great-grandmother, so we might presume her to be well over a century old, and perhaps even immortal.[14] No one in the narrator's family has met her, as she operates entirely by telephone. Given her authority to arbitrate the many *kimari* of the community, it is not unreasonable to suppose her to be their originator as well.

What creates the real conflict in "Kieru" is the narrator's own family *kimari*, apparently unique to them, that their members periodically vanish without warning. They do not run away, nor are they dead, at least in the usual sense; they simply become invisible and intangible. Within the narrative chronology the first to disappear is the eldest son. The narrator, who is his younger sister, knows that he is still present in the household. "I couldn't exactly tell what he did while he was vanished, but I had certain inklings that he had been moving around the place. I would hear a door in the next room rattling even though there was no wind; chopsticks and bowls would become mysteriously dirty; I would get up early and find the dust on the shelves neatly wiped away; it had to be my older brother."[15] Yet he is gone in every practical sense of the word, and while this is perfectly normal within the family, it is nonetheless problematic, for it is his marriage that is being arranged. How can he marry Hiroko if he has disappeared?

The solution to the problem is laughably simple: Hiroko will be married to the second brother, but will not be told of the disappearance of the elder one. Indeed, the narrator's family behaves as though the eldest son of the family had never existed in the first place, and it is left to the narrator, alone, to mourn his disappearance. In the meantime, the second brother takes up the responsibility of wooing Hiroko, which he does by whispering sweet nothings to her over the telephone, while his entire family listens and appraises his skills as a (verbal) lover. Only the narrator slips into her bedroom and remembers her eldest brother fondly, even incestuously.

Clearly, a story like "Kieru" can be read as an intense dream, as a schizophrenic episode on the part of the narrator, or as a bizarre new reality infused with magic. In the end, it does not particularly matter how we choose to read the story, for the narrative says much about the gradual disintegration of traditional values in contemporary Japan, and the real discussion of this involves the narrator herself. We noted earlier that differences exist between the *kimari* of the two families represented in this story, as well as between their *danchi*. In fact, we are apt to be distracted by the extremities of these *kimari*, so much so that it is easy to miss a fundamental fact: there is no real love or attachment in the narrator's household. The family seems to take no notice when one of its number vanishes. The eldest son, who only presents himself to the narrator, expresses his deep sadness at this fact, telling the narrator, "I'm lonely because I have no body. I'm lonely because, even though I'm right here with the family, I'm no longer part of the family."[16] He continues to visit his younger sister, presumably, because she still remembers him and thinks about him, and we sense in her a vaguely erotic attraction to him. "My eldest brother kissed me hard and stroked my arms. As this was done to me, my body swayed, comfortably flabby, feeling like a bag filling with water."[17] This makes more sense to us if we assume that the narrator is dreaming/fantasizing, particularly as she eventually superimposes her fiancé's face onto her brother's; however, it is also possible to imagine that the brother's sudden incestuous passion for her is gratitude for her continued remembrance.

In either event, there is no other path to affection for the narrator, and as her parents arrange her own marriage near the story's end, she can only regard the example of Hiroko's marriage dubiously. Despite their many whispered words of love over the telephone, once Hiroko joins the family as a bride, the second brother simply ignores her. The entire family sleep in hammocks suspended from the ceiling, so this is perhaps not overly surprising (how *does* one make love in a hammock?), but the second brother's dismissive attitude toward Hiroko, who initially tries to be affectionate with her new husband, does not bode well for the narrator's own future prospects.

A number of useful conclusions may be drawn from this darkly humorous narrative. Chief among them is that the contemporary family—or at any rate, the individual within that family—is crushed by a steadily increasing sense of detachment—from family, from neighbors, and from meanings attached to the rituals of the past. In a sense, Kawakami's story suggests, our very souls have somehow been driven into isolation, and while we live within the illusion of a collective society, in actual fact we have no path to reconnect with our collective identity in the contemporary moment. This is presumably why the tale is set in a modern *danchi*, which, as noted above, appears to offer a modern spin on premodern village collectivity, premodern values; at this point, such concepts are performed in name and in form only. We asked earlier why these *danchi* have so many rules and rituals; yet we can never know the answer to this, any more than the inhabitants of these *danchi* can know it. Even "Ten-san," a tangible link with that ancient past, appears to be losing her touch; in the past decade, she laments, not a single one of her arranged marriages has worked out. It was not always so; the narrator's parents note that in their day things were simpler, less heavily ritualistic. Perhaps we should conclude that Ten-san's continual adding of layers of ritual is a compensation for the loss of meaning within those rituals. Perhaps it is her way of attempting to regain what has been lost.

The traditions of family have fared no better, as we have seen. The vows of love exchanged by the second brother and Hiroko are certainly proof of that. During their courtship, which takes place entirely on the telephone, the second brother declares that "my love is as deep as a swamp, and as high as a pile of rubble," perhaps a new twist on the traditional Confucianist saying, popular in the premodern era, that "one's obligation to one's parents is as deep as the ocean and as high as a mountain" (*go-fubo no on wa umi yori mo fukaku, yama yori mo takai*).[18] Here we see slightly less uplifting examples. And when Hiroko asks what will be found at the bottom of that swamp, she is told, "family."[19] If the narrator's family is anything to judge by, this may be the truest line in the story. Family is no longer significant, for it is an empty sign, merely an outdated word that is devoid of the power and meaning it once contained.

This is the emptiness, the absence, that we noted at the start of this chapter: the emptiness of meaning, of signification, within the highly ritualized existence of modern Japanese even now. One image that stands adjacent to this sense of absence is the contrast between sound and silence in this piece. We have noted that Ten-san carries out her work via the telephone; no one meets her. We have also pointed out that, prior to the actual marriage, nearly all the "courtship" that occurred between the narrator's two brothers and Hiroko took the form of whispered words of love that were, as we have seen, somewhat absurd. Yet it is through sound that true absence is made manifest in "Kieru." It is the eldest brother's words to his sister that make his presence known, and through the disembodied and nonsensical magical words of "Goshiki" that the narrator begins her unexplained engorgement. Hiroko's shrinking begins, too, with the cries of cranes, though only Hiroko can hear them, just as only the narrator can hear her eldest brother. The meetings between the two families, also, are marked by various incantations, though their meanings appear incomprehensible to members of the other side.

But not all sound is equal. How does one compare heartfelt words of love to the tongue-twisting nonsense of Goshiki? How can the sadness of the vanished eldest brother be translated by prayers in a language so ancient it can no longer be understood? The point is that sound, while an indication of existence, in this story works toward the erasure of meaningful presence. In its place there persists only meaningless noise, from Ten-san's absurdly complex rituals to the "ancient" Shintō prayers offered by both families, but quite probably understood by neither. When Hiroko offers her opinions, such as voicing her opposition to the "human sacrifice" of her fiancé and his father to the marauding insects at the summer festival, she is quickly informed that she has no right to speak in this place. Yet her voice, we eventually realize, is the voice of truth, almost of reality. Is it any wonder then, as she faces the sheer absurdity of the *kimari* into which she has married, that she simply shrinks into nothing?

This is the terrifying undercurrent of this story. An implicit choice faces the eldest brother, Hiroko, and probably the narrator herself: to exist meaninglessly in this family and this *danchi*, or to vanish meaningfully, leaving only an absence in place of their individual identity. We have already seen that this is the fate of the eldest brother and Hiroko, who are simply erased, forced into total silence. They speak without being heard, touch without being felt, exist without being acknowledged. The only lingering question is what will happen to the narrator; but is there really any question?

"Kieru" is certainly tongue-in-cheek; summer festivals in which two members of the community must sacrifice their bodies for others, and strict rules about how many people make up a family, are plainly absurd, and even humorous. Yet they serve as metaphorical representations of other aspects of contemporary Japanese life—unquestioning loyalty to one's group, strict obedience to authority, an emphasis on tradition and ritual—that are quite real. In Kawakami's allegorical tale, all characters seem to be interchangeable with one another; is postindustrial Japan any different? A worker is a worker, a husband is a husband, a brother is a brother.

If genuine, meaningful social attachments, once the cornerstone of Japanese social structure, are no longer possible amongst humans, perhaps the answer lies in attachments between humans and animals. The narrator's greatest desire is thus to transform; if human attachment can no longer be found, she will, if possible, become a *nekoma*, a small, apparently cat-like animal "with hair on its arms, legs and back, and whiskers."[20] She has a memory of having been held by her eldest brother "long ago" and stroked while he murmured, "nekoma, nekoma" to her and she purred contentedly. Might this "long ago" (*mukashi*) be more distant than a mere childhood memory? Might it not equally indicate reversion to a primordial relationship between Man and Beast? The *nekoma* is apparently a mythic beast, not unlike the *kudagitsune* ("pipe fox"), for which we are told that the narrator's mother once desperately longed, but in vain. Perhaps detachment amongst modern Japanese is not so recent a thing after all.

If human attachment has been sacrificed to the needs of the modern era, then what has been gained by contemporary Japanese individuals in exchange? The answer, no doubt, is a tranquil, prosperous, homogeneous society, or at least a reasonable facsimile thereof. But was it worth it? Can love truly exist in such a scenario? Can feeling, independent thought, passion? Can a meaningful life be lived under those conditions? These, like an affectionate brother or loving bride, merely fade away in Kawakami's narrative, to be forgotten more rapidly than they should. They end up little more than a dream fantasy, preserved only in the narrator who, the reader is uneasily aware, will likely disappear herself once her marriage contract is concluded. And none of it will make any difference to anyone. This is the tragic reality hidden in the allegorical, magical realist narrative space of "Kieru."

## THE RAPTURE AND RUPTURE OF UNBEARABLE DIVINITY

Many of the key elements noted above in "Kieru" may also be found in "Kamisama" (1994; "God Bless You"). Once again we see the peculiar, yet casually depicted juxtapositioning of a modern housing unit (though perhaps not a bona fide *danchi*), and the admixture of human and animal society. Kawakami casually pulls her readers into a modern, everyday setting—complete with apartments, neighbors, highways, and vehicles in the background—but with the magical rupture of a bear living in the narrator's building who speaks extraordinarily refined Japanese, performs the traditional ritual of distributing gifts of *soba* (buckwheat noodles) and *hagaki* (greeting cards) so often neglected now, and claims the connection of some having had some service performed by a distant relative of the narrator. Whether this is true or merely an excuse, Bear (for he will go by no other name) makes this an excuse for extending extraordinary courtesy to the narrator, in the finest traditions (now largely extinct) of an earlier Japanese society. In short, he constructs an obligation for himself, and then sets out to fulfill it. The narrator is less certain, but impressed nonetheless: "It was the sort of connection that might or might not be there, but Bear was deeply moved by what he kept referring to as our 'karmic bond' and the like."[21]

Whatever his motivation, Bear invites the narrator out for a stroll to a nearby river. Upon their arrival they find many people swimming and fishing.

Two men accompanied by a child approach. All three seem surprised by Bear, the child crying out again and again, "It's a bear" and the older men agreeing, "Yes, it's a bear." The child, in the typical fashion of small Japanese boys (and perhaps all boys), pulls at Bear's fur, kicks at him several times, and finally cries "Yaa, *punch*!" and wallops Bear in the stomach. After the boy has run away, followed by the two adults, Bear merely remarks, "There is no malice in children."[22] The narrator's silence ("I said nothing to this") seems to indicate her disagreement.

Bear's mild response to the child's violence, and the fact that the adults neither greet him nor offer a word of apology at the child's behavior, suggests Bear's sense of otherness to those around him, despite his obvious attempts to fit in to their society. Indeed, we might read Bear's character as a sort of emissary, an ambassador, to the world of humanity. In response, with the exception of the narrator, who accepts Bear but does not fully comprehend him or his existence here, humanity treats him as an oddity devoutly to be ignored. Given the story's title, "Kamisama," it does not seem far-fetched to suggest that Bear performs a role not unlike other prophets in human history—Buddha, Christ, Mohammed—who offered a connection to the divine, only to be rejected by the majority of those they met.

And what divinity has Bear come to express? Clearly, he represents the divinity of Nature itself, and all it contains. His task, whether self-appointed or heaven-sent, is to establish what Tamaki Tomita refers to as a "bond" (*kizuna*) between humanity and Nature. Unfortunately, in this corrupt and decadent age, "there is no longer a place for real *kizuna*."[23]

But why should this be? Simply put, it is because humanity has grown arrogant and dismissive of Nature as it has progressed technologically. We may still fear, and even respect, the fury of natural disasters—typhoons, earthquakes, tsunamis, volcanic eruptions—but that respect does not extend to the living creatures with whom we share the earth. Having relentlessly driven our fellow animals into hiding, out of their natural habitats in pursuit of minerals, timber, energy sources, we imagine ourselves superior. Having mastered light-speed communication technology, we have no use for the signals sent us by Nature and her emissaries. We do not "read" the melting of the polar ice caps; we do not hear the words of Bear. At best, he is an oddity to be punched and laughed at; at worst, he is an obstacle to further "progress."

Over the course of the story it becomes clear that the narrator is impressed by Bear's manners and his solicitude; he catches fish from the river with expert eye and lightning-quick paws, then cleans, salts, and dries them for her while she naps beneath a blanket he has brought along for her. He even offers to sing her a lullaby to help her fall asleep (what would that sound like, we wonder?). And yet, even she cannot escape his sense of otherness. From the start she is uncertain what sort of bear he might be—an Asian black bear, a brown bear, even a Malaysian bear?—but she is also concerned that to ask might be impolite. At the end of their walk, Bear makes one further demand on her sensibilities:

> "Could I persuade you to exchange hugs with me? Bear said.
>
> "It's the custom in my hometown when parting with a close friend. That is, if you are not averse to it."[24]

While the narrator does not refuse, she is unprepared for this gesture. As Bear wraps his arms around her, she remarks to herself on the sensation of receiving a real "bear hug":

> He took a step toward me and, spreading his arms wide, wrapped them around my shoulders, rubbing his cheek against my cheek. He smelled of bear. Then he rubbed his opposite cheek against mine, and once again squeezed me around the shoulders with his arms. His body was cooler than I had expected.[25]

And he finishes by invoking the bear god, wishing that its blessings might rain upon her. This piques the narrator's curiosity, and before sleeping, she tries hard to imagine what sort of god the "bear god" might be, but to no avail. Even her slightly more enlightened gaze cannot penetrate that far into the primordial mists of ancient spiritual tradition.

"Kamisama" is followed by a useful sequel, "Sōjō no chūshoku" (1998; Luncheon on the lawn), in which Bear has invited the same narrator out for a picnic by the same riverbank. It appears he has spent some years living amongst the humans—"I passed my youth here,"[26] he tells the narrator rather wonderingly—but while he has made considerable efforts to fit in with his human neighbors, it seems they have not reciprocated. As he tells the narrator of a recent trip he took to his hometown far in the north, she asks whether he flew or took the train. He surprises her by stating that he drove, but that it was necessary to borrow a friend's car. "He had struggled with whether to buy a motorbike or a car, but when he called the dealerships he'd seen in the used car magazines, as soon as they learned he was a bear, their attitudes became very chilly."[27] Bear has also mastered the art of human cuisine, presenting the narrator with a remarkable series of gourmet dishes and an excellent wine. Asked where he learned to cook like this, Bear responds:

> "I'm self-taught."
>
> You're very good.
>
> "Everything I know is self-taught. It's very hard to get into a school."

Maybe it was all the harder to get into a school if you were a bear. Not just schools, either. He must have had all sorts of difficulties.[28]

The undercurrent of the story, then, is that Bear has failed to integrate with human society, but this was not for want of trying; rather, the reception of Bear that we saw in "Kamisama" has remained unchanged over the years. He will always be an outsider, perhaps tolerated, but never really accepted. In this sense the story can easily be read as an allegory for the lives of non-Japanese (or merely those who are different) within Japanese society, from *Zainichi* (ethnic Koreans residing in Japan) to Okinawans, from Ainu to actual foreigners. It could even be read allegorically to describe the lives of those who are different within the ethnic Japanese community—LGBTQ, the physically or mentally challenged, or even so-called returnees (*kikokusei*), who have spent periods of their lives outside of Japan.

While all of these allegorical readings are both possible and fruitful, one point is explicitly clear from the text: the worlds of humans and other animals can no longer mix. And while the attitude encountered by Bear amongst the humans with whom he interacts is unquestionably superior—they naturally see him as an inferior being—the reader is given opportunity to see something the used car dealers and school heads could not: his vast divinity as an integral part of Nature, the god of all. In the midst of their picnic by the river, a tremendous storm breaks upon them. At first Bear attempts to shield the narrator with an enormous beach umbrella he has brought, but with the lightning and thunder crashing directly over them, he thinks better of this, and instead places his body directly over hers, shielding her from harm. As the fury of the storm increases, and the gap between lightning flashes and thunder peals is reduced to nothing (meaning that the lightning is striking directly above them), "a shock ran through his entire body."[29] At this, Bear finally rises up to join with the storm.

> At the moment the shock ran through him, Bear separated his body from me and roared in a massive voice. Awoooooooooooo! he cried. His voice was more powerful than any thunder. Bear stood upright and roared facing the sky. The air seemed to rip apart with the vibrations. Gaps between the thunder and lightning began to open up.
>
> From deep within his belly Bear roared several more times. This is scary, I thought. Both the thunder and Bear were scary. As though he had completely forgotten my presence, Bear assumed a divine form, and continued to raise up the voice of a beast.[30]

Herein lies the climax of the story—of both stories, in fact—at which the narrator, perhaps for the first time, recognizes in Bear not a clever imitator of humans, but a magnificent part of a natural world to which her species, for all their self-imagined superiority, can no longer truly connect. She realizes that it is not for humanity to accept Bear, but for Bear/Nature to accept humanity. However, we are no longer welcome. Tamaki Tokita reads "Kamisama" and "Sōjō no chūshoku" along a similar line, as Kawakami's ruminations on the fractured relationship between human and nature and the loss of *kizuna* among other traditional Japanese values.[31] For her, Bear's old-fashioned speech and gestures hint at the rapid changes of Japanese society since its modernization.[32] Tokita also notes Bear's return to his hometown as an expression of disillusionment with human society—a modern Japan where, as noted above, "there is no longer a place for real *kizuna*."[33]

This disillusionment is palpable at the end of "Sōjō no chūshoku"; Bear leaves without applying his customary hug, nor does he bestow the blessings of the bear god upon the narrator. He merely stands side by side with her, observing some clouds drifting on the wind in the distance, and says goodbye. He is not angry with her, but sad for them both. He promises her a letter when he has reached his hometown, and he is a bear of his word. His letter informs her that, while he had intended to open a shop of some kind, instead he spends his time fishing and cutting grass. "I am gradually forgetting all the customs of your place," he confides. "I've stopped cooking, and now I wonder how I ever could have done such a thing."[34] Whether this means he has forgotten how, or that he considers such acts to be absurd or even barbarous, the reader is left to decide. What we do know, and that for certain, is that he has returned to the lifestyle proper to himself, and to any who live as part of Nature.

But, as noted just above, this is no longer a viable option for humanity—even the narrator herself. When Bear's letter arrives, there is no return address on the envelope, and the postmark is unreadable. She cannot respond to him, so when she writes her own letter, she writes only her own return address on it, and after she affixes a postage stamp—a ritual offering of sorts—she places her own letter at the back of her desk. This has now the flavor of a prayer, a one-way communication now that Bear—a divine prophet—has returned to his own place. The story's end is delicate and touching: "In my bed, before sleep took me, I prayed to the bear god, and then I prayed a little to the gods of humanity as well. Thinking about the letter to Bear, deep in my desk drawer, I fell into a deep sleep."[35]

Readers are given the intimation that, prior to the picnic, the narrator respected and cared for Bear, perhaps even loved him on some level. We also sense, however, that she never truly grasped his experience, nor his considerable power. So why has Bear selected her as someone to whom he might reveal himself? Perhaps it is because the narrator, like Kawakami herself, is open to that which is divine, to the world Bear represents. She becomes a kind of prophet figure. It is true that Bear frightens her when he unleashes his answering call to the thunder—the Japanese word for which, *kaminari,* is a homonym for "cries of the gods," and probably originates there—but he also awes her. "Even in our high-tech world, in the depths of our souls we all live or die in the darkened domain of mythic archetypes," writes Hino Keizō, commenting not on this story but on Kawakami's Akutagawa Prize-winning "Hebi o fumu" (1996; Stepping on A Snake);[36] but he is really writing about Kawakami herself, whose "world of falsehood" is merely another way of expressing Hino's "darkened domain of mythic archetypes," or Bear's "hometown," or what we are calling here Nature. The narrator of "Sōjō no chūshoku" is attuned to that world, even if she is not always aware of it. She longs for that world, even if she does not know precisely where it is. She hears its voice calling to her, embodied in the violence of Bear's roar, but also in the gentleness of his speech, and the soft refinement of his final letter to her. Hino's term "archetypal" (*genkeiteki*) is useful here as well, for the world Bear inhabits is truly the origin of the narrator and her people, and while Bear has not succeeded in his mission to reawaken humanity as a whole to its origins, he has succeeded in awakening one woman, who might act as his prophet. We cannot but wonder whether that prophet is Kawakami Hiromi herself.

## DON'T TREAD ON ME, DON'T TREAD ON YOU

A quasi-sacred aspect underpins the action in the aforementioned "Hebi o fumu" (1996; Stepping on a snake), for which Kawakami was awarded the Akutagawa Prize. Taking place in a district that seems, as usual, to be perfectly poised between the modern world and that of classical legend, this is a story of how humans and snakes interact meaningfully in that liminal space. At the same time, it is about the narrator, Sanada Hiwako's struggle to determine who she is, and where she belongs.

The story begins without preamble: "While pushing through a grove on my way to Midori Park, I stepped on a snake."[37] Whereupon the snake complains, "Once you get stepped on, it's all over" and changes into the form of "a woman around fifty years old."[38] But this is not the quasi-sacred part; it lies in the peculiar work Hiwako does, as an assistant to "Kosuga-san," a middle-aged man (and perhaps an early model to "Nakano" in *Kodōgu: Nakano shōten*) who, with his wife Nishiko, makes Buddhist prayer rosaries to sell around the nearby temples. This invocation of temples—and particularly, Buddhist temples—is a clear and tangible connection to the other world of the dead, and it is not by chance that the priest to whom Kosuga sells his rosaries in the story is married to a snake changeling. Kosuga, for his part, has a snake in his life through his wife. Thus, even before stepping on the snake in the opening line of the story, we see that Hiwako has been living between the worlds of snakes and humans the whole time.

Snake changelings are not uncommon in Japanese legend, from ancient tales popularized in medieval collections like the *Konjaku monogatari* (ca. twelfth century, tales of times now past) to Edo period (1603–1868) Kabuki plays. This is not limited to snakes, of course; Beata Kubiak Ho-Chi notes that animals and other nonhuman protagonists are ubiquitous in premodern Japanese tales and legends, for "anti-anthropocentrism seems to constitute, in contrast to the Western homocentric civilization, a permanent trait of Japanese culture." Anyone familiar with Japanese folklore is accustomed to the fox changeling, often taking on the appearance of a helpless young woman, who draws the amorous attention of lonely young men. Yet snakes are a type of animal, perhaps for obvious reasons, that take on a particularly erotic symbolism. Akemi Takizawa (2002) writes convincingly of the powerful sexual imagery of snakes in *Konjaku*, in which she highlights numerous examples of male serpents penetrating—and even impregnating—young women; she even notes an instance of a female snake fellating a monk while he sleeps.[39] Yet in nearly all of these tales, the animal perishes as a result of its liaison with humans, frequently with the result of its attaining Buddhist enlightenment. The most famous of such stories is surely that of "Dōjōji," in which a woman, overcome with lust for a monk who has put her off, hunts him down and burns him to cinders with her fiery breath as he hides from her beneath a temple bell. Eventually, both the monk and the serpent-woman are redeemed by the prayers of an aged priest.[40]

In Kawakami's tale we find subtle hints of this sexual—or at least sensual—nature of snakes. There is the obvious attractiveness of the priest's wife—"superb in nighttime matters," says the priest—but even Hiwako is drawn to the snakes she meets.[41] Her own, who claims to be her mother, has moved in with her, and when the changeling wraps herself around Hiwako, she finds the experience pleasant.

> Her cheek was cold. It was a feeling of completeness, like holding a cherished pet animal, or being totally enveloped by some huge thing. While rubbing her cheek against mine, she wrapped both her arms around me. Her enfolding arms were also cold, and the ends of her fingers were slightly snake-like. Even as she changed back into a snake, it was not displeasing. Quite the reverse, her snake form was more comforting.[42]

For all the thinly veiled (and potentially incestuous) erotic interplay between Hiwako and her snake/mother, the true seduction concerns not sexual contact but an effort to bring Hiwako over to the snake world for good. Her "mother" attempts daily to convince Hiwako that she would be so much happier living in the world of snakes. Hiwako, for her part, is not particularly attracted by the idea, but neither is she repelled. Kosuga's own wife confides to her that she faced a similar choice years ago; "Why didn't I go into the snake world then? I was invited. You'll be invited too, Sanada-san. The snake invites us again and again. But I refused again and again. Their path is so twisted, I thought it wouldn't do."[43] But what she is really doing is nudging Hiwako herself toward the world of the snakes.

But what *is* the "world of the snakes" here? As in our previous tales, we may read it literally, as a realm in which serpents maintain their own serpentine society; and Hiwako might, presumably, become one of them. Perhaps this is how changelings are made. On a deeper level, however, we may also read this allegorically, as a spiritual cult of sorts, always eager for new members. That Kawakami wrote this story only a year following the so-called sarin incident (*sarin jiken*) of March 20, 1995, in which members of the infamous Aum Shinrikyō cult released nerve gas in the Tokyo subway system during the morning rush hour, killing a dozen people and injuring thousands more, makes such a reading particularly possible.

And yet, the snake world might also be understood simply as a world of adventure and mystery in the mythic sense, which would also connect it to the realm of the unconscious, insofar as the realm of adventure, or what Joseph Campbell called the "Zone of Magnified Power," may also be linked to the archetypal sphere of shared experience and memory that Jung called the collective unconscious (*das kollektive Unbewusste*). For Jung, the collective unconscious was more than mere memory; it was a manifestation of the Platonic notion of the *kósmos noetós*, or "realm of forms," in which the origins (*archē*) of all things in the material world reside. Katrin Amann inclines to this approach:

> In "Hebi o fumu," numerous binary oppositions, such as physical/external vs. spiritual/internal, real vs. illusory, individual vs. the community, are dismantled. The central symbol of the snake cannot be explicated within the limits of a single meaning. The snake may be interpreted as an alter-ego concretized from the protagonist's internality/unconscious, or it may be considered as an actualization of various mythic archetypes vis-à-vis the collective unconscious.[44]

Wada Tsutomu, on the other hand, while agreeing that the snake symbolically represents "the elusive other," also insists that it "continues to exist as an "entity possessing reality," that is, a real thing in Hiwako's life.[45] This is not inconsistent with an archetypal reading of the snake, insofar as its real and physical manifestation evokes—or actualizes—something deeper within Hiwako that is simply dying to escape her inner self. This might be her sexual desire (as noted above, a common trope for serpents in literature, especially in Japan), but it could also suggest her desire to be away from the human world itself, to enter her own inner world, Kawakami's "world of falsehood." The story thus tests which is stronger: Hiwako's inertia, or her urge to flee.

We might note here that the arrival of the snake (or, quite possibly, Hiwako's *conjuring* of the snake) coincides with a low point in Hiwako's life; she has recently quit her job as a schoolteacher, largely because "I sensed that they wanted something from me, but I ended up giving them all sorts of things they didn't want," and so "I got burned out."[46] She has been in relationships, but cannot connect with her partners. Even with her family she finds it impossible to connect, for "there was always a wall, sometimes thin and other times thick, and because of that wall, we could talk."[47] But for Hiwako, clearly, talking is not the same as connecting; in fact, one senses almost that the more she talks, the less she is able to connect, as though the words themselves form a barrier between herself and others. However, "[b]etween the snake and me, there was no wall."[48]

Logically speaking, if Hiwako is incapable of connecting with those in the outside world, and if this condition is exacerbated by her attempts to communicate with people in that world, then her only remaining option is to turn inward and connect with whatever lives *within* herself. Having reached this point, are we content to assume that her snake has appeared before her in that grove outside Midori Park by chance? Surely there is ample reason to suppose that the snake is *summoned*, its role to break Hiwako out of her inertia and draw her into the inner reaches of her own mind. The snake, then, is only her "mother" in the most abstract sense; it is herself, and its role is to draw her more deeply into a place that is truly her own.

To term this an "escape" would be misleading; the world offered to Hiwako by her inner snake is akin to Campbell's "call to adventure," an opportunity to explore a world whose interior space, like the dreamscape in "Atarayoki," is much larger and richer than its exterior. It is a space in which Hiwako might meet her greatest fears, yet also fulfill her deepest desires. It may even be the world of death, of eternity. Its only rules will be those she makes herself. It is, in short, the pure imaginary. And while her beguilingly slithering "mother" may now assume the form of a snake—again, an archetypal manifestation, but almost certainly of *something else*—what Hiwako will truly find in the inner space she is offered may end up being the very essence of herself. We cannot know whether the snake represents the archetype of sexual desire, of physical connection (viz. the image of snakes intercoiled), of mischievous deceit (considering the serpent in the Garden of Eden), or something entirely different. But none of this really matters; what does matter is that Hiwako needs to accept this call to adventure if she is to be complete and fulfilled as a person.

In the end, however, she does not elect to go. Heedless of the seductive purring of her "mother," and the regrets of Nishiko's cautionary tale, Hiwako battles with the snake in a scene reminiscent of the dreamscape. As they fight one another, Hiwako's apartment fills with water, and they float away, passing the rosary shop on the way. Hiwako continues to deny the existence of the snake's world, and herein lies the real issue: she cannot place her faith in this inner world that is offered her. Unlike the narrator of "Kamisama," Hiwako is determined to maintain her hold on the material world, to remain as she is.

But will she?

"Hebi o fumu" concludes without concluding. If Hiwako loses her struggle with the snake, it will mean that her inner voice has succeeded in pulling her into the other world; if she wins, she will remain in the material world, forever doubting, yet perhaps always reminded, as Nishiko is daily reminded, of what she has given up. In this sense, she will forever occupy a liminal space in between the two worlds, a quasi-sacred space occupied and understood only by those whose role is to mediate between life and death. And who can say that, even if she remains in the material world of the living now, she will not give in and join the world of eternity at some later point? If she does, she will no doubt encounter the vanished eldest brother from "Kieru," along with "pipe foxes" and a girl who magically transforms into the "Night Horse."

## CONCLUSION: MIND THE GAP

The secret of Kawakami Hiromi's successful use of the magical imaginary space in her works is that they take place in what we have been calling the "gap"—the liminal space poised neatly and precisely between the magical and everyday worlds. For readers this can be a challenge, because the two worlds actually spill over into one another, leaving us unsure where we are. What saves the experience from descending into the kitschy "with-it-ness" of postmodern self-absorption is the author's wholly un-self-conscious employment of her liminal space; the reader briefly obsesses over the weirdness of it all, but Kawakami blithely charges ahead, heedless of the weird, almost as though she were unaware of it. She is not, of course, truly unaware; "When I'm writing one of my 'false stories' it really shows on my face that I'm lying,"[49] she writes, and we can well believe it. She is, rather, playing a game of chicken with her readers, constantly raising the stakes, implicitly asking her readers, "Can we go one step further? Are you still with me?"

But to what end does she pull her readers into this narrative space that is something between a daytime drama and a really intense acid trip? As we have sought to show in this chapter, the point comes down to maintaining connections: those between people, and the more tenuous, increasingly strained connections between humanity and the natural world. And both are severely threatened by the encroachment of modernity.

To speak of the isolated individual in the modern world is to indulge in cliché, yet how else are we to describe it? Even admitting that the nostalgic image of Japan as an enclosed, homogeneous collection of small, close-knit communities is at best quaint, and quite possibly an Orientalist fantasy, we cannot but reflect on the fact that the isolation and the separation from past connections seems to be getting worse. Even within the home, family members exist alone, together. Even in the rural spaces outside the megalopolis of Tokyo, an emissary from the natural world is brushed aside, ignored. Even stepping on a snake is not enough to bring us to heel; the world of the gods calls to us, in all our modern glory, but no one can hear it because we have our earbuds in.

All of this is perhaps easy to miss, because Kawakami's voice is not that of a strident activist, but rather the tongue-in-cheek voice of a born storyteller. But the story she tells is serious. As a species, modern humanity is not just in danger of wiping out what is left of the natural world, nor even just of destroying the environment to the point that the planet earth becomes uninhabitable; rather, we are literally in danger of forgetting who we are, where we came from, how we got here. Maybe this is why, when she rewrote "Kamisama" two months after the nuclear meltdown in Fukushima in March–April of 2011, she sounded less like an environmentalist than a mythologist. "2011. I wrote 'Kamisama 2011.' But I had absolutely no notion of puffing myself up to warn everyone about the dangers of using nuclear power. Rather, it was to note with surprise how daily life would continue, but some big changes might well occur in our daily lives."[50] She says something a bit more telling near the beginning of that essay, however: "I'm not necessarily one of those who believes in the myriad gods living amongst us, but as I go through these mornings without heat because of the power conservation efforts, and then the sun shines warm through my windows, I catching myself thinking, 'ah, this truly is the divine sun,' and I sense the Japan of old."[51] There was a time, she suggests, when we took the light and warmth of the sun more seriously, as a blessing and a privilege. Now we have forgotten why the sun was divine in the first place. And having forgotten the origins of the sun's divinity, are we thus doomed to forget both its power and its wrath as well? All natural phenomena, all natural disasters, are today explained through scientific analysis; is there not something just a little prudent about acknowledging that we have pissed off the gods of old as well?

That is the gap Kawakami writes about, often so subtly that her message is obscured by the really fun story in which she embeds it. It is a gap between ancient and modern, between belief and contempt, between humanity and the natural world humanity so determinedly rejects or ignores. Kawakami, who was a biology major at university, may be uniquely positioned as a writer to probe modern humanity's approach to the natural world. As she commented to an interviewer less than a year after the nuclear disaster:

> What I think about when I'm writing a novel is, what on earth *are* human beings? What's going to happen when there are so many of them, including me? What is happening to our human relations? I'm always thinking about that as I write. We can consider that from a literary perspective, but in biology we explore the question of how humans function as living beings within the natural world, how they relate to other animals and plants, by what kinds of systems they are made, and how they move about in nature. In a certain sense these kinds of questions come through when I'm writing novels as well.[52]

Humanity's sense of superiority over nature is no doubt related to the egotism of modernity, yet the quasi-biological approach from which Kawakami examines the human subject is forced to acknowledge the insignificance of the human ego in and of itself, for it gains its true meaning chiefly through the context of its interactions with the natural world: "the [human] 'I' is just a tiny speck from nature's point of view, and whether our ego exists or does not exist, the world will continue to turn."[53]

Thus, modern humanity's contempt for the natural world, as we might sense from the stories discussed above, may well be matched by the natural world's contempt for us. We ignore this at our peril, for the natural world beyond the gap, of snakes and bears and changelings and disembodied divine voices, is precisely where our origins lie, in the ancient tales, the archetypal knowledge that defines us and makes us complete. In our current, fragmented state, divorced from our roots, we cannot even make sense to ourselves, let alone to others. This is the ongoing tragedy of modern humanity, and it is only partially alleviated by the faint songs of ancient festival dances and rituals drifting up from the deepest reaches of Kawakami's "world of falsehood." Surely there has never been a more ironically named place.

## NOTES

1. Kawakami Hiromi, "Atogaki," in *Hebi o fumu* (Tokyo: Bunshun Bunko, 1999), 172.
2. Ibid., 172–173.
3. Cécile Sakai, "La littérature féminine au Japon, ou comment apprivoiser les fantômes," *Fantômes dans l'Extrême-Orient d'ier et d'aujourd'hui-Tome 2*. 2017, 269–277, 275.

4. Ninomiya Tomoyuki, "Kawakami Hiromi 'Atarayoki' ron: Komyunikēshon to jikozo," In *Kindai Bungaku Shiron* (Hiroshima: Hiroshima Daigaku Kindai Bungaku Kenkyūkai, 2004), 107–108.

5. Kawakami, "Atarayoki," in *Hebi o fumu*, 107.

6. Ibid., 167.

7. Kawakami, "Atogaki," 172.

8. For a very general introduction to the emergence of *danchi* in the 1960s see Hoshino Ikumi, "Apartment Life in Japan" in the *Journal of Marriage and Family* 26.3 (1964), 312–317; for discussion of more recent effects of *danchi* life on various demographic units of contemporary Japan, see Verdrana Ikalović and Leonardo Chiesi, "A Dynamic Sense of Home: Spatio-Temporal Aspects of Mobility of Young Tokyo Residents" in *Urbani Izziv* 30.1 (2019), 101–114; Sukenari Yasushi, "Housing Estates as Experimental Fields of Social Research" in *Development and Society* 45.1 (2016), 69–87; and Anne Imamura, "A Window On Her World: The Relevance of Housing Type for the Urban Japanese Housewife" in *Ekistics* 52.310 (1985), 34–44.

9. Oda Mistuo, *Kōgai no tanjō to shi* (Tokyo: Seikyūsha, 1997), 238–239.

10. Ibid., 239.

11. Wakabayashi Mikio, "Kōgai nyūtaun to chiiki no kioku—shūgō-teki kioku no toshi shakai-gaku shiron," *Nihon toshi shakai gakkai nenpō* 27, 2009, Nihon toshi shakai gakkai. 12.

12. Kalman Applbaum, "Marriage With A Proper Stranger: Arranged Marriage in Metropolitan Japan," *Ethnology* 34.1 (1995), 37–51.

13. Kawakami, "Kieru," in *Hebi o fumu*, 76.

14. Ibid., 71.

15. Ibid., 69.

16. Ibid., 81.

17. Ibid., 98–99. The English translation of this text mistranslates the word *ude* for "breasts," which would suggest a more serious level of intimacy.

18. Ibid., 86.

19. Ibid.

20. Ibid., 85.

21. Kawakami, "Kamisama," in *Kamisama* (Tokyo: Chūkō Bunko, 1998 [1994]), 10.

22. Ibid., 12–13.

23. Tamaki Tokita, "The Post-3/11 Quest for True Kizuna—Shi no Tsubute by Wagō Ryōichi and Kamisama 2011 by Kawakami Hiromi," *The Asia-Pacific Journal* 13.7.7 (2015): 1–13, 8.

24. Kawakami, "Kamisama," 17.

25. Ibid.

26. Kawakami, "Sōjō no chūshoku," in *Kamisama* (Tokyo: Chūkō bunko, 1998), 183.

27. Ibid., 177.

28. Ibid., 180.

29. Ibid., 186.

30. Ibid., 187.

31. Tokita, "The Post-3/11 Quest for True Kizuna—Shi no Tsubute by Wagō Ryōichi and Kamisama 2011 by Kawakami Hiromi," 8.
32. Ibid.
33. Ibid.
34. Kawakami, "Sōjō no chūshoku," 189–190.
35. Ibid., 192.
36. Hino Keizō, "Tatakai no monogatari" in *Bungei Shunjū* 74.11 (Sept. 1996), 431.
37. Kawakami, "Hebi o fumu," 9.
38. Ibid., 10.
39. See Akemi Takizawa, "Translations and Psychoanalytical Interpretations of Selected Tales from *Konjaku Monogatari-shū*," Master's Thesis, University of British Columbia, May 2002, esp. 46–50.
40. See *Tales of Times Now Past*, trans. by Marian Ivy (Berkeley: University of California Press, 1979), esp. 93–96.
41. Kawakami, "Hebi o fumu," in *Hebi o fumu*, 54.
42. Ibid., 36–37.
43. Ibid., 42.
44. Katrin Amann, *Yugamu karada: Gendai josei sakka no henshintan* (Tokyo: Senshūdaigaku shuppankyoku, 2000), 135.
45. Wada Tsutomu, "Kawakami Hiromi ron," *Kyūshū sangyō daigaku kokusai bunka gakubu kiyō* no.38 (2007), 1–13. 3.
46. Kawakami, "Hebi o fumu," 19–20.
47. Ibid., 29.
48. Ibid.
49. Kawakami, "Atogaki," 172.
50. Kawakami Hiromi, "Atogaki," in *Gunzō* 66.6 (June 2011), 114.
51. Ibid., 113.
52. Kawakami Hiromi and Numano Mitsuyoshi, "Sekai wa yuragi, genjitsu to gensō no sakaime mo yuraide iru: Nihon bungaku no honyakukatachi to shōsetsu "kazabana" o kataru." *Web Magazine: Wochi Kochi* (January 24, 2012), https://www.wochikochi.jp/topstory/2012/04/jbn2.php (Accessed July 4, 2021).
53. Ibid.

## WORKS CITED

Amann, Katrin. *Yugamu karada: Gendai josei sakka no henshintan*. Tokyo: Senshūdaigaku shuppankyoku, 2000.
Applbaum, Kalman. "Marriage With a Proper Stranger: Arranged Marriage in Metropolitan Japan," *Ethnology* 34.1 (1995), 37–51.
Hino Keizō. "Tatakai no monogatari" in *Bungei Shunjū* 74.11 (Sept. 1996).
Kawakami Hiromi. "Kamisama," in *Kamisama*. Tokyo: Chūkō bunko, 1998.
———. "Sōjō no chūshoku," in *Kamisama*. Tokyo: Chūkō bunko, 1998.
———. "Hebi o fumu," in *Hebi o fumu*. Tokyo: Bunshun Bunko, 1999.
———. "Kieru," in *Hebi o fumu*. Tokyo: Bunshun Bunko, 1999.

———. "Atarayoki," in *Hebi o fumu*. Tokyo: Bunshun Bunko, 1999.
———. "Atogaki," in *Hebi o fumu*. Tokyo: Bunshun Bunko, 1999.
Kawakami Hiromi and Numano Mitsuyoshi, "Sekai wa yuragi, genjitsu to gensō no sakaime mo yuraide iru: Nihon bungaku no honyakukatachi to shōsetsu "kazabana" o kataru." *Web Magazine: Wochi Kochi* (January 24, 2012), https://www.wochikochi.jp/topstory/2012/04/jbn2.php (Accessed July 4, 2021).
Ninomiya Tomoyuki. "Kawakami Hiromi 'Atarayoki' ron: Komyunikēshon to jikozo," In *Kindai Bungaku Shiron*. Hiroshima: Hiroshima Daigaku Kindai Bungaku Kenkyūkai, 2004. 107–108.
Oda Mistuo. *Kōgai no tanjō to shi*. Tokyo: Seikyūsha, 1997.
Sakai, Cécile. "La littérature féminine au Japon, ou comment apprivoiser les fantômes," *Fantômes dans l'Extrême-Orient d'hier et d'aujourd'hui-Tome 2.* 2017, 269–277.
Tokita, Tamaki. "The Post-3/11 Quest for True Kizuna—Shi no Tsubute by Wagō Ryōichi and Kamisama 2011 by Kawakami Hiromi," *The Asia-Pacific Journal* 13.7.7 (2015): 1–13.
Wada Tsutomu, "Kawakami Hiromi ron," *Kyūshū sangyō daigaku kokusai bunka gakubu kiyō* no.38 (2007), 1–13.
Wakabayashi Mikio. "Kōgai nyūtaun to chiiki no kioku—shūgō-teki kioku no toshi shakai-gaku shiron," *Nihon toshi shakai gakkai nenpō* 27, 2009, Nihon toshi shakai gakkai.

# Index

3/11 triple disaster (2011), 3, 6, 10, 185

Abe, Kōbō, 3
abjection, 9, 115, 117–127, 129–131
Akutagawa Prize, 36, 38, 74, 96, 180
Aum Subway Sarin Attack (1995), 3, 6, 182

Barthes, Roland, 58, 68n19
birth: of characters, 119, 137, 140, 142, 152, 154, 169; in Kojiki, 2; childbirth, 17, 38, 40–41, 74, 77, 90n42; rebirth, 7, 23–25, 27, 28n11, 169; birth rate, 72, 77–78, 90n42
body: and space, 1–2, 8–9, 17, 23, 39–40, 43–45, 60–61, 64, 82–83, 96–98, 100, 102–104, 108–109, 118–119; and mind, 18–20, 23, 57, 61, 99–102, 104; bodily sacrifice, 59; illness, 9, 95–114; pregnancy, 33, 36–41, 43–44, 72, 81, 84–85, 90n42

Campbell, Joseph, 23, 25–27, 183
cannibalism, 9, 71–94
consciousness, 5, 9, 15–16, 18, 22, 25, 27, 42, 58, 98, 100, 102–103, 106, 108, 110, 151–152; subconsciousness, 6, 168–169
Creed, Barbara, 8, 34–35, 38

*danchi*, 165, 170–175, 187n8
death, 7, 9, 17–19, 22–25, 27, 28n11, 34, 36–38, 44, 51–52, 56, 59, 75, 81, 83, 96–97, 99, 101, 105–110, 112n41, 120, 126, 128, 142–143, 150, 155, 168–169, 183–184
dystopia, 74

exile, 9–10, 139–157

fertility. *See* birth
folklore, 73–74, 85, 165, 181
food, 1, 53, 60–61, 71–93, 119, 168–169
Freud, Sigmund, 31, 34, 37, 169

gender, 31–49, 71–93; and fantasy, 4; and shōjo, 31–32; and the uncanny, 34–35; gender-specific experience, 33, 44–45

hallucination, 96, 100–103, 106, 143
Hino, Keizō, 9, 95–113, 180;
history, 8, 16, 21–23, 33, 85, 98, 102, 151, 153, 170
home: as a symbol, 8, 31, 34–38, 42, 44–45, 72, 80, 82; homeland, 9, 124, 128, 152, 156; hometown, 177, 179–180

identity, 1, 3, 8–9, 18, 20, 31, 33–40, 57, 71, 115–120, 122, 127, 129–131, 132n24, 144–145, 154–155, 169, 173; alter-ego, 63, 120, 182; collective identity, 173; individual identity, 20, 174
*isekai*, 6–7
*iyashi*, 5–7

Jung, Carl Gustav, 17, 25–27, 27n1, 168, 182

Kafka, Franz, 3, 143, 155
Kanai, Mieko, 3, 5, 6, 51–69
Karatani, Kōjin, 2
Katō, Norihiro, 22–23
Kawakami, Hiromi, 4, 10, 28n15, 32–33, 165–189;
*kizuna*, 176, 179
Kōbe Earthquake (1995), 3, 6
Kojiki, 1
Kristeva, Julia, 117–118. *See also* abjection

landscape, 2–3, 7, 17, 32, 95, 119, 169
language, 2, 10, 52, 57–60, 62–64, 118, 127, 138–151, 165–166
liminal space, 32, 52, 57, 61–64, 82–83, 147–148, 180, 184

Maeda, Ai, 2
magical realism, 3, 166
memory, 3, 7, 16, 23, 25, 35, 52–54, 60–61, 81, 95, 98, 116, 117–118, 130, 140, 145, 174, 182; collective memory, 7, 98; individual memory, 7, 98
Miyadai, Shinji, 3
Murakami, Haruki, 3–8, 10, 15–29, 32, 42, 131n1, 165–166;
Murakami, Ryū, 4–5, 9, 115–135;
Murata, Sayaka, 4, 9, 71–93;
myth, 1, 23–27, 28n11, 71–72, 143, 153, 165, 167–169, 175, 180, 182, 185

Napier, Susan, 4, 32
nostalgia, 8, 31, 33–34, 36–37, 41, 98–99, 104
nothingness, 97, 104–105, 107

Occidentalism, 122, 130, 132n24
Ōe, Kenzaburō, 37
Ogawa, Yōko, 1, 4–6, 8, 10, 31–49, 82, 165–166;
Okonogi, Keigo, 32
Ōoka, Makoto, 116
Orientalism, 122, 130, 132n24
Oyamada, Hiroko, 38, 42

parallel world, 3, 5, 15
Plato, 16–17, 19, 25–26, 28n15, 38, 182
pregnancy. *See* body

reality: and cognition, 9, 95–96, 101, 104–105, 109; and fantasy, 4–5, 7, 10, 26, 51–61, 64, 137–138, 165, 172, 174; and *shōjo*, 32–33, 35; rebel against, 120, 124–125, 130
reproduction, 8–9, 31–49, 71–93. *See also* birth and gender

Said, Edward, 122
self: Self and Other, 34; self-consciousness, 106, 184; self-identity, 1, 33, 40
sexuality: and language 58; asexual, 81; female sexuality, 85–88; heterosexual economy, 32, 34, 37–38, 42, 44, 74, 78, 86, 147; sexual abuse and violence, 82, 88, 150; sexual acts, 1, 19, 57–58, 74, 75–77, 79–80, 87, 131–132n8; sexual desire and imagery, 142, 169, 181–183; sexual difference, 35; sexual fantasy, 59, 147; sexual liberation, 85, 91n53; sexual transgression, 118; sexual victimization by society, 73, 83
*shōjo*, 8, 31–49, 168–169

Slaymaker, Douglas, 67n17, 141–143, 149, 154
Sontag, Susan, 108
space: definition of fantastical space, 5–7; dreamscape, 41, 166–169, 183–184; other world or otherworld, 5, 6, 31, 37, 73, 116, 124, 167
Strecher, Matthew, 3, 7–8, 10, 15–29, 98, 165–189
student movements (the 1960s–1970s), 3, 23, 116, 129

Tawada, Yōko: 4, 10, 42, 137–161, 165; time, 6, 7, 8, 16–18, 21–23, 26, 31, 33–34, 37, 39, 41, 44, 52, 54–55, 60–63, 81–82, 96, 98, 100, 145, 152–153, 165

Tokyo, 2–3, 9, 16–17, 19, 97–103, 106–107, 109–110, 117–121, 123–124, 126, 128, 130, 185
transgression, 7, 40, 58–59, 118
trauma, 3, 6, 9, 59, 80, 82–84, 88, 147, 150
Treat, John Whittier, 3, 31–32

United Red Army, 116
utopia, 73–74, 85

violence, 18, 59, 115–118, 123, 125, 127–131, 148–150, 154, 169, 176, 180. *See also* sexual abuse and violence

World War II, 58, 96, 124

Yoshimoto, Banana, 6, 32, 131–132n8

# Index of Works

**Hino, Keizō**
"Dansō ni yurameku shiroku te no hira no mine," 99, 108, 112n40
"Hashigo no tatsu machi," 95–99
"Okujō no kage-tachi," 99
"Tōkyō tawā ga suita," 99–104
"Unkai no sakame," 104–107
*Yume no shima*, 96

**Kanai, Mieko**
"Ai no seikatsu," 51–57, 59, 60, 63
"Akashia kishidan," 56, 62–64
"Boshizō," 59, 68n23
"Ei'en no koibito," 60
"Kotoba/genjitsu/nikutai," 57
"Kūki–otoko no hanashi," 60–61
"Nikutairon e josetsu dai'ippo," 58–59
"Puratonteki na ai," 63–64
"Usagi," 5, 59, 61–62, 64

**Kawakami, Hiromi**
"Atarayoki," 167–170, 183
"Hebi o fumu," 180–184
"Kamisama," 175–179, 184–185
"Kamisama 2011," 185
"Kieru," 170–175, 184
"Sōjō no chūshoku," 177–180

**Miyuki, Ono**
"Pyua," 72, 84–88

**Murakami, Haruki**
*1973-nen no pinbōru*, 17
*1Q84*, 17
*Hitsuji o meguru bōken*, 17, 22, 24
*Kishidanchō-goroshi*, 17–18, 25
*Sekai no owari to hādo-boirudo wandārando*, 17, 20, 24
*Nejimakidori kuronikuru*, 16–18
*Umibe no Kafuka*, 16–19, 22

**Murakami, Ryū**
*Hantō o deyo*, 124–126, 128, 130
*In za miso sūpu*, 120, 122–123, 130
*Kagirinaku tōmei ni chikai burū*, 116–117, 120, 130
*Kibō no kuni no ekusodasu*, 126–129, 131
*Koinrokkā beibīzu*, 118–120, 123–124, 128, 130
*Topazu*, 120–122, 130

**Murata, Sayaka**
*Chikyū seijin*, 72, 74–75, 80–84
"Satsujin shussan," 74
"Seimei-shiki," 74–80

*Shōmetsu sekai*, 74

**Ogawa, Yōko**
"Daiweingu pūru," 36
"Danjiki katsutsumuri," 1
"Domitorī," 31, 33, 41–44
*Hoteru airisu*, 44
*Mīna no kōshin*, 32

"Ninshin karendā," 38–41
"Samenai kōcha," 36–38

**Tawada, Yōko**
"Inu muko iri," 144
"Kakato o ushinakute," 42
*Yuki no renshūsei*, 137–161

# About the Contributors

**Mina Qiao** teaches Japanese literature at Tokyo University of Foreign Studies. She is the author of *Women in the Maze: Space and Gender in Kirino Natsuo's Writings* (2019). She has published articles on space in literature, sadomasochism in literature, and urban culture in *Japan Forum*, *U.S.-Japan Women's Journal*, and *Japanese Language and Literature*.

**Matthew C. Strecher** is professor of Japanese Literature at Sophia University in Tokyo. In addition to numerous books and articles on Murakami Haruki, he has published articles on Japanese literary history, "poison women," and literary journalism in Japan. When he's not busy professing things, he enjoys kayaking and composing music.

**Anthony Bekirov** has completed his MA thesis on Kanai Mieko at University of Geneva and is a prospective doctoral student. His research interests include interactivity in art forms, Japanese literature, and new media. He has published several articles on cinema studies in peer-reviewed academic journals and culture magazines in French. He is also the organizer and speaker of the symposium "Visual Contagions Through the Lens of New Media" (2021).

**Kazue Harada** is an assistant professor of Japanese at Miami University, Ohio, and earned her PhD from Washington University in St. Louis in 2015. Her research focus is contemporary Japanese speculative and science fiction with an exploration of gender and sexuality. She is the author of *Sexuality, Maternity, and (Re)productive Futures: Women's Speculative Fiction in Contemporary Japan* (2021). Her articles have appeared in *U.S.-Japan Women's Journal*, *Japanese Language and Literature*, and *Japanese Studies*.

**Amanda C. Seaman** teaches at the University of Massachusetts Amherst, where she is a professor of modern Japanese language and literature. A scholar of modern women's literature, genre fiction, and gender studies, she is the author of *Bodies of Evidence: Women, Society and Detective Fiction in 1990s Japan* (2004) and *Writing Pregnancy in Low-Fertility Japan* (2017).

...er other publications include translations of Japanese women's literature, writings on Japanese popular culture, and Japanese food culture. Her current research explores the representation of illness and the afflicted in postwar Japanese literature, film, and popular media.

**Francesca Bianco** is a prospective doctoral student at Waseda University, developing a comparative analysis of postwar Japanese poets on MEXT scholarship. She completed her MA thesis on atomic bomb poet Kurihara Sadako's first collection of poems *Kuroi tamago* (Black Eggs) at University of Naples "L'Orientale." Her main research interest is "crisis of the self" of the generation that survived the war and the atomic bomb and its effects on the Japanese literary tradition.

**Barbara Hartley** has written extensively on issues related to girls and women in modern Japan, particularly in the literary studies context. She also researches visual representations of these women and girls, and representations of Asia and Asian women in modern Japanese narrative and visual material. Recent publications include "Sakai Magara: Activist Girl of Early Twentieth Century Japan," published in *Girlhood Studies*, 13, no. 2 (Summer 2020): 103–118 and "Intertextuality, Sex, and the Hollow Life in Kore'eda Hirokazu's *Air Doll*" forthcoming in the *Australasian Journal of Popular Culture*. She is currently an honorary researcher with the University of Queensland in Australia.

www.ingramcontent.com/pod-product-compliance
Lightning Source LLC
Chambersburg PA
CBHW020744020526
44115CB00030B/917